AF594803

MYTH & MARBLE

ANCIENT ROMAN SCULPTURE FROM THE TORLONIA COLLECTION

MYTH & MARBLE

Edited by
Lisa Ayla Çakmak and
Katharine A. Raff

With essays by
Silvia Beltrametti, Lisa Ayla Çakmak,
Katharine A. Raff, and Salvatore Settis

The Art Institute of Chicago
Torlonia Foundation

Distributed by Yale University Press,
New Haven and London

Contents

8 Foreword
10 From the President of the Torlonia Foundation
16 Acknowledgments
19 Note to the Reader

20 **The Torlonia Family Tree**

24
Roman Art and the Torlonia Collection
Lisa Ayla Çakmak and Katharine A. Raff

40
Talking Statues: Antiquity and Cosmopolitanism
Silvia Beltrametti

46
Portraits

72
Funerary Art

84
Gods and Goddesses

110
Reliefs

118
Ideal Forms

128
A Collection of Collections:
The Torlonia Museum and Its Antiquities
Salvatore Settis

140 Exhibition Checklist
151 Selected Bibliography
155 Contributors
156 Index

LEAD SUPPORT for *Myth and Marble: Ancient Roman Sculpture from the Torlonia Collection* at the Art Institute of Chicago is provided by Shawn M. Donnelley and Christopher M. Kelly.

Major funding is contributed by the Jaharis Family Foundation, the Boshell Family Foundation, Dwyer Brown and Nancy Reynolds, Marion Cameron-Gray, and two anonymous donors.

Members of the Luminary Trust provide annual leadership support for the museum's operations, including exhibition development, conservation and collection care, and educational programming. The Luminary Trust includes an anonymous donor, Karen Gray-Krehbiel and John Krehbiel, Jr., Kenneth C. Griffin, the Harris Family Foundation in memory of Bette and Neison Harris, Josef and Margot Lakonishok, Ann and Samuel M. Mencoff, Sylvia Neil and Dan Fischel, Cari and Michael J. Sacks, and the Earl and Brenda Shapiro Foundation.

THE TORLONIA FOUNDATION expresses its thanks to key partners who have made this exhibition possible. The works of the Torlonia Collection have been restored by the Torlonia Foundation with the support of Fondazione Bvlgari. Chiomenti provides crucial support for the Foundation's core activities.

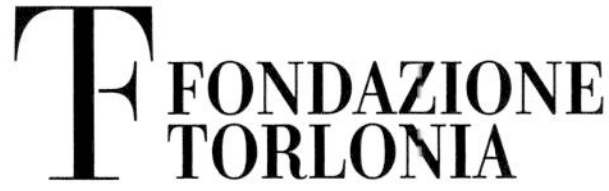

FONDAZIONE
BVLGARI

CHIOMENTI

Foreword

MYTH AND MARBLE: Ancient Roman Sculpture from the Torlonia Collection brings to North America, for the first time, works from one of the largest private collections of ancient Roman sculpture in the world. Thanks to the stewardship of the Torlonia Foundation, its founders, and its president, Alessandro Poma Murialdo, this storied group of sculptures embarks on its inaugural transatlantic tour from Rome to Chicago, Fort Worth, and Montreal.

This exhibition encourages museumgoers across North America to experience this stunning collection of Roman sculpture and to connect it, in ways both prosaic and profound, to the visual culture of today. Sculptures played a role in nearly all the spaces of everyday Roman life—including public forums and monuments as well as cemeteries, libraries, bathhouses, and domestic gardens and shrines. The marble works and single bronze in the Torlonia Collection range from portraits of emperors and their wives to funerary monuments that celebrate the deceased for eternity, to depictions of the gods and goddesses and heroes of Greco-Roman myths. Each sculpture conveyed messages of power, authority, or Roman identity to ancient individuals through a specific visual language. Carved, buried, remade, and restored, these same statues have proven revelatory to countless audiences from the fall of Rome through the nineteenth century and beyond—and they continue to resonate in the present.

The Torlonia Foundation and the Art Institute have long shared a dedication to the dual—and at times paradoxical—ideals of celebrating the ancient world while embracing a dynamic, ever-changing avant-garde. Alessandro Torlonia (1800–1886) founded his eponymous museum of sculpture in the late nineteenth century with the explicit intention of preserving and displaying these works for his country. Across the Atlantic in those same decades, workers in the young Midwestern city of Chicago carved the names of ancient artists into the neoclassical entablature of the city's new art museum building, constructed in 1893: Phidias, Ictinus, Praxiteles, and Apelles. By choosing to name these artists, the museum's founders underscored the foundational role these ancient artists played in creating the visual vocabulary that succeeding generations would repurpose, advance, reject, and remake.

In the ensuing decades, like many growing museums, the Art Institute jump-started its collection of Greek and Roman art by acquiring nearly 500 plaster-cast reproductions of ancient sculptures or architectural fragments, along with a small number of marble sculptures. These works allowed the museum to teach its students about classical art and introduce Chicago's audiences to the artistic achievements of the ancient Mediterranean world. In the same vein, this catalogue aligns with the Art Institute's long-standing educational mission to invite the public into the world of Roman sculpture, with the aid of the exceptional holdings of the Torlonia Collection. This moment finds the Art Institute coming full circle and realizing its founders' ambitions to bring audiences closer to ancient art, on a greater scale than ever before in the museum's nearly 150-year history.

As lead supporters of this exhibition at the Art Institute, Shawn M. Donnelley and Christopher M. Kelly have made this historic display possible. Shawn has served on the advisory committee to the Arts of Greece, Rome, and Byzantium since 2011, and she has served as chair since 2022. Major funding is contributed by the Jaharis Family Foundation, the Boshell Family Foundation, Dwyer Brown and Nancy Reynolds, Marion Cameron-Gray, and two anonymous donors.

As director of the Torlonia Foundation, Carlotta Loverini Botta has been instrumental in the realization of this project, and her passion for both the Torlonia Collection and its history has been essential to its success. Lisa Çakmak, Mary and Michael Jaharis Chair and Curator, Arts of Greece, Rome, and Byzantium, has valiantly led this endeavor, the department's first major exhibition since it was established in 2010, alongside Katharine Raff, Elizabeth McIlvaine Curator, whose expertise in ancient Roman sculpture has led to new discoveries.

Special thanks must be expressed to Eric Lee, Director, and George Shackelford, Deputy Director, both of the Kimbell Art Museum, for their partnership and early involvement in the formation of this exhibition, without which it would not have been possible. Thanks are also due to Stéphane Aquin, Director, and Mary-Dailey Desmarais, Chief Curator, of the Montreal Museum of Fine Arts, for their eager embrace of this joint venture.

The works in the Torlonia Collection speak to us today in the present tense. These objects have been consistently reinterpreted, lived with, and reworked in their long lives; not a single sculpture in this exhibition exists as it did when it left the ancient artist's workshop. We are proud to present their vital stories here, doing what we do best: encouraging visitors to connect a complex ancient past with our own complicated present. Our work affirms the urgent relevance of these objects, now and always.

James Rondeau
President and Eloise W. Martin Director
The Art Institute of Chicago

From the President of the Torlonia Foundation

THE FORWARD-THINKING collecting approach of the Art Institute of Chicago, driven by the tension between building a historical collection and embracing the avant-garde, results in a museum with unparalleled masterpieces. The same ethos lies at the heart of the Torlonia Museum. Originally intended to adorn the Torlonia Family's estates, the Torlonia Collection was transformed into a museum thanks to the vision of Prince Alessandro Torlonia (1800–1886). This radical shift from private holdings to a museum paved the way for the cultural evolution that ultimately led to the modern public museum. With an enduring passion for antiquities, the Torlonia Family has handed down these artworks through generations. It is the same passion that now inspires museum patrons to support institutions as perpetual sources of cultural enrichment.

Myth and Marble: Ancient Roman Sculpture from the Torlonia Collection is the result of the dedication of art leaders who have enabled the world's most important private collection of Roman sculptures to cross the Atlantic for the very first time. This remarkable achievement—driven by the vision of James Rondeau, President and Eloise W. Martin Director, and curators Lisa Çakmak and Katharine Raff of the Art Institute of Chicago—is further enhanced by the commitments of the Kimbell Art Museum and the Montreal Museum of Fine Arts, which will bring the Collection to audiences across North America. The leaders of these institutions, including Director Eric Lee and Deputy Director George Shackelford of the Kimbell Art Museum, and Director Stéphane Aquin and Chief Curator Mary-Dailey Desmarais of the Montreal Museum of Fine Arts, have encouraged this celebration of the Torlonia Collection, to affirm ancient art's role as an essential element of rich and diverse community life.

At the heart of the exhibition are fifty-eight representative sculptures, including twenty-four newly presented works that have recently been restored in the Torlonia Laboratories, thanks to support from Fondazione Bvlgari. The extraordinary array of busts, reliefs, statues, and sarcophagi attests to the evolution of art and culture over the centuries. The penetrating gaze of the Giustiniani resting goat, restored by Bernini, and the striking hues of the two statues of Isis in *bigio morato* marble will enthrall the public with their evocative charm. The Torlonia marbles invite the beholder to reflect on the visual culture that permeated every aspect of ancient Roman society as well as our own; the messages, art, and myths of ancient Rome have shaped human identities for millennia. The last great aristocratic Roman art collection thus recounts the fascinating history of ancient sculpture while illuminating key aspects of our modern world through the history of archaeology and collecting practices.

The Torlonia Collection is not just an ensemble of extraordinary ancient sculptures; it is also a collection of historical collections. The body of works was assembled through acquisitions from the most important Roman patrician collections, along with sculptures excavated on the Family's own land. By the end of the nineteenth century, when the holdings had grown to include an impressive number of ancient marbles, Prince Alessandro Torlonia decided to open the Museo Torlonia in a former grain warehouse on Via della Lungara in Rome. He set out to display 622 works, highlighting the cutting-edge scientific practices of the time through careful curation. A testimony of this endeavor is the 1884–85 catalogue edited by Carlo Ludovico Visconti, which reproduced the complete Collection using a pioneering phototype technique.

The Torlonia Foundation, envisioned by Prince Alessandro Torlonia (1925–2017), has deep historical roots and reflects the founder's love for art. It was established with the aim of preserving and promoting both the Torlonia Collection and the Villa Albani Torlonia, a quintessential expression of eighteenth-century taste. Together, they constitute a cultural heritage of the Family for humanity, to be handed down to future generations. The Foundation has devoted significant attention to its mission through a continued joint effort between the public and private sectors, following a tradition dating back to the Renaissance. The conservation of the Collection is overseen by the Ministry of Culture, which allows these gems of Italian heritage to be admired worldwide. This mission is further supported by our partners: our long-standing collaboration with Fondazione Bvlgari—which has been the main sponsor of the restoration project since its inception in Rome and throughout the global tour—and the invaluable support of Chiomenti for the Foundation's core activities. This important array of initiatives is made possible by the committed Foundation team—in particular, Director Carlotta Loverini Botta, Collection conservator Anna Maria Carruba, project manager Bianca Malitesta, and registrar Giovanni Vincenzo Sergio—along with the Foundation's Scientific Coordinator Carlo Gasparri, the Scientific Advisory Board's President, Salvatore Settis, and the Board's members: Gabriele Galateri di Genola, Filippo Modulo, Carlo Ratti, and Xavier Francesco Salomon.

The Torlonia Foundation promotes its heritage broadly through publications and exhibitions, inspiring further study and research by leveraging the most advanced technologies available. These efforts honor the academic aspirations of Prince Alessandro Torlonia and reflect the cosmopolitan spirit that has always characterized the collection of antiquities.

Alessandro Poma Murialdo
President
Torlonia Foundation

FROM ROME TO THE UNITED STATES AND CANADA, once more we are proud to be at the side of the Torlonia Foundation on this unique journey of artistic rediscovery that brings back to light the unrivaled beauty of the world's most important private collection of ancient Greek and Roman sculptures.

Following an extraordinary exhibition at the Musée du Louvre in Paris in June 2024, the Torlonia marbles are now traveling outside Europe for the first time since the Collection was formed by esteemed Roman patrons in the nineteenth century, reaching some of the most prestigious cultural institutions in the United States and Canada, two countries particularly fascinated with the ancient arts.

The path from the Eternal City to a global tour of this historical significance was laid out when Bvlgari—driven by its commitment to preserving Rome's artistic and cultural legacy for future generations—made an agreement with the Torlonia Foundation to support the restoration of a selection of statues from the Torlonia Collection. The fruits of this collaboration were proudly presented in 2020 with the exhibition *The Torlonia Marbles: Collecting Masterpieces* at the Capitoline Museums in Rome and at Gallerie d'Italia in Milan, where more than ninety newly restored statues finally returned to the public eye after seventy years. This first milestone increased our desire to scale up our commitment to supporting long-term initiatives of this caliber.

With fifty-eight masterpieces from the Collection, of which twenty-four have never before been displayed in modern times, this new exhibition not only demonstrates how the enduring collaboration between the Fondazione Bvlgari and the Torlonia Foundation has brought to light new treasures, but it also testifies to the richness of this magnificent collection, which can be discovered and rediscovered from ever-changing perspectives. Indeed, with each new journey, the Collection allows us to explore fresh interpretations in a sort of eternal rebirth. In this new stage, for example, there is a strong presence of female busts that tell us about the key roles women played in the ancient imperial dynasties.

Furthermore, this tour in the United States and Canada will see Fondazione Bvlgari as the official partner of Torlonia Foundation for the first time. Established in early 2024, Fondazione Bvlgari perpetuates and amplifies a mission that was already an integral part of the Maison Bvlgari: the commitment to building a magnificent future for the environment and society in the fields of art and patronage, education, philanthropy, and inclusion. In these areas and more, our collaboration with the Torlonia Foundation finds fertile ground to continue to elevate life through the search for beauty.

Jean-Christophe Babin
Bvlgari Group CEO and Fondazione Bvlgari President

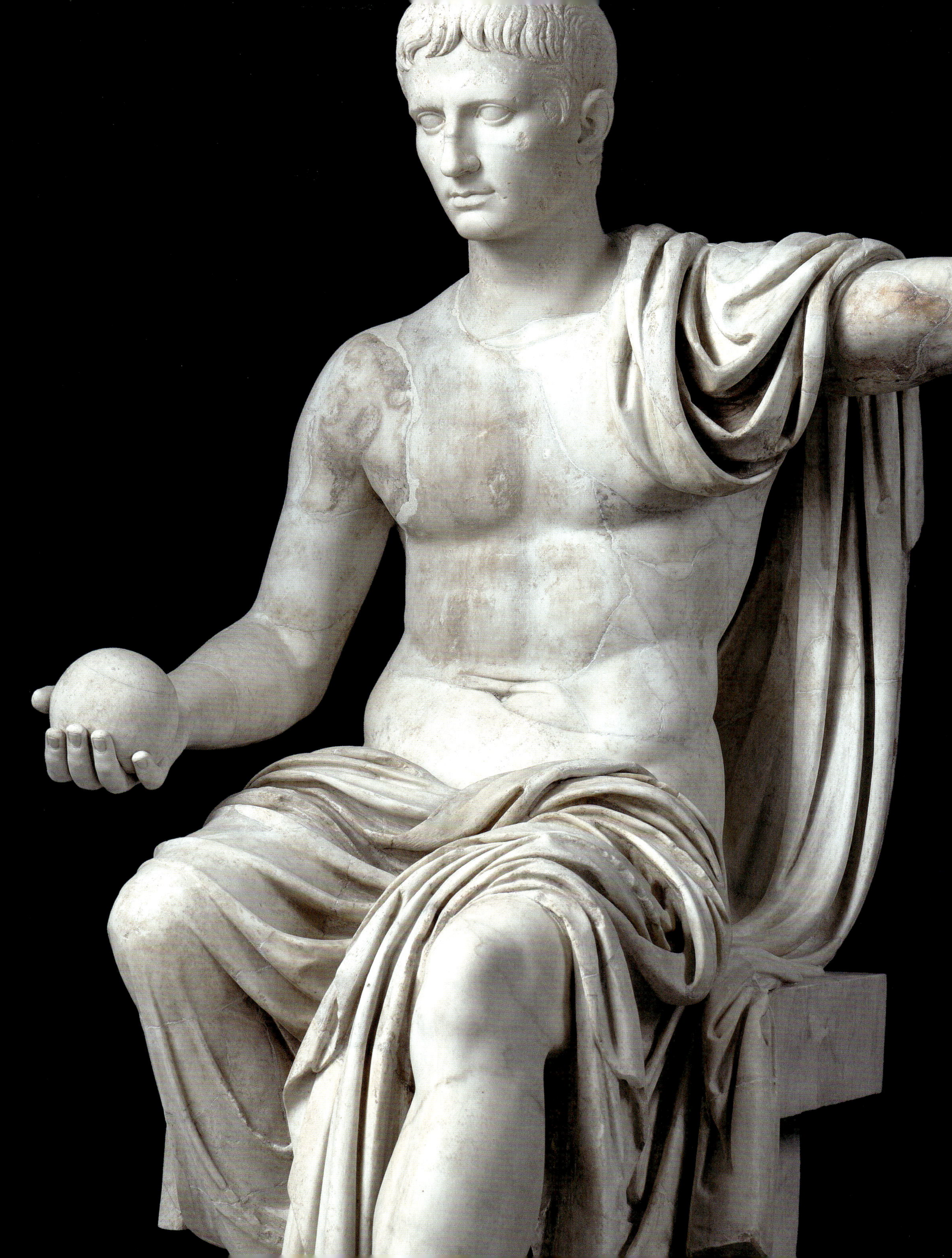

IT IS A GREAT HONOR to introduce this catalogue dedicated to the Torlonia Collection, a remarkable testament to our shared cultural heritage and to the enduring legacy of ancient art. This extraordinary collection, renowned as one of the most significant private assemblages of ancient Roman marble sculptures in the world, embodies the rich history of artistic expression. It is a testament to the dedication of the Torlonia Family members who have preserved these treasures.

As we celebrate the Torlonia Collection in the United States, we reflect on Italy's pivotal role in the preservation and celebration of art. Ancient Roman art holds profound relevance in our modern world, serving as a bridge that connects people around the globe to our shared history and cultural roots. These sculptures remind us of the enduring values of creativity, innovation, and human expression that have shaped our civilization and transcend time. They are not merely relics of the past; they are vibrant reminders of the values we cherish and the importance of preserving our art for generations to come.

Developed over centuries through acquisitions from prominent Roman patrician families and excavations on the Family's estates, this Collection features a diverse array of objects, including large-scale, intricately designed sarcophagi and lifelike busts. It displays striking portraits of individuals and members of the imperial family alongside sculptures of gods and heroes. The artworks in the catalogue profoundly deepen our understanding of the Roman civilization and its extraordinary influence on today's society, from its legal systems and institutions to its art, literature, and cinema. The opening of this display of ancient Roman sculptures at the Art Institute of Chicago and the exhibitions at the Kimbell Art Museum in Fort Worth, Texas, and the Montreal Museum of Fine Arts mark a historic moment, as these masterpieces dating back nearly 2,000 years cross the Atlantic for the first time.

In sharing these treasures with the world, we reaffirm our commitment to cultural diplomacy and the belief that art knows no borders. It is through such exchanges that we foster mutual understanding, strengthen ties between nations, and celebrate our friendship.

Mariangela Zappia
Ambassador of Italy to the United States

THIS EXHIBITION will be the first-ever presentation of the Torlonia Collection outside of Europe. It is only fitting that it would be hosted at three prestigious North American institutions: the Art Institute of Chicago, the Kimbell Art Museum, and the Montreal Museum of Fine Arts.

The depth and strength of the Torlonia Collection ensures that no exhibitions of the Collection are ever quite the same. In the North American show, many recently restored sculptures will be presented for the first time as the result of new curatorial research, complete with new interpretations of the objects and original exhibition and catalogue designs. The Ministry of Culture, through the Special Superintendency of Rome, played a central role in this ambitious project by safeguarding the Collection and providing support for the recent exhibitions in Rome, Milan, and Paris. These exhibitions were the result of an ongoing joint cooperation between the public and private spheres; this work now moves beyond European borders and heads across the Atlantic.

The legal protection of cultural assets has a long tradition in Europe, originating in Italy as early as the sixteenth century. The artist Raphael is said to have initiated the practice after the Pope entrusted him with the task of safeguarding the immense heritage of Rome, including its artworks, architecture, and archaeological treasures. These activities are still carried out today. The long journey to protect the Torlonia Collection's priceless cultural heritage began in 1910 and culminated in March 2016 with the agreement for the protection, conservation, and promotion of the Collection between the Torlonia Family—represented by the Torlonia Foundation created at the behest of Prince Alessandro Torlonia (1925–2017)—and the Ministry of Culture, through the Director General for Archaeology, Fine Arts, and Landscape and the Special Superintendency of Rome.

Over the past decade, the efforts of the Torlonia Foundation and the Special Superintendency to preserve and further enhance this unique "collection of collections" have never ceased. The specific task of the Superintendency, thanks to the expert contributions of its archaeologists and art historians, lies in the supervision of restoration projects, carried out with the support of Fondazione Bvlgari; the handling of the works; and the management of the authorization process for their transportation, both around Italy and internationally. This touring exhibition offers the chance to admire a collection of ancient sculptures, and also to learn more about the passion for antiquities at the heart of European museums between the eighteenth and nineteenth centuries, a passion that would give rise to the discipline of archaeology and the conservation of ancient artifacts.

Daniela Porro
Special Superintendent of Rome
Ministry of Culture, Italy

Acknowledgments

MANY PEOPLE made *Myth and Marble: Ancient Roman Sculpture from the Torlonia Collection* happen; their hard work and collaboration enabled us to bring these storied ancient Roman sculptures on their first journey to North America. Above all, the Torlonia Foundation in Rome demonstrated tremendous partnership over the course of this project. We are indebted to the founders Paola, Francesca, and Giulio Torlonia, along with Alessandro Poma Murialdo, for embracing the project, and we thank Carlotta Loverini Botta for her spirited support. We also extend our thanks to the Foundation's Scientific Coordinator, Carlo Gasparri, the President of the Scientific Advisory Board, Salvatore Settis, and the Board members: Gabriele Galateri di Genola, Filippo Modulo, Carlo Ratti, and Xavier Francesco Salomon. Bianca Malitesta provided essential research assistance, Anna Maria Carruba restored the works in the show, and Giovanni Vincenzo Sergio handled logistical coordination.

We also thank the authors of the conservation reports on the twenty-four recently restored sculptures, on view for the first time in this exhibition: Laura Buccino, Lucilla de Lachenal, and Stefania Tuccinardi. We are grateful to the Foundation team members who keep the organization running: Alberto Sabatini, Alfonsina Sciarrillo, and Silvia Iacoangeli; and Lara Facco and Marianita Santarossa at the Lara Facco Press and Communication Office.

The Museum Box, including David Gramazio, Anna Bursaux, Naomi Remes, and Tim Moore, were essential intermediaries, coordinating logistics and contracts. The Superintendent Daniela Porro and Antonella Bonini at the Special Superintendence, Archaeology, Fine Art, and Landscape of Rome, supported this major international collaborative endeavor. In the United States, we were fortunate to work with excellent teams at the two venues for this historic tour: at the Kimbell Art Museum, Eric Lee, Director; George Shackelford, Deputy Director; Susan Drake, Nicole Chism Griffin, and Jennifer Casler Price; and at the Montreal Museum of Fine Arts, Stéphane Aquin, Director; Mary-Dailey Desmarais, Amélie Lapointe, Michèle Meier, Carolina Calle Sandoval, and Laura Vigo.

At the Art Institute, James Rondeau, President and Eloise W. Martin Director, enthusiastically endorsed this project from its earliest stages, along with Sarah Guernsey, Deputy Director and Senior Vice President for Curatorial Affairs, and Sarah Kelly Oehler, Vice President of Curatorial Strategy and Field-McCormick Chair and Curator, Arts of the Americas. David Nacol, Senior Vice President, Philanthropy; Katie Rahn, Senior Vice President, Marketing and Communications; Emily Benedict, Vice President, Campus Operations; Amy Allen, Vice President, Engagement; and Aaron Andersen, Associate Vice President, Financial Planning and Analysis, have also been essential supporters of this undertaking.

Our colleagues in the Arts of Greece, Rome, and Byzantium were crucial to realizing the department's first major exhibition since its formation in 2010. Jeffrey Nigro offered steadfast curatorial assistance from the very beginning, tackling every research question with enthusiasm and writing for the catalogue. Eric Warner expertly oversaw art movement and installation, while Elizabeth Hahn Benge, Stephanie Caruso, Simone Chagoya, Acassia Ferreira Da Cunha, Lorien Yonker, and Andrew Crocker provided additional logistical, administrative, and research support. Karen Manchester struck up the initial conversations that set the exhibition into motion.

Many scholars lent their expertise to this volume. Essays by Salvatore Settis and Silvia Beltrametti offer insights into the history of the Torlonia Collection while illuminating its ability to inspire and encourage new ideas that have global resonance. Laura Buccino, Lucilla de Lachenal, and Stefania Tuccinardi conducted extensive art historical research on the twenty-four sculptures that were newly conserved for this exhibition; their scholarship forms the basis of the checklist in this catalogue. Carlo Gasparri shared his insights gleaned over more than four decades studying the Torlonia Collection and its rich history. We are also deeply indebted to Elaine Gazda for being a lifelong source of inspiration and profound guidance on all things related to Roman art, especially sculpture.

This book was creatively designed by James Goggin and Shan James of Practise, who embraced our request for a modern presentation of these sculptures and produced a publication more visually compelling than we could have ever imagined. Our colleagues in Publishing, led by Katie Reilly, were dedicated collaborators: Nora McGreevy, with the support of Lisa Meyerowitz, skillfully shaped and edited the book's contents; Elizabeth Upenieks, with Lauren Makholm, steered its production; Josephine Yanasak-Leszczynski capably coordinated images and image rights; and Isella Sandoval handled administrative needs. Juliet Clark proofread the text, and Theresa Duran crafted the index.

The exhibition was likewise a team effort. In Exhibitions, led by Becca Schlossberg and assisted by Aylin Corona, Kate Weinberg deftly managed complex logistics and kept the project running smoothly. To develop his striking exhibition design, Richard J. Ferrer drew inspiration from ancient Roman architecture. In Visual Design, led by Michael Neault and Christine Zavesky, Salvador Cruz Jr. created a vibrant graphic treatment for posters, labels, and visuals, with Vitalii Emelianov, Kristin Best, and Kari McCluskey. Erin Clark Fenton oversaw production. In Collections and Loans, led by Cayetana Castillo, Timothy Campos and Erin Gordon managed the tricky shipments of these often heavy and fragile objects, while Michael Henri Hall, Jessy Williams, and their teams ran an organized and efficient installation. In Finance, Jessica Applebee and Dawn Koster assisted with the budget and key financial details.

Museum staff across many departments helped us interpret these objects and their stories for a general audience. In developing both the catalogue and the exhibition labels, Ginia Shubik Sweeney, Marielle Epstein, and Sam Ramos in Interpretation, led by Emily Fry, deeply engaged with these sculptures and their meanings and developed a narrative for the show; we warmly thank them for their commitment to making these ancient artworks relevant to the audiences of today. Kirill Mazor, Gina Giambalvo, Alex Quintanilla, and Logan Chappe brought the Portus Relief to life through video and produced a compelling audio guide that links the stories presented across the modern and historic wings of the museum. Rebecca J. Long and Jacquelyn N. Coutré in Painting and Sculpture of Europe and Leslie M. Wilson and Jill Bugajski in the Research Center helped develop content and programming around the exhibition. In the Ryerson and Burnham Libraries and Archives, Violet Jaffe, Autumn L. Mather, and the circulation team obtained critical research materials. In Conservation and Science, led by Francesca Casadio, Rachel Sabino, Katharine Shulman, Giovanni Verri, and Andrew Talley brought their expertise to bear on the installation of select objects.

The following colleagues promoted *Myth and Marble* in Chicago and beyond: in the Office of the President and Director, Kate Tierney Powell; in Public Affairs and Marketing and Communications, Lauren Schultz, Jen Nelson, Megan Michienzi, Nora Gainer, Shannon Burke, Nadine Schneller, Salina Tsegai, Sadie Schwarm, Elizabeth Dudgeon, Paul Jones, Rainn Thomas, Meg Fertig, and Calley Oresick; in Philanthropy, George Martin, James Allan, Arielle Jacobi, Eve Jeffers, Mary DeYoe, Jen Oatess, Anna Maria Carvallo VanMeter, and Sam White; in Legal, Carolyn Boies and Troy Klyber, led by Leslie Darling; in Engagement, Stephanie Henderson, Joe Iverson, Miguel Perez, Frances McMahon Ward, Court Tan, and Mel Harris; in Visitor Engagement, Peter Smiler and Joe Maxwell; on the Retail team, Heather Reinholtz, Jennifer Evanoff, Melissa Dishunts, and Kaleb Sullivan. This ambitious project was realized across three museum exhibition spaces with the aid of Thomas Ryan and the Facilities and Logistics team. Laticia Annison-Romano and our Buildings and Grounds colleagues, and Lucio Ventura, Corey Burrage, and the Protection Services team, ensured visitors' safety and comfort during the run of the show.

Numerous colleagues outside the museum contributed to aspects of this exhibition, including Antonio Addari, Floriano Fornasier, Giuseppe Mastropietro, and the staff at Arterìa; Sam Clapp; Chris Rockey; Crispin Corrado; Bernard Frischer, Mohamed Abdelaziz, Albert Prieto, and Lasha Tskhondia at Flyover Zone.

We extend our gratitude to the individuals and organizations who have generously supported this exhibition, including lead supporters Shawn M. Donnelley and Christopher M. Kelly, the Jaharis Family Foundation, the Boshell Family Foundation, Dwyer Brown and Nancy Reynolds, Marion Cameron-Gray, and two anonymous donors. Members of the Luminary Trust provide annual leadership support for the museum's operations, including exhibition development, conservation and collection care, and educational programming. The Luminary Trust includes an anonymous donor, Karen Gray-Krehbiel and John Krehbiel, Jr., Kenneth C. Griffin, the Harris Family Foundation in memory of Bette and Neison Harris, Josef and Margot Lakonishok, Ann and Samuel M. Mencoff, Sylvia Neil and Dan Fischel, Cari and Michael J. Sacks, and the Earl and Brenda Shapiro Foundation. We also thank the United States Department of State for endorsing our application for immunity from seizure as we transported these objects across the Atlantic.

Finally, and most importantly, we thank Prince Alessandro Torlonia (1925–2017), the founder of the Torlonia Foundation. His strong belief in the importance of promoting, researching, and displaying the Torlonia Collection is what enables us to continue his work today, bringing audiences across the world closer to these exceptional works of ancient art.

Lisa Ayla Çakmak
Mary and Michael Jaharis Chair and Curator,
Arts of Greece, Rome, and Byzantium
The Art Institute of Chicago

Katharine A. Raff
Elizabeth McIlvaine Curator,
Arts of Greece, Rome, and Byzantium
The Art Institute of Chicago

Note to the Reader

English-language titles were written by the volume editors with the Torlonia Foundation.

Dates are Common Era unless otherwise specified. The volume editors date the Roman Empire from 27 BCE, when Augustus came to power as the first emperor, to 476 CE, when the Western Roman Empire fell.

Measurements are given in centimeters for an entire object as it exists today, including its base, its ancient components, and all later restorations, unless otherwise noted. Dimensions are listed in the order of height then width then depth.

The abbreviation MT ("Museo Torlonia") prefaces unique identification numbers for works in the Torlonia Collection; this numbering system derives from Carlo Ludovico Visconti's 1884–85 illustrated catalogue (see page 151 for a complete reference).

Key Roman Imperial Figures

Augustus, the first emperor: 63 BCE–14 CE; reigned 27 BCE–14 CE

Trajan: 53–117; reigned 98–117
Plotina: before 70–122/123
Marciana: about 50–112
Matidia: before 68–119

Hadrian: 76–138; reigned 117–138
Sabina: mid-80s–137

Antoninus Pius: 86–161; reigned 138–161
Faustina the Elder: about 97–140

Marcus Aurelius: 121–180; reigned 161–180
Faustina the Younger: about 130–175/176

Lucius Verus: 130–169; reigned 161–169
Lucilla: 148/150–182

Commodus: 161–192; co-reign with Marcus Aurelius 177–180, solo reign 180–192
Crispina: birth year unknown–by 191/192

Septimius Severus: 145–211; reigned 193–211
Julia Domna: about 170–217
Caracalla: 188–217
Geta: 189–211

THE TORLONIA FAMILY TREE

THERE ARE MOMENTS when the fate of objects and the destinies of human beings combine to shape the course of events. Artifacts do this all the time; in this sense, they are far from passive objects—they are living entities, constantly evolving and interacting with human history.

This is particularly true for the Torlonia Collection, a "collection of collections" encompassing three centuries of antiquities heritage. It reflects not only the history of the artworks themselves but also the legacies of their many owners: the centuries-old Roman aristocracy, acclaimed restorers, and visionary collectors.

Over the course of nearly a century, **Prince Alessandro Torlonia** (1800–1886) embraced these diverse artistic legacies that had converged within his family, restoring and reshaping them in ways that were as relevant in his day as they would prove to be for future generations. Alessandro played a pivotal role in forging the Family's legacy. Ultimately transforming the last great princely holdings of Rome to establish the Torlonia Museum in 1876, he imposed a decisive turn onto his already unique collection, paving the way for the cultural evolution that led to the concept of the modern public museum.[1]

The extensive estate of the renowned restorer Bartolomeo Cavaceppi (1716–1799), who defined the purist style of restoration inspired by the theories of Johann Joachim Winckelmann, also stands as a final testament to some of Rome's oldest collections.[2] Upon his death, Cavaceppi bequeathed his legacy to the Accademia di San Luca, one of the many cultural institutions supported by the **Duke Giovanni Torlonia** (1754–1829), who acquired it, thus saving it from dispersal. Giovanni was the second son of **Marino Tourlonias** (1725–1785), the founding patriarch of the Family and the first to settle in Rome from the region of Auvergne, France. He skillfully navigated twists of fate as the century unfolded to become a banker both for the Papal States of Pope Pius VI and the Bonaparte family. Throughout his life he gained noble titles and acquired the vast Torlonia real estate portfolio, including among others the estate of Civitella Cesi (1814), which granted him the title of *Prince*.[3] He also acquired Villa Torlonia (1797), which was restored by the architect Giuseppe Valadier in collaboration with the sculptors Antonio Canova and Bertel Thorvaldsen; and Palazzo Bolognetti in Piazza Venezia (1807).

In 1800, the same year that his third son Alessandro was born, Giovanni purchased the monumental sculpture *Hercules and Lichas* (1795–96) by Canova and displayed it as the centerpiece of the new residence in Piazza Venezia. A number of sculptures from Cavaceppi's studio were also incorporated into

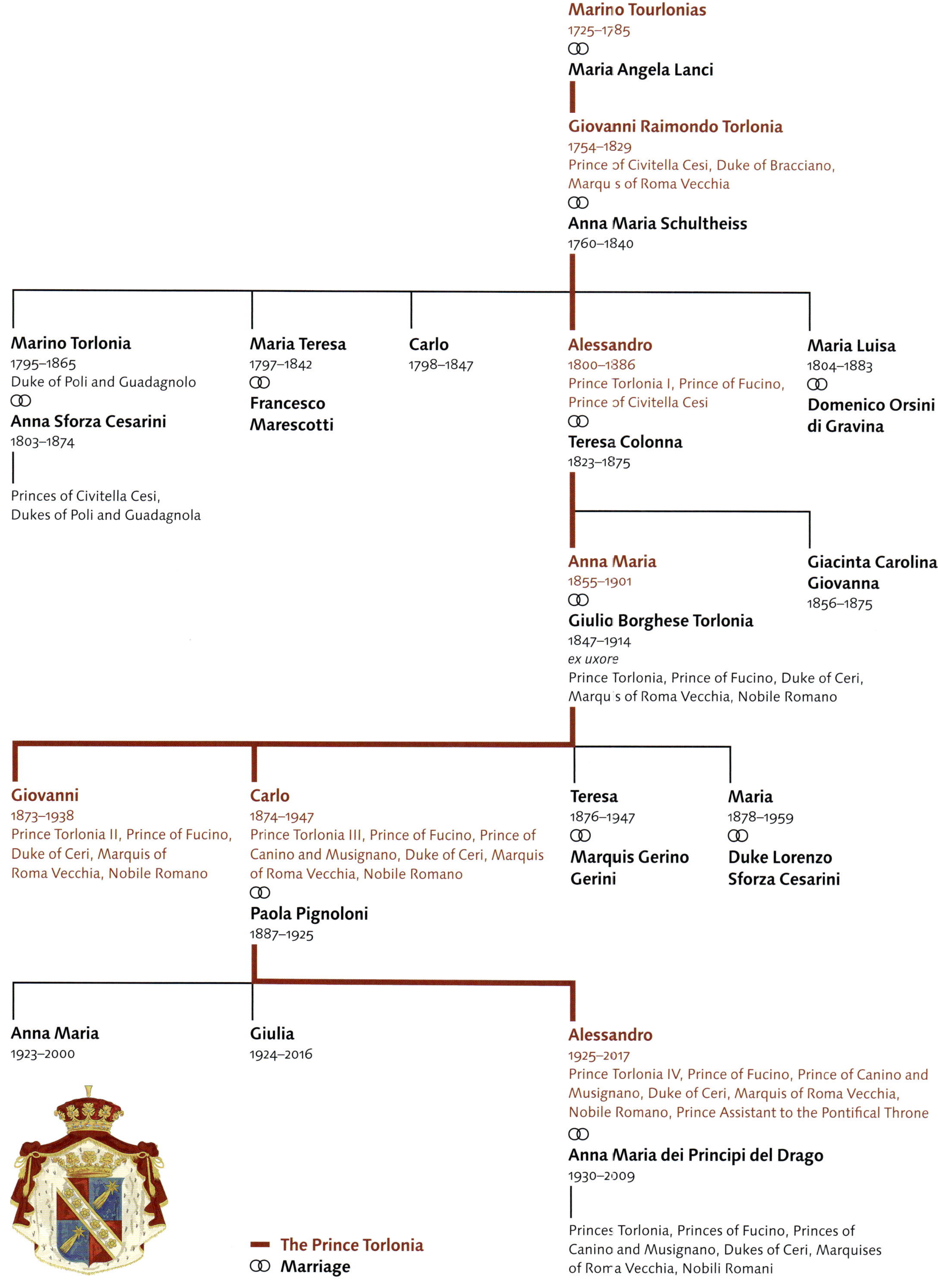

Marino Tourlonias
1725–1785
Maria Angela Lanci
Giovanni Raimondo Torlonia
1754–1829
Prince of Civitella Cesi, Duke of Bracciano,
Marquis of Roma Vecchia
Anna Maria Schultheiss
1760–1840
Marino Torlonia
1795–1865
Duke of Poli and Guadagnolo
Anna Sforza Cesarini
1803–1874
Princes of Civitella Cesi,
Dukes of Poli and Guadagnola
Maria Teresa
1797–1842
Francesco
Marescotti
Carlo
1798–1847
Alessandro
1800–1886
Prince Torlonia I, Prince of Fucino,
Prince of Civitella Cesi
Teresa Colonna
1823–1875
Maria Luisa
1804–1883
Domenico Orsini
di Gravina
Anna Maria
1855–1901
Giulio Borghese Torlonia
1847–1914
ex uxore
Prince Torlonia, Prince of Fucino, Duke of Ceri,
Marquis of Roma Vecchia, Nobile Romano
Giacinta Carolina
Giovanna
1856–1875
Giovanni
1873–1938
Prince Torlonia II, Prince of Fucino,
Duke of Ceri, Marquis of
Roma Vecchia, Nobile Romano
Carlo
1874–1947
Prince Torlonia III, Prince of Fucino, Prince of
Canino and Musignano, Duke of Ceri, Marquis
of Roma Vecchia, Nobile Romano
Paola Pignoloni
1887–1925
Teresa
1876–1947
Marquis Gerino
Gerini
Maria
1878–1959
Duke Lorenzo
Sforza Cesarini
Anna Maria
1923–2000
Giulia
1924–2016
Alessandro
1925–2017
Prince Torlonia IV, Prince of Fucino, Prince of Canino and
Musignano, Duke of Ceri, Marquis of Roma Vecchia,
Nobile Romano, Prince Assistant to the Pontifical Throne
Anna Maria dei Principi del Drago
1930–2009
Princes Torlonia, Princes of Fucino, Princes of
Canino and Musignano, Dukes of Ceri, Marquises
of Roma Vecchia, Nobili Romani
The Prince Torlonia
Marriage

the Palazzo's grand decoration, which became the heart of the Family's lavish social life. Ancient sculpture soon became a significant element of the Prince's extensive assets: the Torlonia Family had by this time become powerful bankers, yet their name would remain forever intertwined with art.

In 1816 a set of about 260 sculptures from the collection of Vincenzo Giustiniani (1564–1637)—an Italian nobleman, banker, and one of the most influential art collectors of his time—was offered to Giovanni Torlonia as collateral for a large loan. The collection included the famous sculpture known as the "resting goat," the head of which had been restored by illustrious artist Gian Lorenzo Bernini (1598–1680) himself. This treasure trove became part of the Torlonia Collection in 1825.[4]

Upon the death of his father in 1829, Prince Alessandro Torlonia became Giovanni's principal heir. Alessandro had been educated in London and Paris, and was to play a pivotal role in shaping the Family's fortune by adding an international dimension to the bank's activities. Indeed, soon after taking the helm of the Torlonia bank, he was made a partner of Maison Rothschild in Paris. At the same time, he invested in cultural projects in Rome and promoted the advancement of agricultural ventures throughout the region. Alongside his brothers, he oversaw the construction of a family chapel in the Basilica of Saint John Lateran, where his parents' tomb was placed. Alessandro's business strategy focused on securing large public tenders while significantly extending the holdings inherited from his father, becoming one of the largest landowners of the rural area around Rome (the so-called *agro romano*).[5] He also underwrote the colossal effort to drain Lake Fucino in central Italy, thereby earning the title of Prince of Fucino in 1875.

In 1840 he married Teresa Colonna (1823–1875), a member of the oldest Roman aristocracy. Over these years he radically renovated the Family mansions, bestowing them with an opulence unparalleled in Rome at the time.[6] But his vision extended beyond traditional patronage, and while negotiating the purchase of Villa Albani in 1866, he also came up with a radical new approach to the Family's collection—one that would ultimately lead to the founding of the Torlonia Museum.

Villa Albani now stands as a sublime testament to the antiquarian taste that emerged in the mid-eighteenth century, a taste for which Rome became a key destination on the Grand Tour. The nephew of Pope Clement XI and a skilled diplomat, Cardinal Alessandro Albani (1692–1779) was a collector and a great promoter of Neoclassicism. The Villa was, above all, a cultural powerhouse, designed in the mid-eighteenth century by architect Carlo Marchionni to host his prestigious art collections, and the project was deeply influenced by Johann Joachim Winckelmann and his illustrious intellectual circle known as the *Cenacolo di Villa Albani*.[7] Alessandro embraced Cardinal Albani's Neoclassicist dream and restored the Villa to its former glory. Tall umbrella pines became part of the garden landscape; he replenished the art collections depleted by looting during the Napoleonic wars and relocated about fifty sculptures of portraits, animals, and decorative elements which had once stood in the Villa's gardens to the eponymous museum that he was in the process of building.

Throughout the second half of the nineteenth century, the Torlonia Family carried out excavations on their own properties, several of which were located on the sites of ancient imperial residences. These yielded discoveries such as the portrait of a young woman known as the "Maiden of Vulci" and a third-century relief depicting the Roman imperial harbor found in Portus. The Family gathered an impressive collection of ancient marble sculptures, but for Alessandro, this was not merely about the accumulation of wealth, but rather about crafting a lasting cultural legacy to uphold the self-representation tradition rooted in the Roman aristocracy: he decided to open the Torlonia Museum in 1876.

Sculptures that had formerly been preserved in the great Roman noble collections came together once more in a former warehouse on Via della Lungara near Palazzo Corsini. The path through the museum—overseen by two descendants of the most famous dynasty of antiquarians, Pietro Ercole Visconti (1803–1880) and his nephew Carlo Ludovico Visconti (1828–1894)—ended with a spectacular display of imperial busts. Alessandro Torlonia's academic ambitions were evident in the exceptional quality of his sculptures, arranged into thematic groups such as the "Room of the Muses," as well as through the creation of a groundbreaking phototype catalogue, distributed freely to European academic institutions. The catalogue reproduced the complete Collection in a modern fashion, forever defining its outline and bequeathing it to history.[8]

The Torlonia Museum closed in the wake of World War II, and its sculptures remained unseen by the public until the 2020 exhibition at the Capitoline

Museums, the result of a fruitful agreement with the Ministry of Culture. The highest expression of this passion for art, which grew as it was passed down through the various generations of the Family, is today the Foundation. Established at the behest of Alessandro's descendant of the same name, **Prince Alessandro Torlonia** (1925–2017), it came into being with the aim of preserving and promoting the Torlonia Collection and Villa Albani Torlonia. Together, as well as comprising an exceptional source of artistic heritage, they reflect some of the key moments of our civilization, the history of collecting, and the history of archaeology and restoration.

Today, the series of recent exhibitions organized by the Foundation, in partnership with renowned institutions, are part of this collecting enterprise. They exemplify the "contemporary act" of a long-standing principle underpinning the Torlonia Family's practice of artistic patronage—for through art, people find their destinies to be intertwined, shaping not only what we see but also who we become.

Carlotta Loverini Botta
Director
Torlonia Foundation

Notes

1 For more on the history of the Torlonia Family, see Carlo Gasparri, "The Torlonia Museum: The Last Roman Collection of Antique Sculpture," in *The Torlonia Marbles: Collecting Masterpieces*, ed. Salvatore Settis and Carlo Gasparri, exh. cat. (Milan: Rizzoli Electa, 2021), 30–47.

2 Such as the collections—dating back to the sixteenth and seventeenth centuries—of Pio da Carpi, as well as the Caetani and Cesarini Families.

3 These include lands in Roma Vecchia and Porto (purchased in 1797), the Bracciano holdings (1803), and the estate of Civitella Cesi (1814).

4 This was documented in the illustrated inventory *Galleria Giustiniana del Marchese Vincenzo Giustiniani*. See p. 140 for a complete citation of this volume in English.

5 Notably, Alessandro acquired the duchy of Ceri in 1833 and later the principality of Canino, purchased from the heirs of Lucien Bonaparte.

6 The mansions included Borgo Palazzo Giraud, Palazzo Bolognetti in Piazza Venezia, and Villa Torlonia on Via Nomentana.

7 The circle featured key figures such as Giovanni Battista Nolli, Giovanni Battista Piranesi, Anton Raphael Mengs, Bartolomeo Cavaceppi, and Johann Joachim Winckelmann.

8 Carlo Ludovico Visconti, *I monumenti del Museo Torlonia di sculture antiche riprodotti con la fototipia* (Rome: Stabilimento Fotografico Danesi, 1884–85).

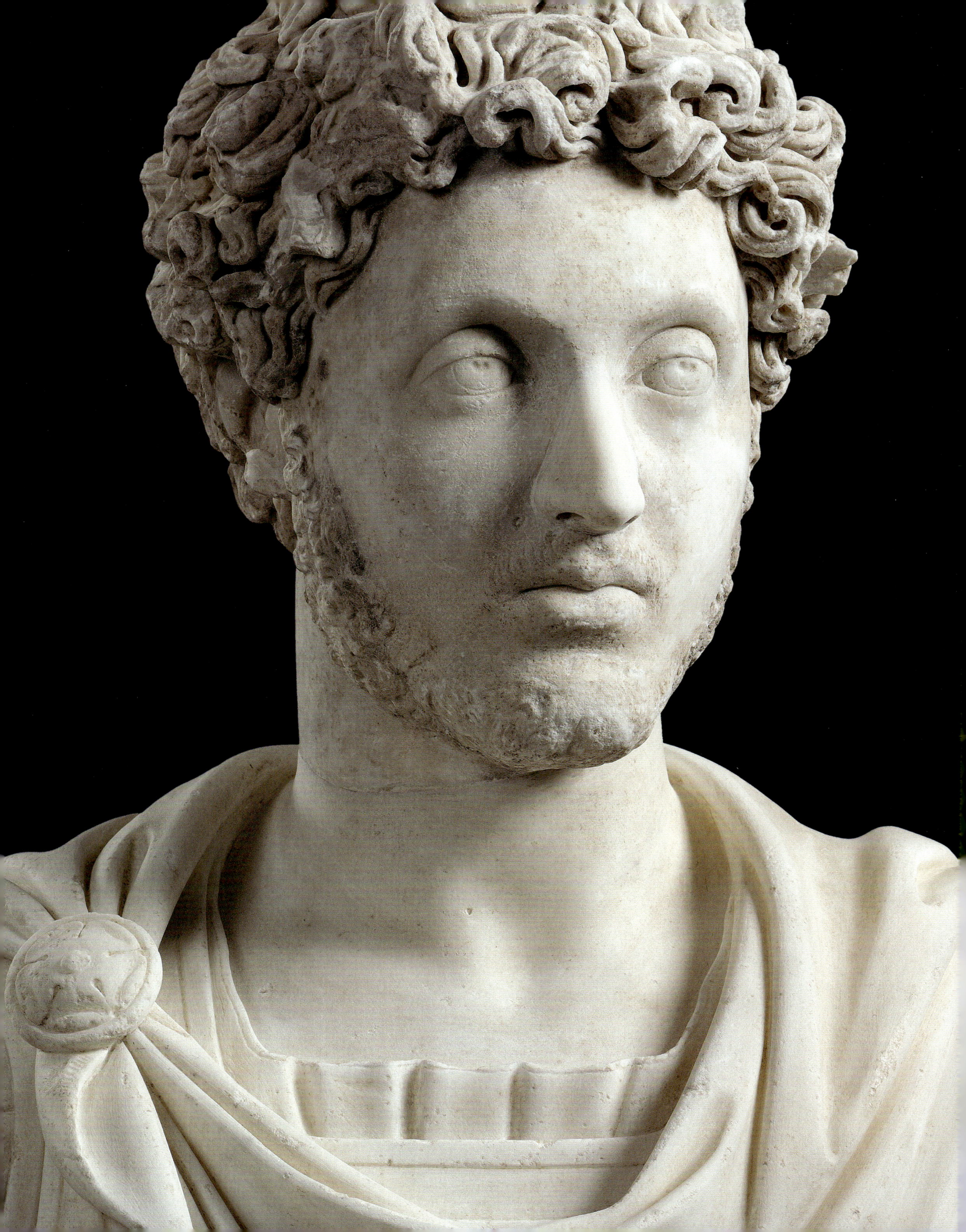

Lisa Ayla Çakmak and Katharine A. Raff

ROMAN ART & THE TORLONIA COLLECTION

IN A LETTER DATED BETWEEN 145 AND 147, the Roman tutor Marcus Cornelius Fronto wrote to his former student Marcus Aurelius (see cats. 13–14), briefly describing the experience of moving through the ancient urban landscape:

> You know how in all money-changer's bureaus, booths, bookstalls, eaves, porches, windows, anywhere and everywhere there are likenesses of you exposed to view, badly enough painted most of them to be sure [. . .] yet at the same time your likeness, however much a caricature, never when I go out meets my eyes without making me part my lips for a smile and dream of you.[1]

Fronto's note offers a window into the visually saturated world of the ancient Roman Empire at the height of its power in the second century. By the time Fronto wrote this letter, Marcus Aurelius had been selected as the heir apparent, and sculptures of the future emperor were already displayed in Roman cities.[2] Second-century audiences would have seen countless images of the imperial family in the visual landscape, in addition to depictions of gods, myths, mortals, and animals. These images were rendered in a range of media, materials, and sizes, from paintings to mosaics—but Romans valued sculpture as the highest art form, and they demonstrated a particular preference for works carved from marble.[3]

As the primary medium available to and experienced by everyone across the social spectrum, marble sculpture provided ancient Romans with a common visual vocabulary. Sculptures employed recognizable personal attributes, iconographies, and motifs to communicate everything from political propaganda to subtler messages of power, authority, and identity to the diverse audiences of a vast empire. Today, scholars look to these elements as clues to decipher the layered and complex visual language used by ancient sculptors and their patrons—especially the emperor, his family, and the elite classes who commissioned the greatest number of these works. This essay introduces some key aspects of this visual vocabulary as seen in the works in the Torlonia Collection, one of the most important and extensive private collections of Roman marble sculptures in the world.[4]

Sculpture in Roman Visual Culture

By the early second century CE, the Roman Empire encompassed parts of three continents: Europe, Africa, and Asia (see fig. 1). The empire's geographic expanse across its many provinces brought culturally, ethnically, religiously, and linguistically diverse populations under a unified rule. Most people living within the empire's borders could not read, and many also did not speak the primary languages of the administration: Latin in the west and Greek in the east. As a result, the best way to communicate with the broader population was through images, which functioned as a visual language that would have been instantly understandable to Roman audiences.[5]

Sculptures appeared in nearly every context imaginable in ancient Rome: baths, gymnasiums, libraries, theaters, amphitheaters, public forums, and temples.[6] Sculptural production reached its peak in the second century, when works were needed to adorn the new civic and religious buildings of the growing empire. Romans bedecked these structures with multistory pairs of columns, between which they displayed sculptures of deities, mythological figures, and heroes, often related to a specific theme (see fig. 2). They also commonly featured portrait statues representing members of the imperial family, local elites, and benefactors. Artworks were selected according to a building's function, following the Roman aesthetic principle of *decorum* or appropriateness.[7] A statue of Aphrodite (cat. 29), a goddess known for her birth from the sea, might have graced a public bath complex, while a work such as the Torlonia Collection's statue of a nude male athlete (cat. 54) would have been at home in a gymnasium. Similarly, a statue of Apollo (cat. 36), the god of music, poetry, and prophecy, could have been displayed in an amphitheater.

Emperors often commissioned monuments or other public sculptures to celebrate their military prowess. Emperor Trajan (reigned 98–117) successfully carried out two military campaigns against Dacia—the region north of the Danube River in present-day Romania—during his reign, after which Dacia became a Roman province. He memorialized his conquests through the construction of the Forum of Trajan, which he adorned with full-length

1 Map of the Roman Empire, about 31 BCE to 330 CE.

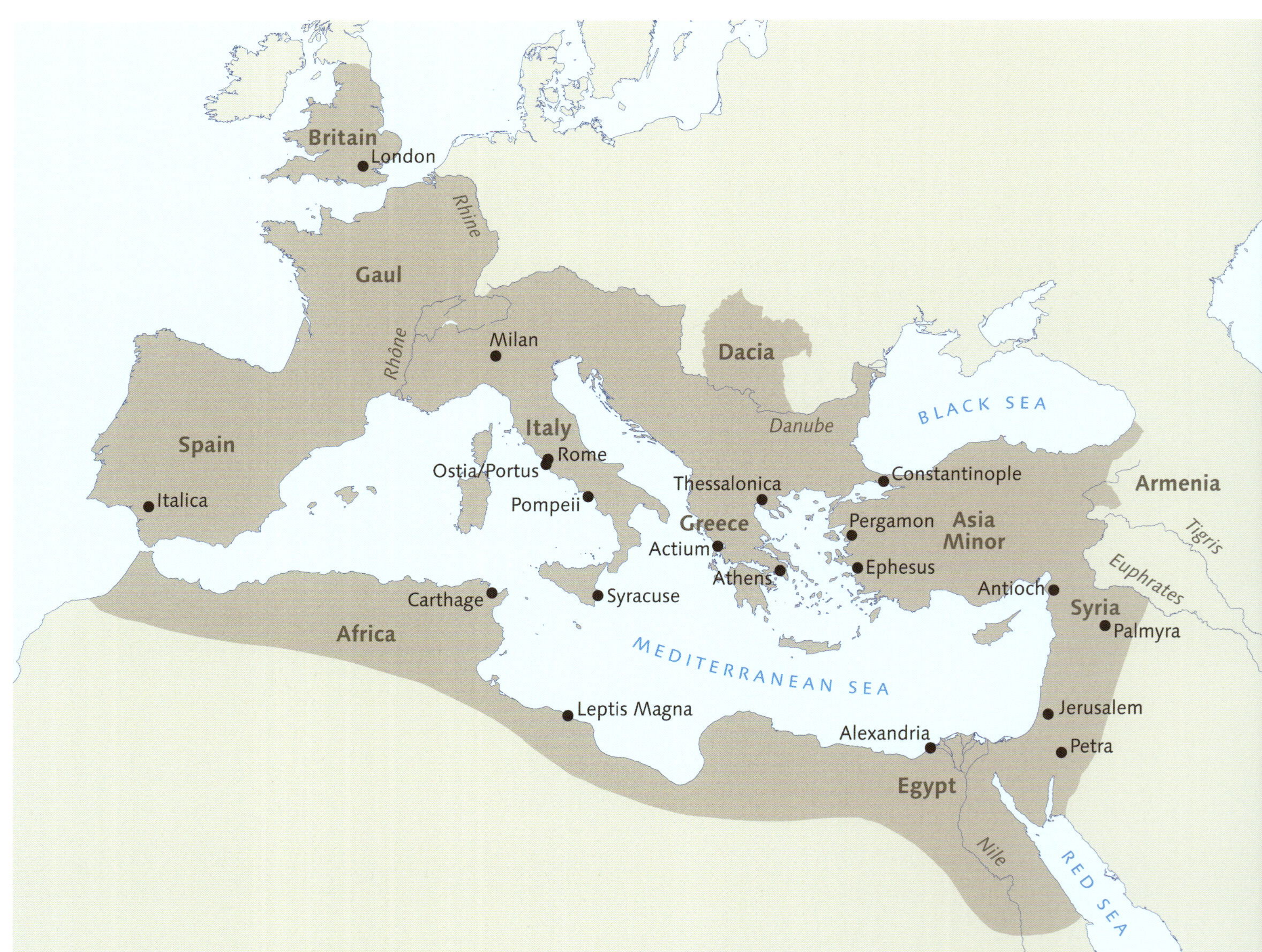

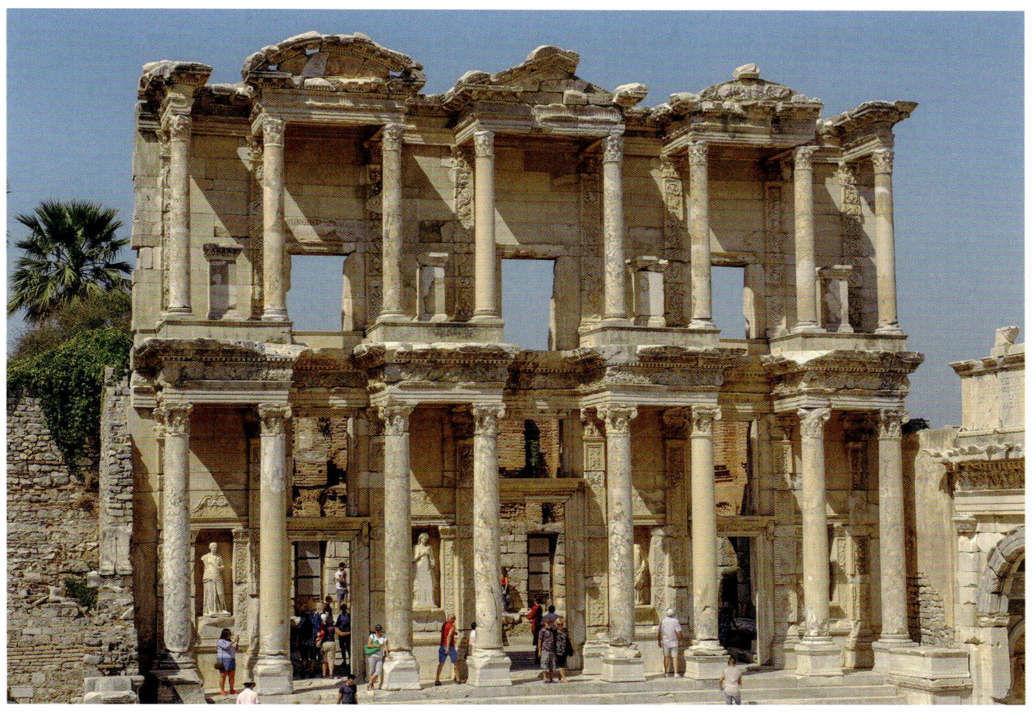

2 Sculptures once decorated the exterior niches of the Library of Celsus in ancient Ephesus (present-day Turkey).

statues of Dacian warriors. The towering statue of a male prisoner from Dacia (cat. 51) in the Torlonia Collection is unfinished, but it might have been intended to stand in Trajan's Forum.[8] The figure wears a non-Roman costume with loose-fitting pants and a soft cloth cap, and his now-missing hands were likely once crossed at the left hip to indicate his defeat. Similar sculptures of Dacians that probably once decorated Trajan's Forum were moved, nearly two centuries later, to the Arch of Constantine in Rome, where they can still be seen today (fig. 3).[9]

At home, many Romans employed small-scale statuettes of deities, typically made from bronze, in private religious practices conducted at household shrines known as *lararia*.[10] Among elite Romans, the house or *domus* was an intimate but public space where patrons would engage in social rituals, from meeting with clients in the morning to hosting banquets in the evening.[11] In a richly appointed home, sculptures in marble and bronze were part of a multimedia array of wall paintings, stucco reliefs, floor mosaics, furnishings, costly tableware, and other items through which the elite could showcase their wealth and taste.[12] Many Romans also advertised their social

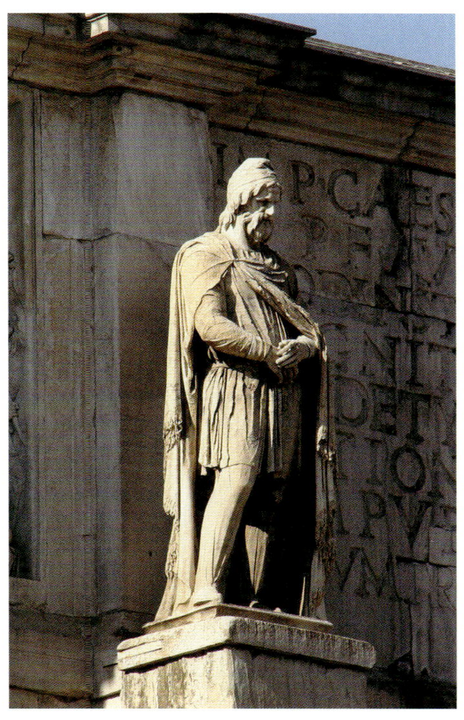

3 A statue of a Dacian prisoner on the Arch of Constantine, present-day Rome.

status through funerary monuments such as reliefs, altars, and burial containers. Such sculptures might be enhanced with portraits, dedicatory inscriptions, or mythological motifs that memorialized the dead, celebrated aspects of the deceased's identity, and promoted the reputations of surviving family members.[13]

Sculptures in stone, and marble in particular, have survived in the greatest numbers from the ancient world to today because of their ubiquity and durability. Ancient sculptors also cast some of the largest, most famous sculptures of antiquity in bronze, a prestigious and expensive material; however, relatively few large-scale bronzes survive today because the metal was easily melted down and reused for weapons, coins, or tools.[14] This historical scarcity is reflected in the Torlonia holdings, which consist of 622 works in marble and a single bronze statue (cat. 53). Compared to bronzes, large or life-size stone sculptures were usually less costly. Carving stone—while still a difficult and laborious process—required fewer raw materials than bronze casting, and marble quarries were abundant across the ancient Mediterranean.[15] Sculptors worked collectively in workshops and used tools such as chisels, drills, mallets, rasps, and abrasives to shape slabs of marble.[16] The resulting sculptures could be freestanding (carved "in the round") or reliefs, in which carved figures project from a flat background.

In antiquity, stone sculptures were often richly painted or decorated with gilding and inlays of bone, glass, or gems.[17] For example, the statue of a young woman popularly known as the "Maiden of Vulci" or the "Torlonia Girl" bears holes drilled into the sides of her head and her earlobes, which suggests she would have once worn earrings and a diadem (fig. 4). Artists used naturally available and manufactured pigments, combining them with a binder such as egg or wax for application.[18] But over the centuries, much—if not all—of this original color has been lost. Many ancient pigments and binders naturally degraded over time or were removed by caretakers, either purposefully or unintentionally, during cleaning and restoration processes. In the nineteenth and early twentieth centuries, the apparent absence of color on sculptures from antiquity led some European and North American scholars and artists to believe that the stone had been intentionally left bare.[19] This misinterpretation aligned with the prevailing biases of the era, which idealized whiteness and equated it with beauty and purity.[20] In fact, this perspective would have been foreign to ancient Greeks and Romans.[21]

Some ancient colors can still be seen with the naked eye today. Traces of red pigment are visible on the flames of the lighthouse and parts of the merchant ships in one of the Torlonia Collection's most famous works, a relief depicting the ancient imperial harbor at Portus (cat. 52). The dazzling scene, once painted with various shades of red, yellow, green, and blue, shows the ships, seafarers, and civic and religious monuments that dotted the seaside landscape in the late second to early third century.[22] Viewed up close today, the relief allows contemporary audiences to imagine themselves momentarily immersed in the image-rich world of ancient Rome.

Portraits

Many ancient Mediterranean cultures created portraits, but Romans placed a unique emphasis on portraiture for its ability to convey particular aspects of an individual's identity. Facial characteristics, hairstyles, clothing, and inscriptions offered important signifiers of one's occupation, political inclinations, social status, and religious and cultural affiliations.[23] Anyone who had the financial means to do so could potentially commission a portrait. As a result, we can see images of people from all levels of the Roman social hierarchy, from formerly enslaved freedpersons to members of the working classes and the elite social orders, placed in a range of contexts.[24] Portraits of people outside the imperial family were displayed in public spaces to honor local officials or benefactors, often for good works or public gift-giving. Likenesses of the emperor and the imperial family, meanwhile, were regularly commissioned by both the imperial house and private individuals for their own aims.[25]

From the time that the Torlonia Collection was formed in the nineteenth century, scholars have celebrated its comprehensive collection of portraits, which date from the Republican period to the end of the empire.[26] Three early examples in the Torlonia Collection stand out for their quality and rarity. The portrait of a young woman (fig. 4, cat. 1) is arguably the best-known work in the Collection.[27] Dated to the late Republic, it is renowned among art historians for the uniquely crisp, geometric forms of its idealized facial features and serene expression. A strikingly realistic portrait of an elderly man (cat. 2) wearing an unusual, wide-brimmed hat has historically been identified as a third- to second-century BCE Hellenistic ruler, possibly Euthydemus of Bactria; however, recent examinations have questioned this dating and identification.[28] Finally, another sculpture of an elderly man (cat. 3) is one of the best-known examples of the Roman tradition of veristic or realistic portraiture popular at the end of the Republic. Sculptors working in this style, which is primarily associated with male subjects, would emphasize the physical signs of aging—such as deep-set wrinkles, sagging skin, sunken cheeks, and blemishes—as evidence of an individual's experience, character, and virtues.[29] With its exacting attention to detail in rendering the man's appearance, this work embodies the traditional Republican aristocratic values of maturity and authority.

While the three examples mentioned above are among the earliest individual likenesses in the Collection, the majority of the Torlonia portraits were created after Rome transformed from Republic to Empire. Over the course of a few tumultuous years, Octavian (see cat. 4) installed himself as the first emperor in 27 BCE and ruled until his death in 14 CE. During his reign, Octavian—who became known as *Augustus* (revered one)—established an imperial artistic program carefully crafted to signal a new age of peace and prosperity for Rome. In contrast to the Republican style, which emphasized leaders' aging features, Augustus's portraits presented the emperor as unchanging and eternally youthful to convey the stability of his authority.[30] Subsequent emperors from the first through early third centuries followed Augustus's lead in their commissioned portraits, which underwent only modest physical changes as they aged.

Many of the imperial portraits in the Torlonia Collection date to the second century CE, the period generally considered to mark the height of the Roman Empire. The antiquarians Pietro Ercole Visconti and his nephew, Carlo Ludovico Visconti, compiled the first catalogues of the Torlonia Collection in the late 1800s, and some of their identifications stem from early-modern collecting practices. Inspired by other major museums in Rome, the Viscontis may have been eager to assemble a complete "set" of likenesses of the Roman imperial leaders, including the emperors' wives, sisters, mothers, and other relatives.[31] Notably, Carlo Ludovico's catalogue published in 1884–85 lists the Torlonia holdings as possessing representations of all of the second-century emperors, and he further identifies many Torlonia portraits as the wives and other key family members of the emperors from this period.[32]

Verifying the identities of many male imperial figures in the Torlonia Collection is possible because their unique visages circulated widely through coins, sculptures, and other portable objects, both to establish their

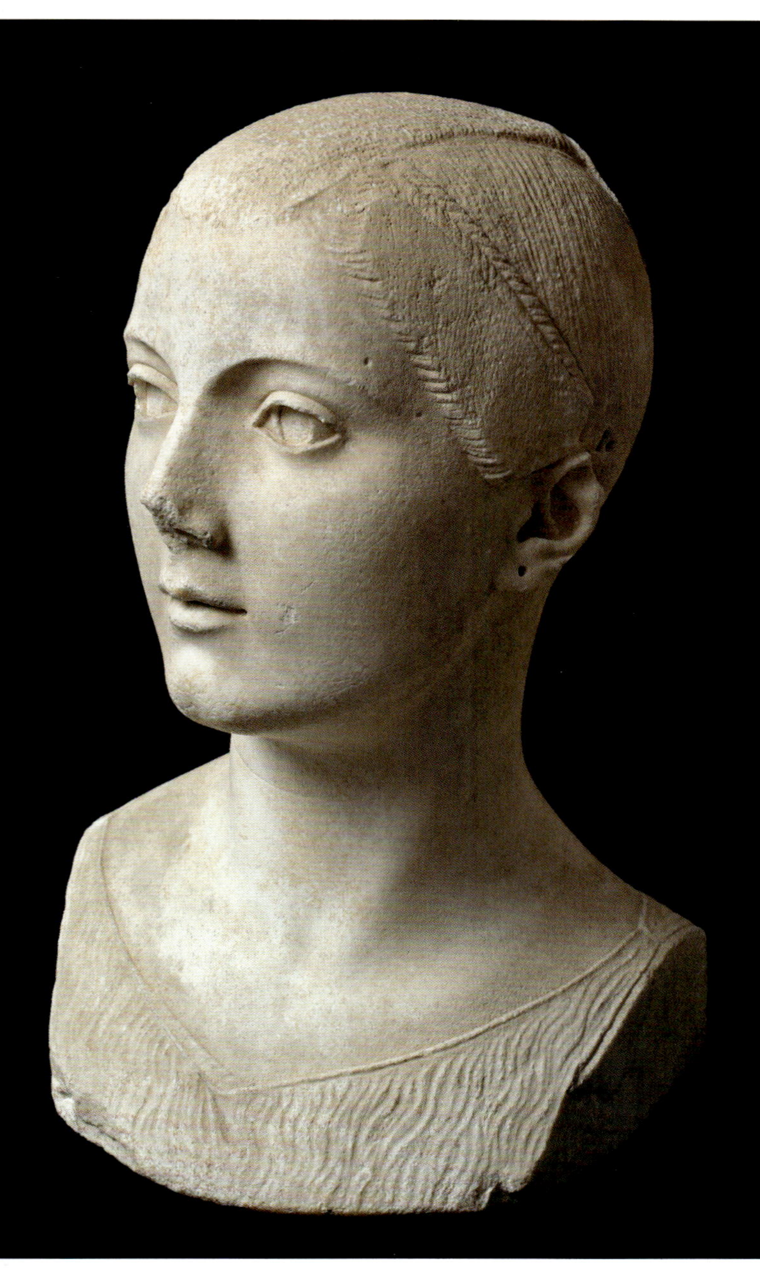

4 Portrait of a Young Woman, known as the Maiden of Vulci, mid-1st century BCE. Roman, late Republican Period. Marble; 34 × 22 × 17 cm. Torlonia Collection, MT 489 (cat. 1).

appearances for the broader population and to promote their social and political agendas.[33] The portrait head of the emperor in particular functioned as a visual substitute for his authority. The majority of the population would have never seen the emperor in person, so it was critical that his image be recognizable to viewers throughout the empire—not only during his lifetime but also after his death.[34]

Portraits of imperial women, on the other hand, exhibit stylistic and formal similarities to those of private women from their respective periods.[35] Elite Roman women were often shown with idealized facial features, including round faces, smooth skin, and wide eyes—all of which evoked the appearance of female deities. Many private women also wore hairstyles resembling those of the wives of the reigning emperors, who were known through sculpture and coinage.[36] As a result, it is often difficult to distinguish between portraits of imperial and private women.[37] This phenomenon applies to the Torlonia holdings: in preparation for the first North American presentation of the Torlonia Collection, conservation treatments and art historical research have led a number of the sculptures once identified by the Viscontis as female imperial family members to be newly reidentified as private portraits of anonymous women.[38]

This significant group of second-century portraits nevertheless offers a rare opportunity to explore the role that portraiture played in visually promoting dynastic succession and legitimizing the reigning emperor's authority.[39] Adoption was common in the Roman world, and nowhere was it practiced with more success than in the imperial dynasties of the second century.[40] When an emperor had no male heir to succeed him, he would select a candidate whom he believed would most capably rule, assuring the continuation of the empire.

Both the emperors and to some extent the women of the imperial court were influential in making these dynastic decisions.[41] There was no Latin equivalent to the term *empress* to describe the wife of the Roman emperor, as the term *emperor* derives from the Latin *imperator*, referring to the commander of the military.[42] Yet, given their proximity to the emperor, the wives, sisters, and daughters of the imperial court appear to have wielded some "soft" power that could impact the establishment and future successes of their respective dynasties. These sources of influence included prominent familial connections; personal wealth and resources, including enslaved people; and

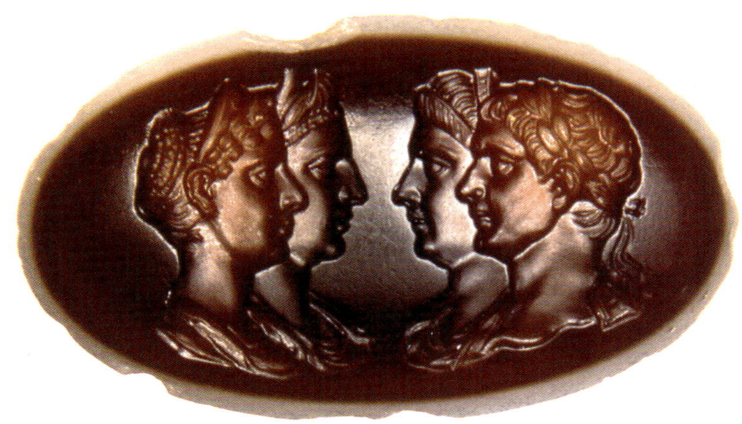

5 Cameo gem showing Emperor Trajan (right) and his wife Plotina (second from right), his sister Marciana (left), and her daughter Matidia (second from left), shown here larger than life. Roman, 2nd century. Agate-sardonyx; 1.9 × 3.3 cm. Museo Archeologico Nazionale di Napoli.

the power to sway imperial court decisions by showing support for or opposition to adoptions and marriages involving the imperial family.[43]

The Torlonia Collection includes a number of depictions of influential imperial women, as well as portraits of elite private women that were restored in the modern era to resemble the wives of emperors—another indicator of nineteenth-century collectors' interest in acquiring portraits of all the members of a given imperial family, not just its patriarch. For example, a large-scale statue of a woman in the Collection was restored to depict Plotina (see cat. 6), the wife of Emperor Trajan (see cat. 5). Ancient literary sources suggest that Plotina helped determine the succession plan for the first imperial family of the second century.[44] Plotina and Trajan had no children of their own, but they had grand ambitions to elevate Trajan's blood relatives.[45] This included promoting Trajan's older sister Marciana (see cat. 7) and her daughter Matidia (see cat. 8) in imperial imagery (see fig. 5).[46] Matidia's daughter and Trajan's grandniece, Sabina (see cat. 10), was also essential to Trajan and Plotina's plan. Around the year 100, Sabina was married to Hadrian, making him the heir apparent and connecting him through marriage to the Trajanic family.[47] Plotina may have facilitated this match even in spite of Trajan's wishes, perhaps due to her great affection for Hadrian.[48]

Through their imperial likenesses, emperors and their wives sought to resemble—or distinguish themselves from—their imperial predecessors.[49] Emperor Hadrian (reigned 117–138) (see cat. 9) deployed Sabina's image in great numbers after 128, the year he granted her the title *Augusta*.[50] A feminized version of *Augustus*, this title similarly meant "revered one" and could be granted to the emperor's wife and high-ranking imperial women.[51] Many of Sabina's imperial portraits showed her wavy locks swept into a simple, nest-like bun. Such a classicizing hairstyle diverged from the tall, crafted coiffures of Trajanic women and instead resembled those of female deities.[52] In a similar break from tradition, Hadrian distinguished himself from the clean-shaven Trajan and previous emperors by wearing a beard.[53]

Perhaps to create the illusion of a true dynastic succession from Hadrian to himself, and to legitimize his own rule, Antoninus Pius (reigned 138–161) (see cat. 11) was also portrayed with a beard, a tradition co-opted by the next several generations of emperors. The Antonine dynasty lasted for more than half a century due to a combination of adoptive and hereditary succession. Antoninus's wife, Faustina the Elder (see cat. 12), who descended from an even higher-ranking family than her husband, died in 140 during the third year of Antoninus's twenty-three-year rule. Even long after her death, she continued to be widely depicted in marble and on coins produced by the imperial house.[54] Sculptures of Faustina the Elder showed her hair parted at the center—perhaps to evoke Sabina's goddess-like coiffure—braided, and arranged in a flat bun atop her head.[55]

Faustina the Elder's oval face, round cheeks, and heavy-lidded, almond-shaped eyes are echoed in the sculpted visage of her one surviving child, Faustina the Younger (see cat. 15), who helped ensure the continuity of the Antonine dynasty during this period. As the daughter, wife, mother, and mother-in-law of four different emperors, Faustina the Younger was the mortar holding the structure of the Antonine imperial house together.[56] From a young age, she was raised to be the wife of the future emperor Marcus Aurelius (reigned 161–180) (see cats. 13–14), whose long beard in his portraits was likely intended to mimic those worn by the Greek philosophers he famously admired.[57] Just about eight years old when her father became emperor, Faustina the Younger was rendered in at least ten known portrait types throughout her lifetime; these likenesses offer the rare opportunity to consider the subtle changes in one ancient person's appearance over approximately thirty years.[58] She gave birth to as many as fourteen children, and imperial imagery widely celebrated her tremendous fecundity, particularly on coins associating her with goddesses of fertility and childbirth, including Ceres, Venus, and Juno (see fig. 6).[59]

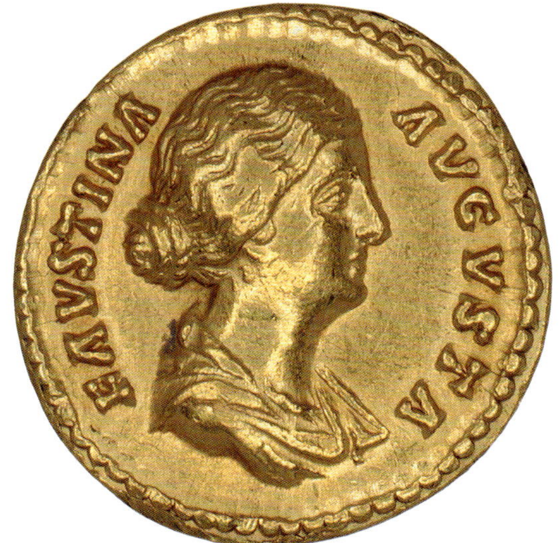

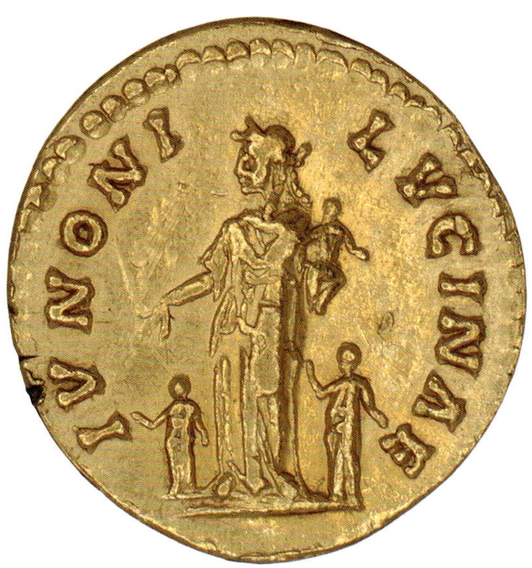

6 Many images of Faustina the Younger celebrated her fertility. This coin, shown here larger than life, includes Faustina's portrait on one side (left) and Faustina or the goddess Juno standing over two children and cradling an infant in her arm on the other side (right). Aureus (Coin) Portraying Empress Faustina the Younger, 161–75, issued by Marcus Aurelius. Gold; diam. 2 cm. Minted in Rome. The Art Institute of Chicago, gift of Martin A. Ryerson, 1922.4877.

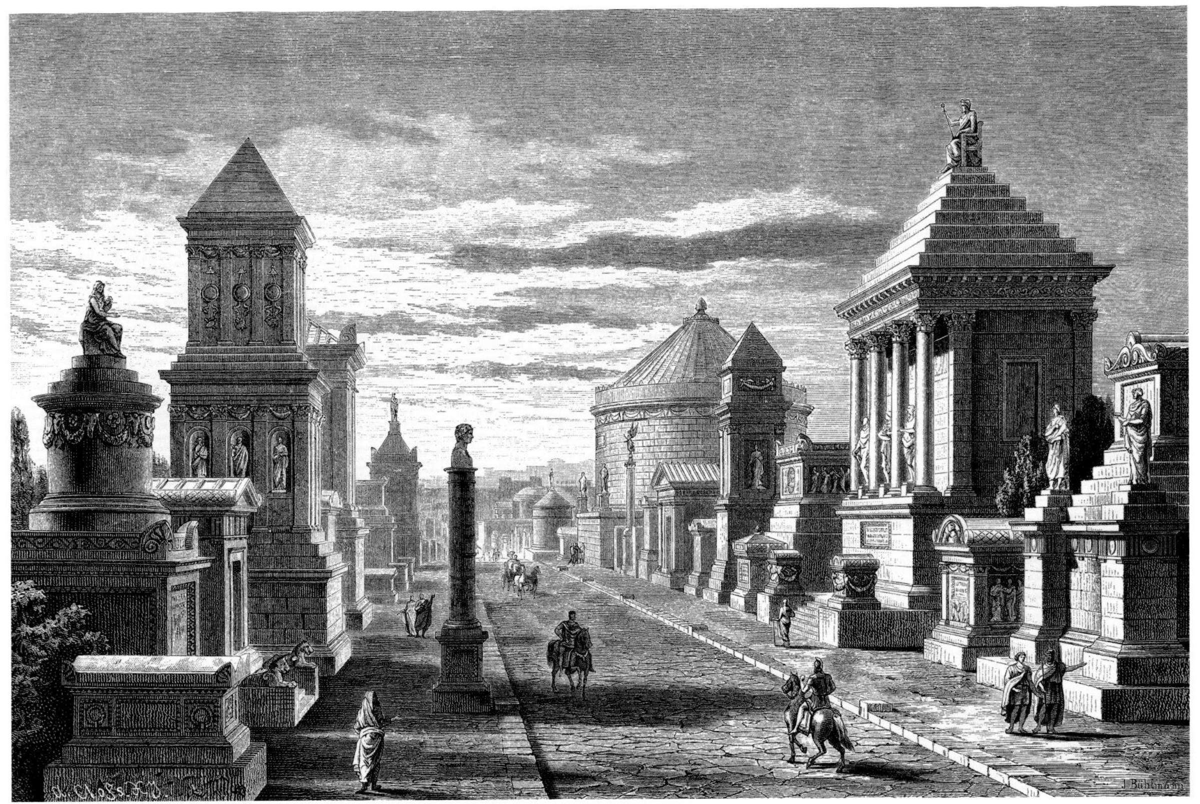

7 Funerary monuments lined the Appian Way, a major ancient road that connected the city of Rome to the empire. Adolf Closs (German, 1840–1894), after Josef Bühlmann (German, 1844–1921). *Via Appia, near Rome*, 1882. Engraving.

Only six of Faustina the Younger's children lived to adulthood, but these children still offered hope for the Antonine dynasty's continuation. Her second eldest daughter, Lucilla (see cat. 17), whose imagery closely resembled her mother, was married to Marcus Aurelius's co-emperor Lucius Verus (reigned 161–169) (see cat. 16).[60] Faustina's only surviving son, Commodus (reigned 180–192) (see cats. 18–19), became the first Roman emperor to be born "in the purple" during his father's reign.[61] Yet despite Faustina's role in this carefully orchestrated succession plan, the Antonine regime came to an abrupt end under Commodus, whose megalomaniacal behaviors, including his self-styling as the hero Hercules, led to his assassination in 192.

Following the chaotic "Year of the Five Emperors" from 192 to 193, in which multiple men vied for the throne, the Roman politician Septimius Severus (reigned 193–211) (see cat. 21) emerged on top. Born in Leptis Magna (present-day Libya), Severus was the first Roman emperor to hail from North Africa.[62] Much like his predecessors, he hoped to establish a long-lasting dynasty for his family and two sons, Caracalla and Geta. In an effort to legitimize his claim to power, Severus had himself and his sons retroactively adopted into the Antonine family in 195. This made Severus both the adopted son of Marcus Aurelius and the "brother" of Commodus, the latter of whom Severus deified in an attempt to rehabilitate the disgraced emperor's image. Visual similarities between Severus's portraits and those of the Antonine men created an intentional—albeit fictitious—family resemblance, particularly in the men's tousled curls and long, wavy beards.[63]

Meanwhile, Severus's wife Julia Domna (see cat. 22), who belonged to a senatorial family from the Roman province of Syria, initially mirrored Faustina the Younger's hairstyle; it was only later in life that Julia Domna adopted her signature wig. Much like Faustina the Younger before her, Julia Domna played a critical role in Severan dynastic planning as the mother of future imperial heirs. She therefore featured prominently in imperial imagery, which stressed such themes as abundance, dynastic unity, and familial harmony.[64] Yet the Severan dynasty came to its own unhappy end after its patriarch's death. Caracalla ordered the murder of his brother Geta in 211; he was assassinated in 217, leading to Julia Domna's death by suicide that same year.

Funerary Sculptures

Romans used sculptures to honor the departed and even link these individuals to the divine realm. Placed outside the city for public health reasons, tombs functioned like modern-day billboards. As people traveled past the city limits, they would have seen statues and monuments of varying sizes lining the sides of roads, declaring the virtues of the deceased while also advertising the social and economic standing of surviving family members (see fig. 7).[65] Funerary monuments housed the remains of the dead, which were interred in a sarcophagus (a stone coffin) or in a cinerary urn if the deceased was cremated. These structures were active sites of mourning: families would gather at tombs on birth or death anniversaries and festivals of the cult of the dead, often leaving food and flowers as offerings for the departed.[66]

Many funerary monuments not only marked someone's resting place but also recorded their appearance. One life-size group sculpture of a husband and wife in the Torlonia Collection (cat. 23) depicts an unnamed couple standing with their right hands clasped in a gesture known as *dextrarum iunctio* (joining right hands), a motif thought to symbolize marital concord.[67] Because this gesture often appears on altars, funerary reliefs, and sarcophagi, it is thought that this husband and wife adorned a sepulchral monument, commemorating the couple and the value that they placed on harmony in their marriage.

Another monument in the Collection, a large marble sarcophagus (cat. 24), depicts a deceased couple reclining on its lid. The body of the sarcophagus is decorated with scenes from the myth of Hercules performing the Twelve Labors, the nearly impossible tasks that the hero completed to atone for killing his family. The fact that the Labors of Hercules appear on another sarcophagus in the Collection (cat. 25) speaks to the popularity of this story in funerary art from the second to fourth centuries CE. The individuals entombed here or their surviving family members might have found Hercules's tale appropriate: he successfully completes the Labors through brute force, determination, and cleverness; when he dies, he joins the gods on Mount Olympus and lives among them as an immortal.[68]

Even the figural motifs on funerary monuments could sometimes contain hints as to the identity of the people they commemorated. One sarcophagus (cat. 26) features a repeated elongated "S" pattern and two lions pinning down beasts of prey: an antelope and a ram.[69] A tamer wrangles each lion, leading scholars to speculate that the tomb's original owner might have been a magistrate who organized *venationes* (animal hunts).

Other works of funerary art in the Torlonia Collection reflect the emotional value that Romans invested in their children during the imperial period.[70] A funerary monument of a boy (cat. 27), identified by an inscription as a fourteen-year-old youth named Gaius Marcius Crescens, bears a bust-length profile of the child wearing a tunic and toga, suggesting his standing as a freeborn citizen.[71] His portrait is set within a crown of wheat and fruit held by two winged cupids. As immortal children whose playful personalities often mimicked those of real human children, cupids were a fitting subject to decorate a child's funerary monument.[72] Another statue of a young girl holding a bird (cat. 39) may have likewise been created to honor a deceased child. The girl's hairstyle, which features a delicate braid that extends from the top of her forehead to the back of her skull, evokes the topknot worn by Venus and Cupid; the hairstyle might have been chosen in an effort to elevate the child from the mortal to the divine realm.[73]

A young boy playing with three dogs (cat. 38), also in the Collection, strikes a less serious tone—not least of all due to his naked, pudgy body resembling that of a wingless cupid. Sculptures of nude children, especially boys with tousled hair and in active poses, were frequently created for display in Roman homes. These playful mythical beings were meant to call to mind the mortal children of a household, who were often underfoot.[74]

Deities, Myths, and More

Often looking back to ancient Greece for inspiration, Romans sculpted deities, heroes, monsters, animals, and other scenes from everyday life—all subjects represented in the Torlonia holdings. Greece became a province of the ever-expanding Roman Republic in 146 BCE, and with this territorial expansion came an explosion of Roman interest in "ancient" Greek art that endured well into the second century CE, by which time Athens and its iconic Acropolis were nearly 700 years old. The presence of one Greek relief from Athens in the Collection (cat. 49) attests to Romans' appetite for ancient Greek art and culture. Manufactured in Greece in the late fifth century BCE, the relief might have originally functioned as a votive offering in a religious setting, perhaps even on the Acropolis. It was imported into Rome centuries later for display in an entirely different context, possibly an elite Roman residence.[75]

As the Roman Empire grew, its leaders and people began to embrace a common history that claimed a Greek cultural past and ancestry for all Romans.[76] Roman artists employed Greek styles and forms to promote Greco-Roman gods, their appearances, and their domains; in turn, these sculptures helped to codify and spread this new cultural identity across the empire. This cultural entanglement is evident in a Roman statue of Cupid and Psyche (cat. 30) in the Torlonia Collection. Based on a late Hellenistic type, the charming couple features two petite figures—Cupid, the *Roman* god of love, with feathered wings; and Psyche, a maiden whose name is the *Greek* word for breath or soul, with butterfly wings—in an intimate embrace. Some works in the Collection pay an even more direct debt to earlier Greek art: the statue of a goddess known as the "Hestia Giustiniani" (cat. 28) is a direct quotation of a fifth-century BCE Greek bronze statue.

To represent idealized or divine beings in their shared system of deities, Roman sculptors often borrowed and innovated on well-established ancient Greek conventions.[77] In their Roman contexts, old subjects could take on new meanings. To many Roman viewers, for example, the Torlonia statue group of Aphrodite and her child Eros (cat. 29) would have immediately called to mind her Roman equivalent, Venus, who was also a goddess of love and sexuality. In contrast to Aphrodite, however, Venus took on an expanded civic role for Romans as the ancestor and protector of the Roman people. The Roman general and statesman Julius Caesar (about 100–44 BCE) claimed Venus as his ancestor and prominently featured the goddess on his coins, so that her image came to symbolize Roman power throughout the Mediterranean world.[78]

Romans also linked Venus closely to martial power and to Mars, the Roman god of warfare and agriculture (and the equivalent of the Greek Ares). Venus and Mars were considered divine ancestors and protectors of the Roman people through separate foundation myths.[79] The Torlonia Collection's head of Mars (cat. 32) wears a helmet that was once adorned with images reinforcing his association with war. The remains of what are likely griffins—a symbol of the god's vengeful nature—appear in relief on the raised cheekpieces. Across the visor, the fragmentary image of an eagle, later restored as a cupid, might have evoked the eagle emblems that crowned the military standards of Roman legions.[80]

Rome's expansion also brought its people into contact with new deities outside the Greco-Roman pantheon. The presence of the Egyptian goddess Isis (cats. 43–44), identifiable by the characteristic "Isis knot" at the center of her dress, in multiple works in the Torlonia Collection attests to the popularity of this goddess in the Roman Empire.[81] Similarly, the relief depicting Mithras (cat. 50), an Indo-Iranian god of justice, contracts, and light, reflects the introduction of Mithraism, a religion that spread across the empire from the first through fourth centuries due to its popularity among Roman soldiers.[82] Mithras wears distinctly non-Roman clothing: a knee-length tunic, pants, closed shoes, and a tall, pointed cap. This relief, which would likely have been displayed in a shrine to the god, depicts Mithras slaying a bull so its blood can be used to fertilize the earth—a ritual his worshippers sometimes reenacted in his honor.

Afterlives

Not a single work in the Torlonia Collection looks today as it did when it left the ancient artist's workshop. While many twenty-first-century viewers are conditioned to appreciate the fragmentary state of ancient Roman sculpture, collectors in the seventeenth to nineteenth centuries favored complete works of art. At the time, artists regularly restored antiquities to earn income and gain experience working with sculpture, adding limbs and heads to ancient torsos (see, for example, cat. 53).[83] Nearly all the artworks featured in this publication were restored in this way, most of them before they entered the Torlonia Collection. Countless sculptors and some renowned artists, such as Italian Baroque sculptors Pietro Bernini (see cat. 31), his son Gian Lorenzo Bernini (see cat. 58), and Bartolomeo Cavaceppi, contributed to these restorations.[84] These artists often exercised considerable creative license in restorations, either spurred by their own ideas or as dictated by their patron. Sometimes modern restorers unintentionally or incorrectly altered how an ancient artwork was interpreted, as with the

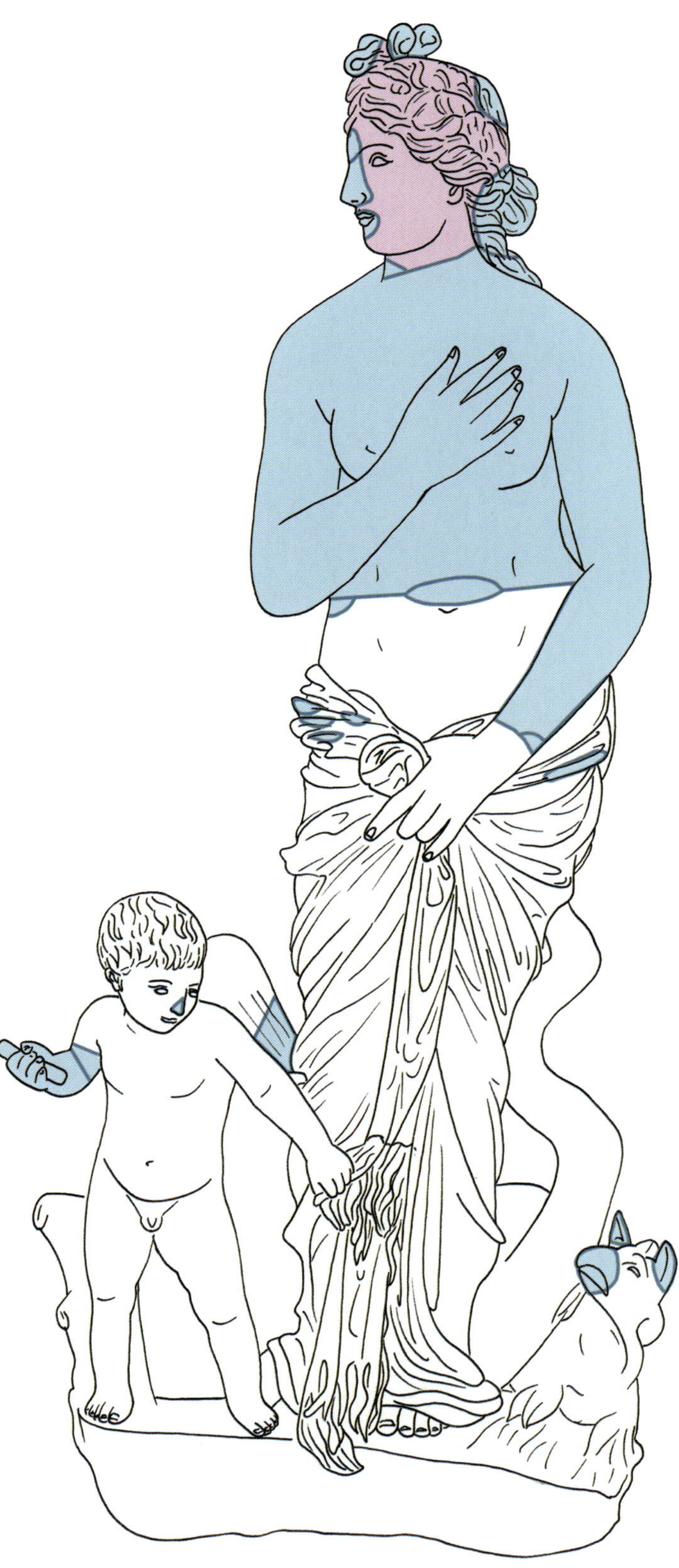

8 Conservation diagram of **Statue of Aphrodite with Eros and Ketos** (cat. 29). White: original ancient marble; blue: modern restorations; pink: ancient marble, unrelated to original.

Torlonia statue group of Aphrodite and Eros (cat. 29). The *ketos*, a serpent-like sea monster, at Aphrodite's feet would have struck an ancient viewer as odd; typically, Aphrodite is accompanied by a dolphin. Recent analysis has revealed that this creature originally took the form of a dolphin; a restorer added the ears and muzzle of the *ketos* centuries later, transforming it into a different beast altogether (see fig. 8).

Artists would also occasionally piece together an entirely new object from disparate ancient fragments, as is the case with two ornamental works in the Collection. One composition (cat. 55) consists of two separate ancient pieces, a head of Medusa and a table leg with a griffin's head—a pairing that might date to the transfer of the Giustiniani Collection to the Torlonia Collection in the nineteenth century. Its collectors later commissioned a mate for the piece: restorers affixed a modern Medusa head, a direct copy of the first work, to an ancient table leg (cat. 56). In the checklist beginning on page 140, readers can learn more about the Torlonia Foundation's ongoing conservation research, which continues to yield new insights into the storied lives that these sculptures have led in the millennia since their creation.

Notes

1 Marcus Cornelius Fronto, *Correspondence*, vol. 1, trans. C. R. Haines, Loeb Classical Library 112 (Cambridge, MA: Harvard University Press, 1919), 207, 4.12.4. For a letter date of 148, see Amy Richlin, *Marcus Aurelius in Love: The Letters of Marcus and Fronto* (Chicago: University of Chicago Press, 2007), 143.

2 Barbara M. Levick, *Faustina I and II: Imperial Women of the Golden Age* (Oxford, UK: Oxford University Press, 2014), 51–56; T. Corey Brennan, *Sabina Augusta: An Imperial Journey* (Oxford, UK: Oxford University Press, 2018), 65.

3 Peter Stewart, *Statues in Roman Society: Representation and Response* (Oxford, UK: Oxford University Press, 2003).

4 Salvatore Settis and Carlo Gasparri, eds., *The Torlonia Marbles: Collecting Masterpieces*, exh. cat. (Milan: Rizzoli Electa, 2021); Stefania Tuccinardi, *Un tesoro di erudizione e arte: Il Museo Torlonia di scultura antica* (Rome: Bardi Edizioni, 2022); Carlo Gasparri, Salvatore Settis, and Martin Szewczyk, eds., *Chefs-d'œuvre de la collection Torlonia*, exh. cat. (Paris: Musée du Louvre, 2024).

5 Jaś Elsner, *The Art of the Roman Empire: AD 100–450* (Oxford, UK: Oxford University Press, 2018), 10–13.

6 Brenda Longfellow, "Architectural Settings," in *The Oxford Handbook of Roman Sculpture*, ed. Elise A. Friedland and Melanie Grunow Sobocinski, with Elaine K. Gazda (Oxford, UK: Oxford University Press, 2015), 343–57.

7 On *decorum*, see Ellen Perry, *The Aesthetics of Emulation in the Visual Arts of Ancient Rome* (Cambridge, UK: Cambridge University Press, 2005), 28–77; Elizabeth Bartman, "Sculptural Collecting and Display in the Private Realm," in *Roman Art in the Private Sphere: New Perspectives on the Architecture and Decor of the Domus, Villa, and Insula*, 2nd ed., ed. Elaine K. Gazda (Ann Arbor: University of Michigan Press, 2010), 74–75.

8 Stefania Tuccinardi, "Unfinished Statue of a Dacian Prisoner," in Settis and Gasparri, *Torlonia Marbles*, 190–91, cat. 33.

9 Diana E. E. Kleiner, *Roman Sculpture* (New Haven, CT: Yale University Press, 1992), 213–14, 445.

10 David G. Orr, "Roman Domestic Religion: The Evidence of the Household Shrines," *Aufstieg und Niedergang der römischen Welt* 2, no. 16.2 (1978): 1557–91.

11 Andrew Wallace-Hadrill, *Houses and Society in Pompeii and Herculaneum* (Princeton, NJ: Princeton University Press, 1994).

12 John R. Clarke, *The Houses of Roman Italy, 100 B.C.–A.D. 250: Ritual, Space, and Decoration* (Berkeley: University of California Press, 1991); Gazda, *Roman Art in the Private Sphere*.

13 Björn C. Ewald, "Funerary Monuments," in Friedland and Sobocinski, *Oxford Handbook of Roman Sculpture*, 390–406.

14 Carol C. Mattusch, *Classical Bronzes: The Art and Craft of Greek and Roman Statuary* (Ithaca, NY: Cornell University Press, 1996). Small-scale bronze statuettes produced in the imperial period survive in considerable numbers from all regions of the empire. See Jens Daehner, Kenneth Lapatin, and Ambra Spinelli, eds., *Artistry in Bronze: The Greeks and Their Legacy* (Los Angeles: J. Paul Getty Museum, Getty Conservation Institute, 2017).

15 Ben Russell, *The Economics of the Roman Stone Trade* (Oxford, UK: Oxford University Press, 2013).

16 Amanda Claridge, "Marble Carving Techniques, Workshops, and Artisans," in Friedland and Sobocinski, *Oxford Handbook of Roman Sculpture*, 107–22. The unfinished statue of a Dacian prisoner (cat. 51) is still attached to a slab at its back, which is why it is classified as a relief in this volume.

17 Mark B. Abbe, "Polychromy," in Friedland and Sobocinski, *Oxford Handbook of Roman Sculpture*, 173–88. Sculptures in terracotta, stucco, colored stones, and bronze were also enhanced with coloristic effects. Scholarship on sculptural polychromy typically involves an interdisciplinary approach that combines art historical and archaeological research with scientific analysis. See Giovanni Verri, Thorsten Opper, and Thibaut Deviese, "The 'Treu Head': A Case Study in Roman Sculptural Polychromy," *British Museum Technical Research Bulletin* 4 (2010): 39–54.

18 Hilary Becker, "Pigment Nomenclature in the Ancient Near East, Greece, and Rome," *Archaeological and Anthropological Sciences* 14, no. 20 (2022): doi.org/10.1007/s12520-021-01394-1.

19 Alfred Emerson (1859–1943), the first curator of classical art at the Art Institute of Chicago, openly disagreed with this opinion. See Alfred Emerson, *Catalogue of a Polychrome Exhibition: Illustrating the Use of Color Particularly in Graeco-Roman Sculpture* (Chicago: Art Institute of Chicago, 1892), 7–8.

20 Margaret Talbot, "The Myth of Whiteness in Classical Sculpture," *New Yorker*, October 22, 2018, newyorker.com/magazine/2018/10/29/the-myth-of-whiteness-in-classical-sculpture.

21 Rebecca Futo Kennedy, *Race and Ethnicity in the Classical World* (Indianapolis: Hackett Publishing, 2013), xiii.

22 Anna Maria Carruba, "Research and Restoration of Some Sculptures in the Torlonia Collection," in Settis and Gasparri, *Torlonia Marbles*, 310–11, fig. 19.

23 Jane Fejfer, *Roman Portraits in Context* (Berlin: De Gruyter, 2008).

24 Fejfer, *Roman Portraits in Context*, 33–63, 239–44.

25 Barbara Kellum, "Imperial Messages," in Friedland and Sobocinski, *Oxford Handbook of Roman Sculpture*, 425–30; Amy Russell and Monica Hellström, eds.,

The Social Dynamics of Roman Imperial Imagery (Cambridge, UK: Cambridge University Press, 2020).

26 Pietro Ercole Visconti, *Catalogo del Museo Torlonia di sculture antiche* (Rome: Topografia Editrice Romana, 1876), 6–7; Carlo Ludovico Visconti, *I monumenti del Museo Torlonia di sculture antiche riprodotti con la fototipia* (Rome: Stabilimento Fotografico Danesi, 1884–85), vi.

27 Stefania Tuccinardi, "Portrait of a Girl," in Settis and Gasparri, *Torlonia Marbles*, 138–39, cat. 1. This portrait and the portrait of a man known as the "Old Man from Otricoli" (cat. 3) were for many years on display in Rome at the Villa Albani, thus making them accessible to scholars. See Elizabeth Bartman, "The Torlonia Marbles: Rescue, Restoration, Rehabilitation," *American Journal of Archaeology* 126, no. 1 (2022): 154.

28 Stefania Tuccinardi, "Male Portrait, Called Euthydemus of Bactria," in Settis and Gasparri, *Torlonia Marbles*, 140–41, cat. 2. On the possibility that it depicts a Roman general, see Anna Maria Riccomini, "Before the Torlonia: Antique Sculptures in the Drawings and Engravings of the Sixteenth and Seventeenth Centuries," in Settis and Gasparri, *Torlonia Marbles*, 63.

29 Stefania Tuccinardi, "Male Portrait on Modern Bust, called Old Man of Otricoli," in Settis and Gasparri, *Torlonia Marbles*, 142–43, cat. 3. On Republican portraiture, see Kleiner, *Roman Sculpture*, 31–42; and Fejfer, *Roman Portraits in Context*, 262–70.

30 Paul Zanker, *The Power of Images in the Age of Augustus*, trans. Alan Shapiro (Ann Arbor: University of Michigan Press, 1988); Karl Galinsky, *Augustan Culture: An Interpretive Introduction* (Princeton, NJ: Princeton University Press, 1996).

31 Pietro Ercole Visconti, *Catalogo del Museo Torlonia*; Carlo Ludovico Visconti, *I monumenti del Museo Torlonia*. On the inclusiveness on the series of portraits, see Stefania Tuccinardi, "The Torlonia Museum," in Settis and Gasparri, *Torlonia Marbles*, 137. See also Mary Beard, *Twelve Caesars: Images of Power from the Ancient World to the Modern* (Princeton, NJ: Princeton University Press, 2021), 122–30, 251. This "collect them all" approach may derive from practices developed during the Renaissance, when collectors were eager to assemble images of the first twelve Roman emperors and their wives.

32 Carlo Ludovico Visconti, *I monumenti del Museo Torlonia*, 386–96.

33 Elsner, *Art of the Roman Empire*, 49–81; Fejfer, *Roman Portraits in Context*, 331–69, 373–429.

34 Kellum, "Imperial Messages," 423–25.

35 See Elizabeth Bartman, "Hair and the Artifice of Roman Female Adornment," *American Journal of Archaeology* 105, no. 1 (2001): 1–25. On the similarities between hairstyles worn by imperial and private women, see Klaus Fittschen, "Courtly Portraits in the Era of the Adoptive Emperors (AD 98–180) and Their Reception in Roman Society," in *I, Claudia: Women in Ancient Rome*, ed. Diana E. E. Kleiner and Susan B. Matheson, exh. cat. (New Haven, CT: Yale University Art Gallery, 1996), 42–52.

36 However, styles that appeared to have originated among private women, such as the so-called "turban coiffure," also appear to have achieved some popularity, albeit not necessarily among imperial women. See Katharine A. Raff, "Portrait Head of a Young Woman, A.D. 130/40," in *Roman Art at the Art Institute of Chicago*, ed. Katharine A. Raff (Chicago: Art Institute of Chicago, 2017), cat. 7, artic.edu/digitalroman.

37 Fejfer, *Roman Portraits in Context*, 351–62. Fejfer has suggested that such similarities might have intentionally created connections between imperial and senatorial women, which in turn helped link the emperor to the senatorial families and other elites whom he depended upon for support.

38 See cats. 7–8, 10, 12, 17, 20.

39 Stefania Tuccinardi, "The Torlonia Museum," in Settis and Gasparri, *Torlonia Marbles*, 137. Since the Visconti catalogues were published, the identifications of certain portraits have been reconsidered, in this essay and elsewhere.

40 On the second-century emperors, see Bowman, Garnsey, and Rathbone, *Cambridge Ancient History: Volume 11*.

41 Maria Grazia Granino Cecere, "Legittimazione e partecipazione al potere: Le donne della domus imperiale durante il principato adottivo," in *Vibia Sabina: Da Augusta a Diva*, ed. Benedetta Adembri and Rosa Maria Nicolai (Milan: Electa, 2007), 39–49.

42 Levick, *Faustina I and II*, 5; Mary T. Boatwright, *Imperial Women of Rome: Power, Gender, Context* (Oxford, UK: Oxford University Press, 2021), 2.

43 Levick, *Faustina I and II*, 19–39. See also Kleiner and Matheson, *I, Claudia*; Brennan, *Sabina Augusta*; Guy de la Bédoyère, *Domina: The Women Who Made Imperial Rome* (New Haven, CT: Yale University Press, 2018); Mary Beard, *Emperor of Rome: Ruling the Ancient Roman World* (New York: Liveright, 2023), 201–5. On the idea that imperial women were still generally powerless despite their proximity to the emperor, see Boatwright, *Imperial Women of Rome*, 281–88.

44 Brennan, *Sabina Augusta*, 17–24.

45 Nicholas Jackson, *Trajan: Rome's Last Conqueror* (Barnsley, UK: Greenhill Books, 2022), 107–8. Trajan was the first emperor from the provinces; he hailed from the city of Italica in the province of Hispania Baetica (in present-day Spain). He deified several deceased family members, including his adoptive father Nerva, his biological father M. Ulpius Traianus, and his sister Ulpia Marciana, thus creating new divine lineage for himself.

46 Boatwright, *Imperial Women of Rome*, 107–9.

47 Sabina and Hadrian likely had a contentious and childless marriage. See Brennan, *Sabina Augusta*, 29–34.

48 Brennan, *Sabina Augusta*, 51–54; Granino Cecere, "Legittimazione e partecipazione al potere," 39–41.

49 On imperial female portraiture, see Annetta Alexandridis, *Die Frauen des römischen Kaiserhauses: Eine Untersuchung ihrer bildlichen Darstellung von Livia bis Iulia Domna* (Mainz, Germany: Philipp von Zabern, 2004).

50 Brennan, *Sabina Augusta*, 86–88.

51 Levick, *Faustina I and II*, 5, 34–36; Boatwright, *Imperial Women of Rome*, 2, 31–36. Augusta was an honorific title, as women were not permitted to hold political or military offices.

52 This may foreshadow Sabina's deification. On deification, see Ittai Gradel, *Emperor Worship and Roman Religion*, Oxford Classical Monographs (Oxford, UK: Clarendon Press, 2002). On Sabina's portrait types, see Andrea Carandini, *Vibia Sabina: Funzione politica, iconografia e il problema del classicismo adrianeo* (Florence: Leo S. Olschki, 1969); Eve D'Ambra, "Is Beauty Divine? A Reassessment of the Portraiture of Sabina," *Memoirs of the American Academy in Rome* 65 (2020): 132–71.

53 On the potential reasons why Hadrian wore a beard, see Katharine A. Raff, "Portrait Head of Emperor Hadrian, A.D. 130/38," in Raff, *Roman Art at the Art Institute of Chicago*, cat. 6, artic.edu/digitalroman.

54 On Faustina the Elder's deification, see Levick, *Faustina I and II*, 119–26. The Temple of Diva Faustina, the first monument to a woman in the Roman Forum, is evidence of Faustina the Elder's prominence after her death. See Margaret L. Woodhull, "Imperial Mothers and Monuments in Rome," in *Mothering and Motherhood in Ancient Greece and Rome*, ed. Lauren Hackworth Petersen and Patricia Salzman-Mitchell (Austin: University of Texas Press, 2012), 241–45.

55 Kleiner, *Roman Sculpture*, 277–78.

56 Levick, *Faustina I and II*, 61–64.

57 On the sculpted and coin portraits of Marcus Aurelius and Faustina the Younger, see Christian Niederhuber, *Roman Imperial Portrait Practice in the Second Century AD: Marcus Aurelius and Faustina the Younger* (Oxford, UK: Oxford University Press, 2022), 8–75.

58 Klaus Fittschen, *Die Bildnistypen der Faustina minor und die Fecunditas Augustae* (Göttingen: Vandenhoeck and Ruprecht, 1982).

59 Levick, *Faustina I and II*, 115–18. For a suggestion that she had as many as 15 children, see Boatwright, *Imperial Women of Rome*, 84–85. On coins depicting Faustina the Younger, see Alexandridis, *Die Frauen des römischen Kaiserhauses*, 322–41, table 23.

60 Portraits of Lucilla and Faustina the Younger so resemble one another that cat. 15 was initially identified as Lucilla; see Carlo Ludovico Visconti, *I monumenti del Museo Torlonia*, 392, cat. 557. For this portrait as an example of Faustina the Younger's eighth portrait type, see Klaus Fittschen, *Die Bildnistypen der Faustina minor*, 60–61, no. 7; Niederhuber, *Roman Imperial Portrait Practice*, 95, no. 10.

61 Anthony R. Birley, "Hadrian to the Antonines," in *The Cambridge Ancient History: Volume 11, The High Empire, A.D. 70–192*, ed. Alan K. Bowman, Peter Garnsey, and Dominic Rathbone (Cambridge, UK: Cambridge University Press, 2008), 186–87, 190–94.

62 Brian Campbell, "The Severan Dynasty," in *The Cambridge Ancient History: Volume 12, The Crisis of Empire: A.D. 193–337* (Cambridge, UK: Cambridge University Press, 2008), 1–4.

63 Julie Van Voorhis and Mark Abbe, eds., *Imperial Colors: The Roman Portrait Busts of Septimius Severus and Julia Domna* (Lewes, UK: Giles; Bloomington, IN: Sidney and Lois Eskenazi Museum of Art, 2023), 43, 128, 132–34; Kleiner, *Roman Sculpture*, 320.

64 Van Voorhis and Abbe, *Imperial Colors*, 57–59, 133–34, 136. See also Kleiner, *Roman Sculpture*, 325–26; Natalie Boymel Kampen, *Family Fictions in Roman Art* (Cambridge, UK: Cambridge University Press, 2009), 82–103.

65 Stewart, *Statues in Roman Society*, 2; Michael Koortbojian, "*In commemorationem mortuorum*: Text and Image Along the 'Streets of Tombs,'" in *Art and Text in Roman Culture*, ed. Jaś Elsner (Cambridge, UK: Cambridge University Press, 1996), 210–33.

66 J. M. C. Toynbee, *Death and Burial in the Roman World* (Baltimore: Johns Hopkins University Press, 1971), 43–64.

67 Laura Buccino, "Group of Husband and Wife," in Settis and Gasparri, *Torlonia Marbles*, 252–53, cat. 69.

68 On sarcophagi depicting Hercules, see Guntram Koch, Hellmut Sichtermann, and Friederike Sinn-Henninger, *Römische Sarkophage* (Munich: C. H. Beck, 1982), 148–49, 392–93.

69 On strigilated sarcophagi, see Janet Huskinson, *Roman Strigillated Sarcophagi: Art and Social History* (Oxford, UK: Oxford University Press, 2015). The "S" pattern resembles a *strigil*, a tool used to scrape oil off the body as a form of bathing. Scholars have described sarcophagi bearing these motifs as "strigilated sarcophagi," although ancient viewers might not have made this connection.

70 See Katharine A. Raff, "Statue of a Young Boy, 1st Century A.D.," in Raff, *Roman Art at the Art Institute of Chicago*, cat. 1, artic.edu/digitalroman.

71 For the Latin inscription and its English translation, see cat. 27. The authors thank Francesca Tataranni and Ryan Platte for their generous assistance with the translation of the inscription.

72 Janet Huskinson, *Roman Children's Sarcophagi: Their Decoration and Its Social Significance* (Oxford, UK: Clarendon Press, 1996), 105–7.

73 On the depiction of divine subjects to bestow some form of immortality on the deceased child, see Janet Huskinson, "Constructing Childhood on Roman Funerary Memorials," *Hesperia Supplements* 41 (2007), 334.

74 On cupids and divine children in Roman art, see Katharine A. Raff, "Statue of a Young Boy, 1st Century A.D.," in Raff, *Roman Art at the Art Institute of Chicago*, cat. 1, artic.edu/digitalroman.

75 Carlo Gasparri, "Attic Votive Relief," in Settis and Gasparri, *Torlonia Marbles*, 174, cat. 25. The carving of the relief lacks the crispness of early imperial Neo-Attic reliefs, suggesting that it is of earlier Greek manufacture. On Neo-Attic sculpture, see J. J. Pollitt, *Art in The Hellenistic Age* (Cambridge, UK: Cambridge University Press, 1986), 169–75.

76 Elsner, *Art of the Roman Empire*, 4–6, 12.

77 Elaine K. Gazda, "Beyond Copying: Artistic Originality and Tradition," in *The Ancient Art of Emulation: Studies in Artistic Originality and Tradition from the Present to Classical Antiquity*, ed. Elaine K. Gazda (Ann Arbor: University of Michigan Press, 2002), 1–24. See also Anna Anguissola, "'Idealplastik' and the Relationship Between Greek and Roman Sculpture," in Friedland and Sobocinski, *Oxford Handbook of Roman Sculpture*, 240–59.

78 Katharine A. Raff, "Fragment of a Statue of Venus, 1st/2nd Century A.D.," in Raff, *Roman Art at the Art Institute of Chicago*, cat. 3, artic.edu/digitalroman.

79 Katharine A. Raff, "Head of Mars, 2nd Century A.D.," in Raff, *Roman Art at the Art Institute of Chicago*, cat. 10, artic.edu/digitalroman.

80 On the griffin's association with Mars and other deities, see Zanker, *Power of Images*, 200.

81 On the veneration of Isis in the Roman Empire, see R. E. Witt, *Isis in the Graeco-Roman World* (Ithaca, NY: Cornell University Press, 1971). See also Hugh Bowden, *Mystery Cults in the Ancient World* (London: Thames and Hudson, 2010), 156–80.

82 On Mithraism, see Bowden, *Mystery Cults in the Ancient World*, 181–97.

83 Janet Burnett Grossman, Jerry Podany, and Marion True, eds., *History of Restoration of Ancient Stone Sculptures* (Los Angeles: J. Paul Getty Museum, 2003).

84 Lucilla de Lachenal, "Antique and not Antique in the Torlonia Marbles: Suggestions for a History of the Restorations from the Seventeenth to the Nineteenth Century," in Settis and Gasparri, *Torlonia Marbles*, 78–91; Tomaso Montanari, "Bernini Father and Son as Restorers for Vincenzo Giustiniani: a Venus and a Goat," in Settis and Gasparri, *Torlonia Marbles*, 92–97.

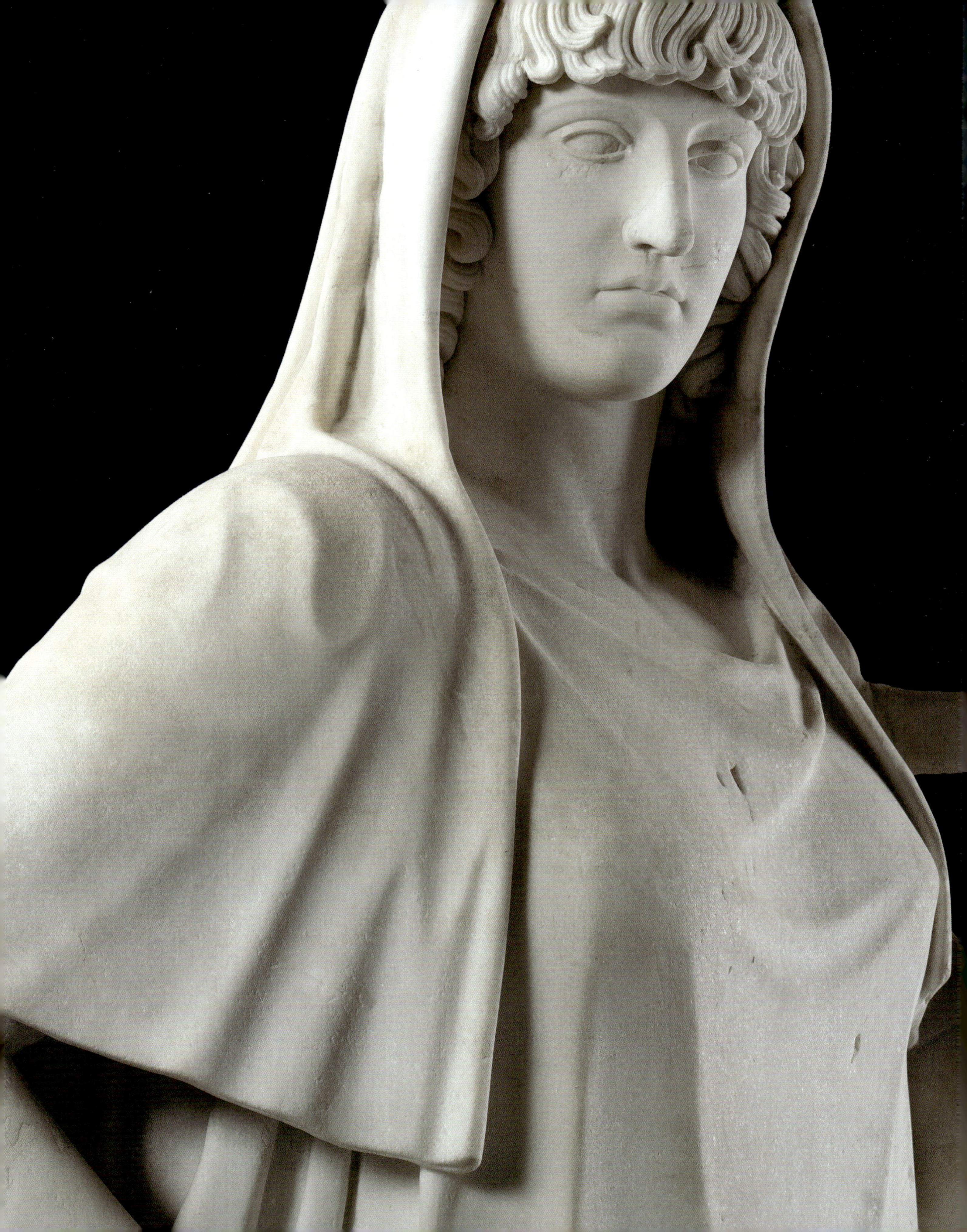

Silvia Beltrametti

TALKING STATUES: ANTIQUITY & COSMOPOLITANISM

ROME, JANUARY 2020. When I stepped into the tucked-away rooms in the Torlonia Laboratories (fig. 1), where most of the Torlonia marble sculptures had been stored for more than a century, my heart skipped a beat. In the dim light, the ancient figures seemed to come alive—and I knew that they had stories to tell that mattered.

The presentation of the Torlonia marbles in the main galleries of a prestigious United States institution is an extraordinary achievement given that Italian patrimony laws, which restrict the export of cultural property, have made it especially difficult for this type of artwork to be displayed abroad.[1] The exhibition of these sculptures at the Art Institute of Chicago is therefore an event to celebrate. By overcoming challenges to the mobility and public presentation of "high-level" antiquities, this exhibition embraces key tenets of cosmopolitanism, the theory that the free movement of art can inspire new ideas that have global resonance.[2]

The antiquities presented here enable contemporary viewers to engage with an array of global debates, among them discussions of liberty, democracy, and emancipation. Examining the meaning of these notions lies at the heart of humankind's universal experience.[3] This inquiry is a dynamic exercise: the definitions of these concepts have evolved over time and will continue to be renegotiated in the future. The real value of this kind of reflection lies in the very concept of change and reevaluation—and in that respect, the visual vocabulary of ancient Rome can provide useful interpretative lessons that span time and geography.

Let's take the issue of the integration of foreigners: an urgent matter in Roman times that also reverberates loudly today. The unfinished statue of a Dacian prisoner (cat. 51), which might have been intended for display in Trajan's Forum, prompts us to consider the Roman practice of turning defeated enemies into citizens in their quest for expansion and new alliances. This sculpture can serve as a springboard for today's viewers to ponder due process and the fair trial of war prisoners; it can also raise questions about citizenship and the integration of people from "foreign" places—two issues that are becoming more pressing as today's migration crisis intensifies across the globe. Considered in this way, this statue becomes a vehicle through which the ancient past speaks to us in new idioms.

Ancient Roman art doesn't only provide templates to think about the world; we can also use the sculptures in the Torlonia Collection to deepen our understanding of the human self. Classicist Mary Beard reminds us that examining the similarities and differences between ancient and contemporary notions of freedom does not just make us better-informed arbiters of propositions on shared power, but also turns us into better observers and analysts of our own societies. She argues that understanding concepts through the artwork and literature of classical antiquity empowers each of us to see in a different light, with the focus on the human self as an enlightened thinker and agent. Choosing the individual as the measuring unit humanizes the process by which histories are framed and allows for diversity of thought.[4]

This process expressly values individualized experiences, as everyone will assess the commonalities between past and present differently. We can look to the Torlonia Collection's exceptional holdings of imperial Roman portraits as an illustration. The sculpture of a seated Augustus (cat. 4) reveals the emperor's strategy to promote his persona and political ideology through the commission of idealized portrayals evoking his success and power—in this instance, through an association with Jupiter, the supreme god of the pantheon. Visitors living in totalitarian regimes might recognize the dangers of such propagandistic images, while others may place the emphasis on the emperor's diplomatic goals and long-term commitment to the prosperity and stability of his people. Another group may wonder about women's rights under Augustus's reign and the ability of the imperial women depicted in the Torlonia Collection, such as Faustina the Younger (see cat. 15) or Julia Domna (see cat. 22), to influence political outcomes through the exertion of "soft power."[5]

The global networks that allow for these marbles to travel around the world enable new narratives to supplement existing ones, thereby creating a broader, international approach to reconsidering history. In framing his definition of cosmopolitanism, philosopher Kwame Anthony Appiah asserts that when ideas—and their embodiments—cross boundaries, their messages are amplified.[6] He reminds us that even if the notion of world citizenship has a long history in Western philosophy, related ideas of universal brotherhood and sisterhood have existed in many continents throughout time. One of the first attempts to define *cosmopolitanism* occurred at the time that many of the pieces in the Torlonia Collection were created, around the second century CE. As Marcus Aurelius, the second-century emperor and dedicated student of Greek philosophy, wrote: "A human being has

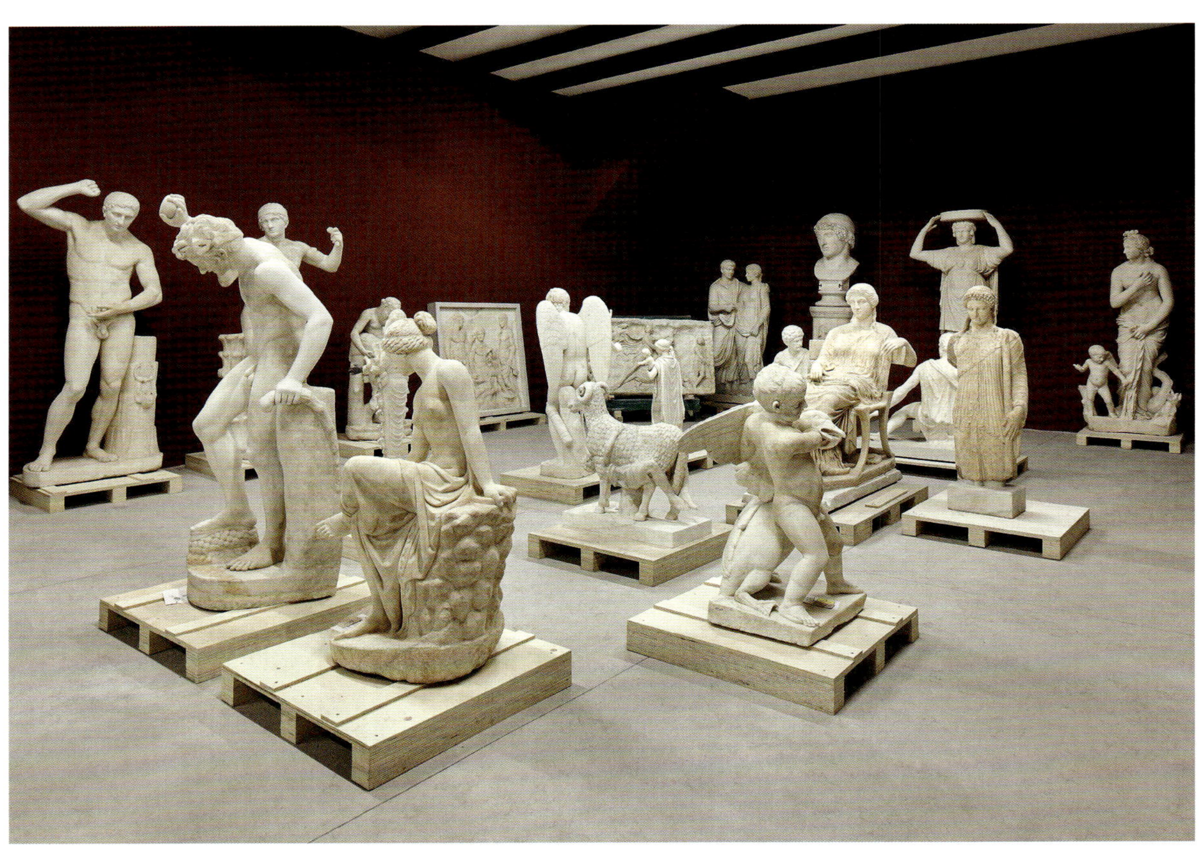

1 Sculptures on display at the Torlonia Laboratories, Rome, Italy.

close kinship with all of humanity—not a bond of blood or seed, but a community of the spirit." He further implied that as concepts translate across societies, intimate connections are made that support the broader human need for answers to questions about justice, identity, and freedom.[7]

The idea of accessing a foreign culture through its art resonates strongly with the Torlonia marbles. Romans extensively collected and reinterpreted artwork from Greece. Greek marble sculptures were extremely sought after and often copied in Republican Rome and the Empire because of their aesthetic qualities as well as their engagement with themes of virtue and morality.[8] Greek artworks reached Rome either as war loot or as the result of market forces. Motivated by financial rewards and other opportunities, Greek artists moved their workshops to Rome in the same way that contemporary artists might relocate today.[9] By the first century CE, during the late Republican period, Rome had a busy art market fueled by local and foreign demand, complete with professional dealers, appraisers, and auctioneers, as well as forgers and copyists.[10]

Many of the sculptures in the Torlonia Collection date from that key window between the first and second century, which coincides with the peak of marble carving in ancient Rome; but the Collection as a whole spans the fifth century BCE to the second half of the fourth century CE. Alessandro Poma Murialdo, the president of the Torlonia Foundation, describes its accumulation as "a collection of collections"—with Rome as a common denominator, anchored in two and a half millennia of cultural stratification.[11] The monumental statue of a goddess known as the "Hestia Giustiniani" (fig. 2, cat. 28) testifies to the former notion by carrying the very name of the prestigious seventeenth-century collection to which it once belonged. This astonishing work was also praised by the revered German art historian Johann Joachim Winckelmann in his foundational 1764 publication *History of the Art of Antiquity*.[12]

The oldest sculpture in the exhibition, an ancient Greek relief (cat. 49) dating to the late fifth century BCE, testifies to the fact that artworks traveled in antiquity. The marble relief depicts a votive scene with a young man bringing offerings to deities at a temple in the acropolis of Athens. It is thought to have been discovered in excavations sponsored by the Torlonia Family in the 1820s in the environs between the Villa of Maxentius and the Mausoleum of Caecilia Metella along the Appian Way, in the former site of a villa owned by the second-century Athenian rhetorician Herodes Atticus.[13] A friend of

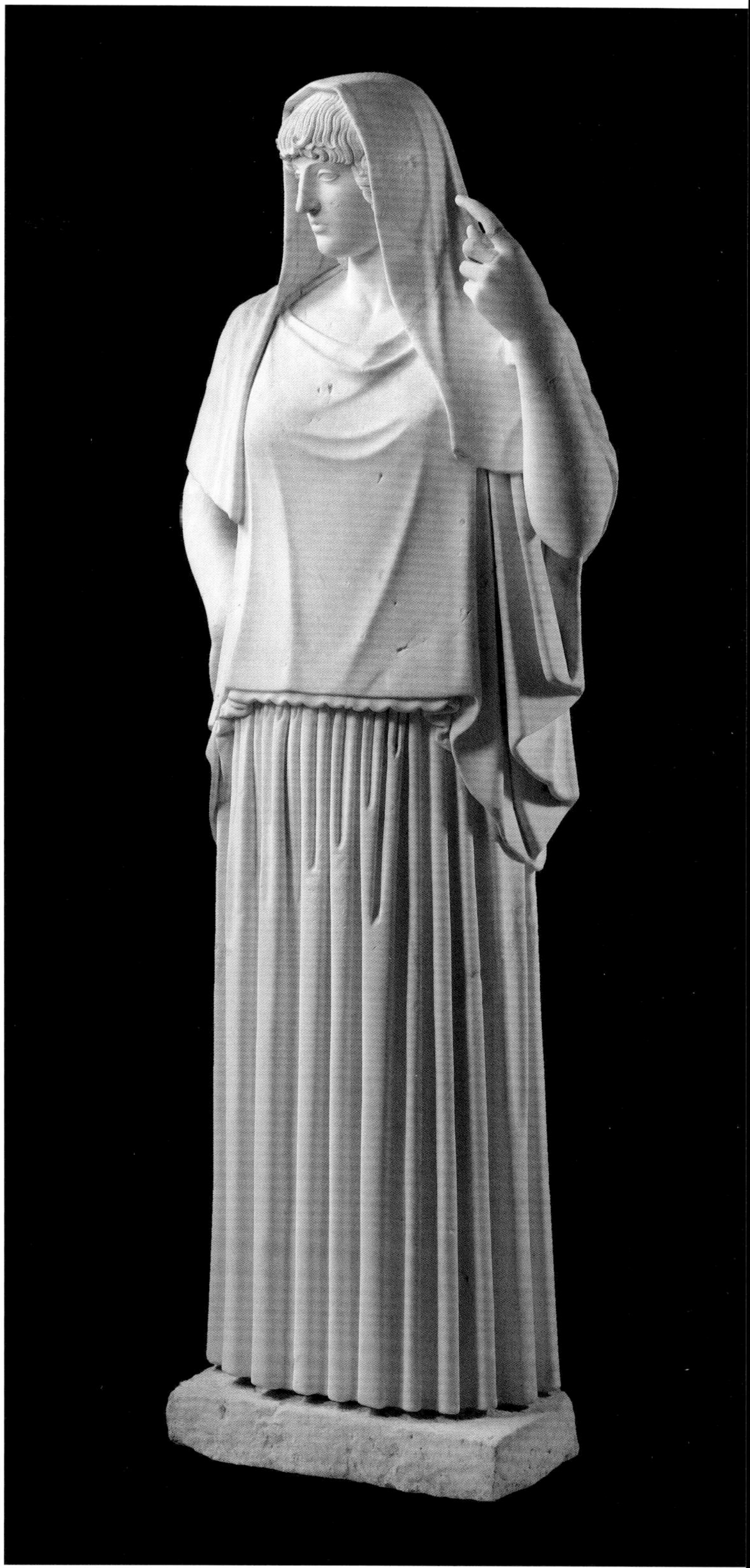

2 Statue of a Goddess, known as the Hestia Giustiniani, first half of 2nd century. Roman, Imperial Period. Marble; 200 × 78 × 53 cm. Torlonia Collection, MT 490 (cat. 28).

Emperor Antoninus Pius (see cat. 11) and the tutor of future emperors Marcus Aurelius (see cats. 13–14) and Lucius Verus (see cat. 16), Atticus may have imported the relief from Athens when he established a residence in Rome to attend to his duties as a senator.[14] Atticus's high-ranking status and wealth would have allowed him to possess and transport this heavy marble relief from Athens to Rome.

The figurative elements of the Torlonia marbles connect us with a visual culture that is not fundamentally different from the one we live in today.[15] Famously, the first-century CE Roman author Pliny the Elder recounts a competition between two prominent Greek painters in the fifth century BCE: Parrhasius and his rival Zeuxis. The artists are called upon to uncover their work publicly in the Athens agora. Zeuxis unveils his painting first, and his depiction of grapes is so realistic that birds fly down and attempt to peck them. When Parrhasius is asked to lift his curtain, however, it becomes apparent that the curtain *was* the artwork: he had rendered a curtain in paint so skillfully that every spectator, including Zeuxis, had been deceived.[16] Illustrations of illusion in art have defined many great artists since, and the tradition has become embedded in our visual culture.

Several examples in the Collection illustrate this paradigm, such as the portrait once identified as Euthydemus of Bactria (cat. 2) and the portrait bust known as the "Old Man of Otricoli" (cat. 3). Both men's likenesses are crafted with such detail that one could imagine them winking and talking. The men's lifelike features and distinctive physical traits also suggest that the artists who sculpted these works were free to exert their creativity and make aesthetic choices. Most sculptures representing emperors and deities adhered to set archetypes and a visual vocabulary that was primarily the product of political strategies: the subject had to be easily recognizable. But when ancient Roman artists worked on private commissions, they were often allowed to unleash their creative skills. The iconic portrait in the Torlonia Collection, known as the "Torlonia Girl" or *la fanciulla di Vulci* in Italian (the maiden of Vulci) (cat. 1), is yet another example that attests to a dimension of freedom of expression present in ancient Rome. Freedom of artistic expression is not only a key criterion of art making today, but also a fundamental value of a cosmopolitanism that celebrates differences in imagination.

Finally, by building links across peoples, times, and places, the Torlonia Collection stimulates conversation about the legitimate ownership of antiquities, a hotly debated topic. Views in this field tend to split in two ways: cultural nationalists acknowledge the decision-making power of sovereign states and maintain that antiquities should remain in the countries where they are excavated; on the other hand, internationalists, often speaking on behalf of collecting institutions, insist that global diasporas require a perspective that can accommodate the movement of people and objects across borders.[17] This international exhibition of the Torlonia marble sculptures illustrates that a golden mean is not only possible but sustainable: when the owners of these unique pieces allow them to circulate freely, the powerful stories they tell can spread exponentially and become the property of humankind. And from that, it becomes clear that all citizens of the world, equally, have an interest in accessing ancient material to explore our common past in order to engage with the present more meaningfully.

Allowing for ownership rights and temporary possession to coexist fosters a true cosmopolitanism that celebrates universality by protecting the integrity of the artworks and emphasizing universal access to these collections. These marbles are much more than an exquisite feast for the eye: they also illustrate how the past informs who we are today, and their relevance to the important questions of our time makes it even more crucial that people across the globe can connect with these works and the shared heritage that these marbles embody. I am overjoyed to bear witness to the stories that these statues will tell as they travel around the world.

Notes

1 Italy, Code of the Cultural and Landscape Heritage, Legislative Decree no. 42 (2004), articles 66 and 67. See also Silvia Beltrametti, "Museum Strategies: Leasing Antiquities," *Columbia Journal of Law and the Arts* 36, no. 2 (2013).

2 James Cuno, *Whose Culture?: The Promise of Museums and the Debate over Antiquities* (Princeton, NJ: Princeton University Press, 2009). See also Kwame Anthony Appiah, "Who Are We? Identity and Cultural Heritage," and Neil MacGregor, "Why Do We Value Cultural Heritage?," both in *Cultural Heritage and Mass Atrocities*, ed. James Cuno and Thomas G. Weiss (Los Angeles: Getty Publications, 2022), 27–58.

3 Kathleen Wren Christian, *Empire Without End: Antiquities Collections in Renaissance Rome, c. 1350–1527* (New Haven, CT: Yale University Press, 2010); Susan Jaques, *The Caesar of Paris: Napoleon Bonaparte, Rome, and the Artistic Obsession that Shaped an Empire* (New York: Pegasus Books, 2020); Erin L. Thompson, *Possession: The Curious History of Private Collectors from Antiquity to the Present* (New Haven, CT: Yale University Press, 2016).

4 Mary Beard, "What Can We Learn from the Classics?," Berlin Family Lectures, University of Chicago, Chicago, IL, April 20, 25, and 26, 2023. See also Mary Beard, *SPQR: A History of Ancient Rome* (New York: Liveright, 2015).

5 Kristina Milnor, *Gender, Domesticity, and the Age of Augustus: Inventing Private Life* (Oxford, UK: Oxford University Press, 2008).

6 Kwame Anthony Appiah, "Whose Culture Is It, Anyway?," in *Cosmopolitanism: Ethics in a World of Strangers* (New York: W. W. Norton, 2006), 115–36.

7 Marcus Aurelius, *M. Antonius Imperator Ad Se Ipsum*, ed. Jan Hendrik Leopold (E. Typographeo Clarendoniano: 1908), 12.26.

8 Salvatore Settis, "Supremely Original: Classical Art as Serial, Iterative, Portable," in *Serial / Portable Classic*, ed. Salvatore Settis, Anna Anguissola, and Davide Gasparotto (Milan: Fondazione Prada, 2015). See also Margarete Bieber, *Ancient Copies, Contributions to the History of Greek and Roman Art* (New York: New York University Press, 1977).

9 See Jaś Elsner, *The Art of the Roman Empire: AD 100–450*, Oxford History of Art (Oxford, UK: Oxford University Press, 2018).

10 Elsner, *Art of the Roman Empire*. See also H. Anne Weis, "Gaius Verres and the Roman Art Market: Consumption and Connoisseurship in Late Republican Rome," in *O tempora, O mores: Römische Werte und römische Literatur in den letzten Jahrzehnten der Republik*, Beiträge zur Altertumskunde 171, ed. A. Haltenhoff, A. Heil, and F. H. Mutschler (Berlin: B. G. Teubner, 2003): 355–400.

11 Arianna Antoniutti, "Come noi Torlonia curiamo i nostri celebri marmi," *Giornale dell'arte*, June 8, 2024, ilgiornaledellarte.com/articolo/come-noi-Torlonia-curiamo-i-nostri-celebri-marmi.

12 Johann Joachim Winckelmann, *History of the Art of Antiquity*, trans. Harry Francis Mallgrave (Los Angeles: Getty Publications, 2006), 236.

13 See Stefania Tuccinardi, "Torlonia Excavations," and Carlo Gasparri, "Attic Votive Relief," cat. 25, in *The Torlonia Marbles: Collecting Masterpieces*, ed. Salvatore Settis and Carlo Gasparri, exh. cat. (Milan: Rizzoli Electa, 2021), 171–72, 174.

14 Gasparri, "Attic Votive Relief," 174. The relief is said to come from near the Tomb of Caecilia Metella, given the history of the Torlonia Family's land assets; however, this information cannot be confirmed.

15 For context see Elsner, *Art of the Roman Empire*, and Jaś Elsner, *Roman Eyes: Visuality and Subjectivity in Art and Text* (Princeton, NJ: Princeton University Press, 2007).

16 Pliny the Elder, *Natural History*, trans. John Bostock (London: Taylor and Francis, 1855), book 35.

17 The "nationalist" versus "internationalist" debate was introduced by the seminal paper of John Henry Merryman, "Two Ways of Thinking About Cultural Property," *American Journal of International Law* 80, no. 4 (Oct. 1986), 831. For representative arguments on the internationalist side, see James Cuno, *Who Owns Antiquity?: Museums and the Battle Over Our Ancient Heritage* (Princeton, NJ: Princeton University Press, 2010). For representative arguments on the side of nationalists, see *Trade in Illicit Antiquities: The Destruction of the World's Cultural Heritage*, ed. Neil Brodie, Jennifer Doole, and Colin Renfrew (Cambridge, UK: McDonald Institute for Archaeological Research, 2001).

PORTRAITS

A YOUNG WOMAN gazes up and slightly to the right with a serene expression. She is depicted with idealized facial features, including an oval face with round cheeks; wide, almond-shaped eyes; and a small mouth with bow-shaped lips. Her arched eyebrows, which gently extend into the bridge of her nose, indicate that the sculptor who created this work may have been influenced by the crisply modeled features of ancient Greek bronze sculpture. The intricate, individual folds of the fabric visible below her neck suggest a finely woven, diaphanous garment.

This portrait, a rare example of late Republican-era female portraiture, is an elegant likeness created by a highly skilled sculptor. Today, however, the work is missing certain elements that would have enhanced its lifelike appearance in antiquity. The figure's delicately carved locks of hair are pulled into a flat bun, but parts of the top and sides of her hairstyle were intentionally left unfinished to accommodate a now-missing hair ornament. Presumably made of metal and embellished with gold leaf and gemstones, it would have been affixed to the head using the holes drilled behind the ears. Holes in the earlobes indicate that this sculpture originally wore earrings made of similarly expensive materials. Her eyes would have been enhanced with inlays of glass, ivory, bone, or rock crystal to create a more individualized likeness.

A wealthy family likely commissioned this costly portrait to honor the young woman, demonstrating her family's love and affection for her as well as their own wealth and social standing. Although the portrait's original display context remains unknown, it might have been created for a tomb setting, perhaps to commemorate the subject's passing before she had reached marriageable age. Alternatively, it might have appeared in a domestic or sacred context, perhaps displayed alongside the likenesses of other distinguished family members.

1

Portrait of a Young Woman, known as the Maiden of Vulci

Mid-1st century BCE

Marble; H. 34 cm

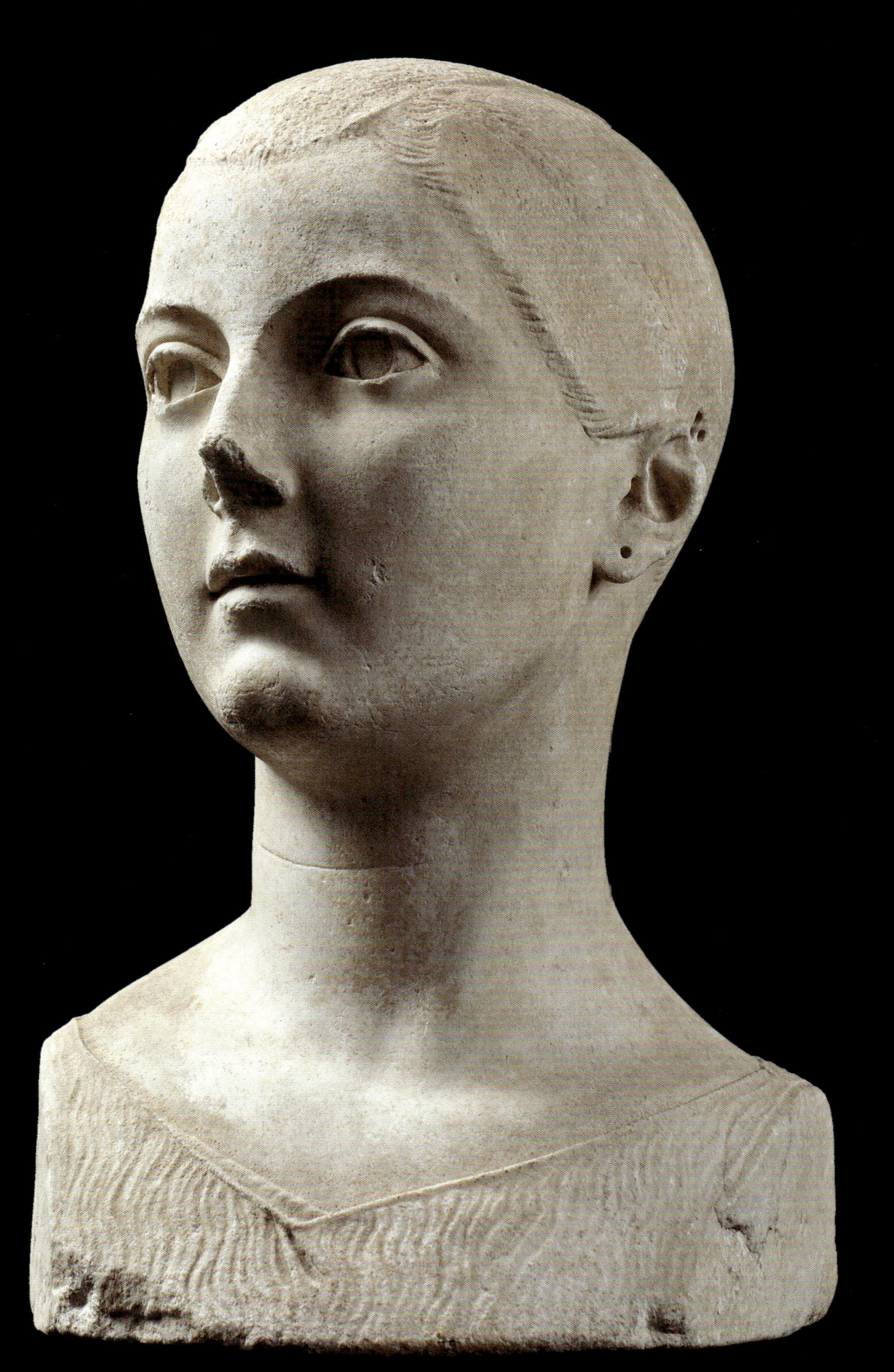

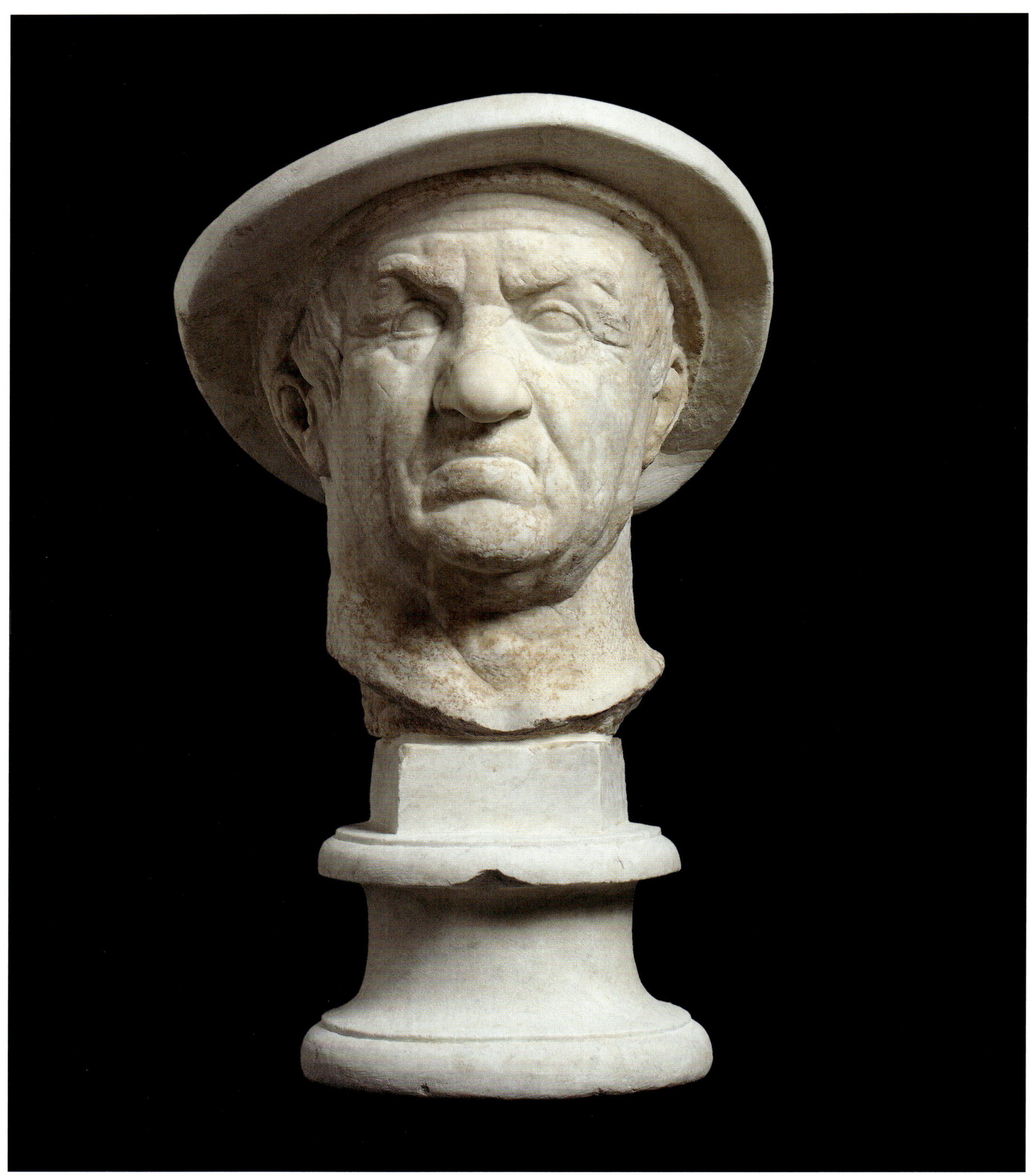

2
Portrait of a Man, known as Euthydemus of Bactria
Late 3rd–early 2nd century BCE
Marble; H. 55 cm

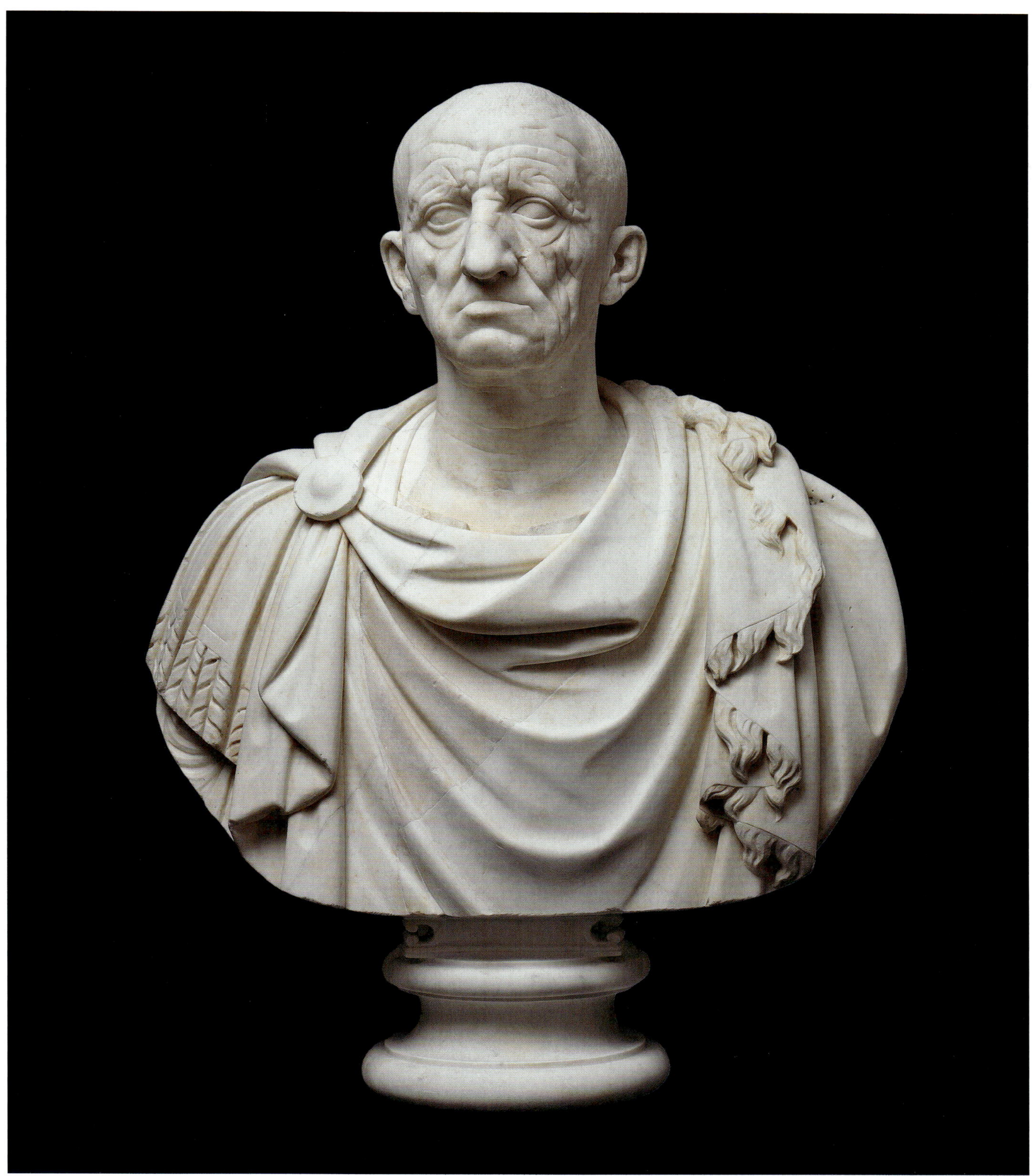

3
Portrait of a Man, known as the Old Man of Otricoli
Mid-1st century BCE
Marble; H. 78 cm

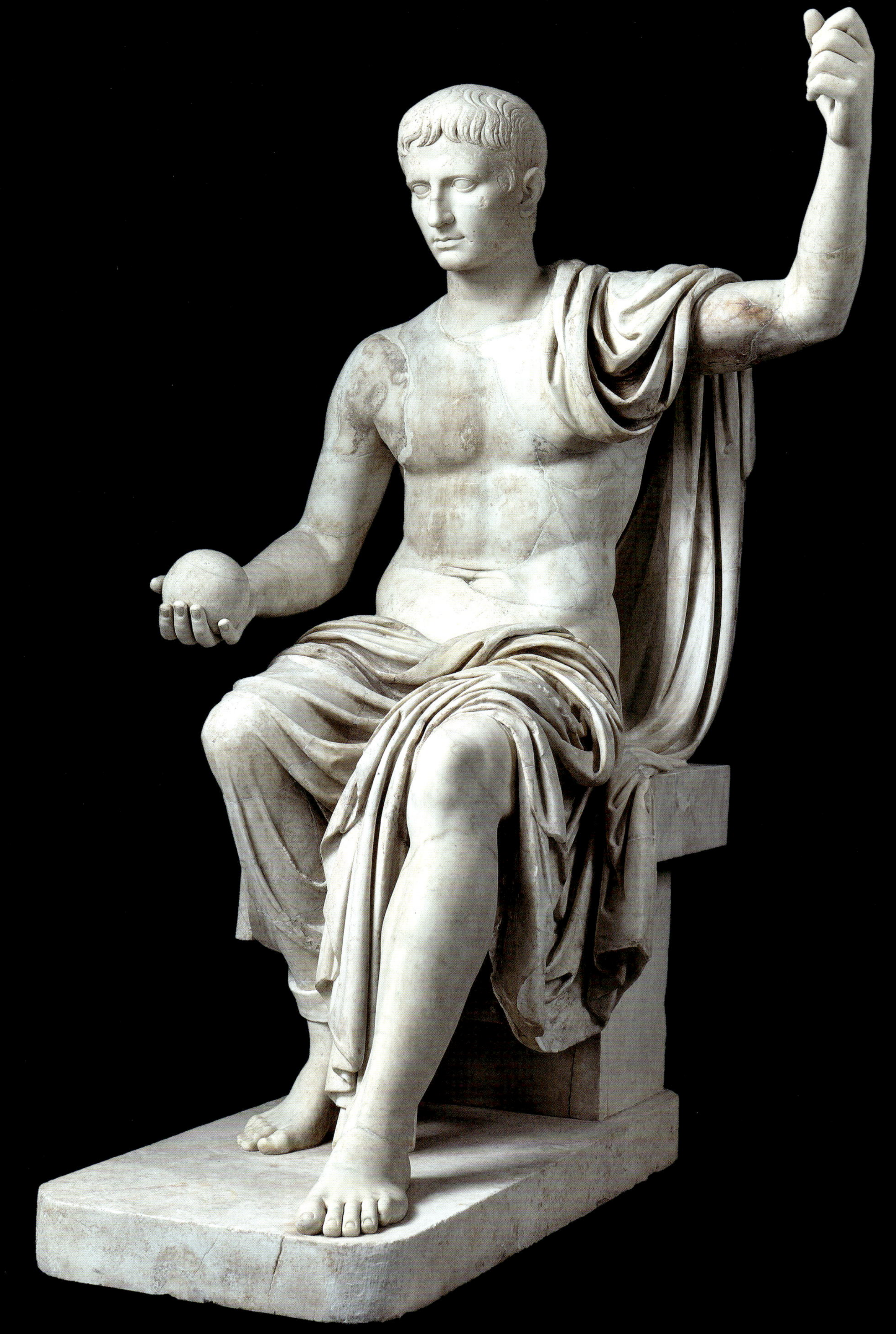

AN EMPEROR sits on a throne, partially nude, with a mantle covering his lower body and left shoulder. This iconography can be traced to a fifth-century BCE statue of the Greek god Zeus at the sanctuary of Olympia; the same pose and symbols were later employed in images of Jupiter, the supreme deity of the Roman pantheon. Recent conservation work tells us that the portrait head of Augustus, the first Roman emperor, was added to this ancient body in modern times. Although we don't know the statue's original identity, its restorers likely chose Augustus as the new subject because he is one of the few emperors known to have been depicted in a seated pose in ancient sculpture.

In 27 BCE, the Senate granted Octavian two titles that would forever alter the course of Roman government. The first title, *Princeps* (first), suggested that he was first among his fellow citizens. The second title, *Augustus* (revered one), was subsequently used as his name and was later adopted by his successors as the emperor's primary title.

Augustus was the first of the emperors to be shown in such a costume and pose, which would have made an explicit visual statement to Roman viewers about the emperor's supreme power, equating his rule over the empire to that of Jupiter over the cosmos. Such a declaration made through the public display of a statue of this type would have clearly contradicted Augustus's own attempts to present himself as "first among equals"; in his lifetime, he carefully crafted his image and persona to avoid the appearance of elevating or aggrandizing himself as a ruler. For this reason, the few portraits of seated Augustus that survive today are thought to have been created after his death and deification, when allusions to his divine authority would have been entirely appropriate.

4
Statue of an Emperor on a Throne with a Portrait of Augustus
1st century
Marble; 164 × 51 × 101 cm

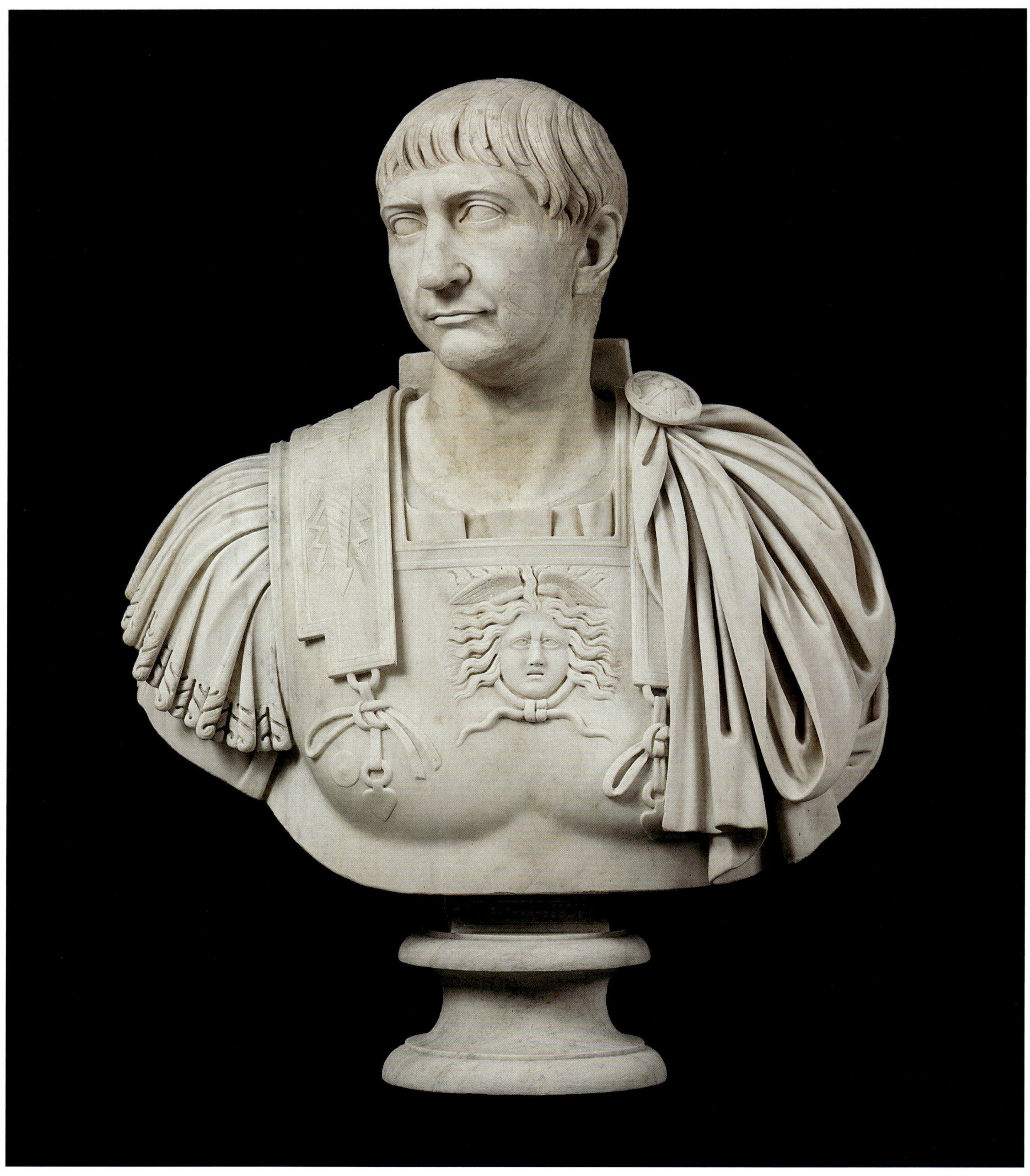

5
Portrait of Trajan
17th–18th century
Marble; H. 85 cm

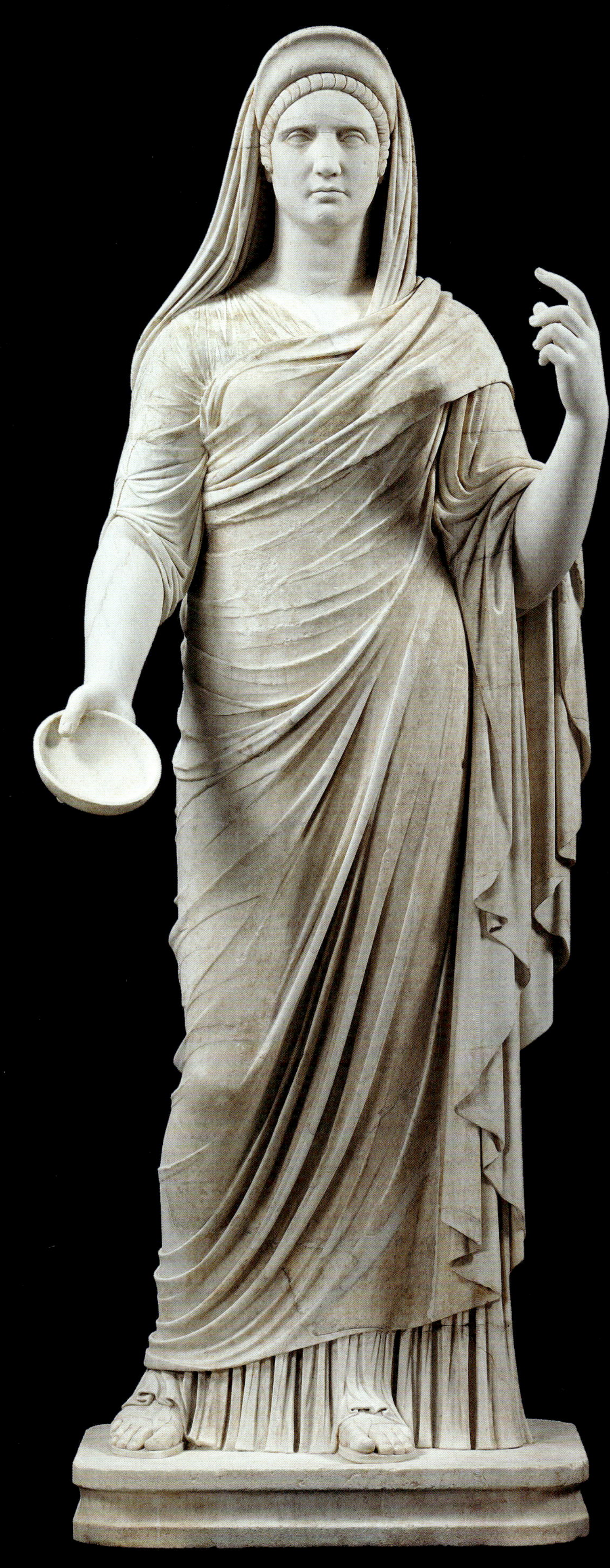

6
Statue of a Woman, restored as Plotina
Late 1st–early 2nd century
Marble; 206 × 78 × 81 cm

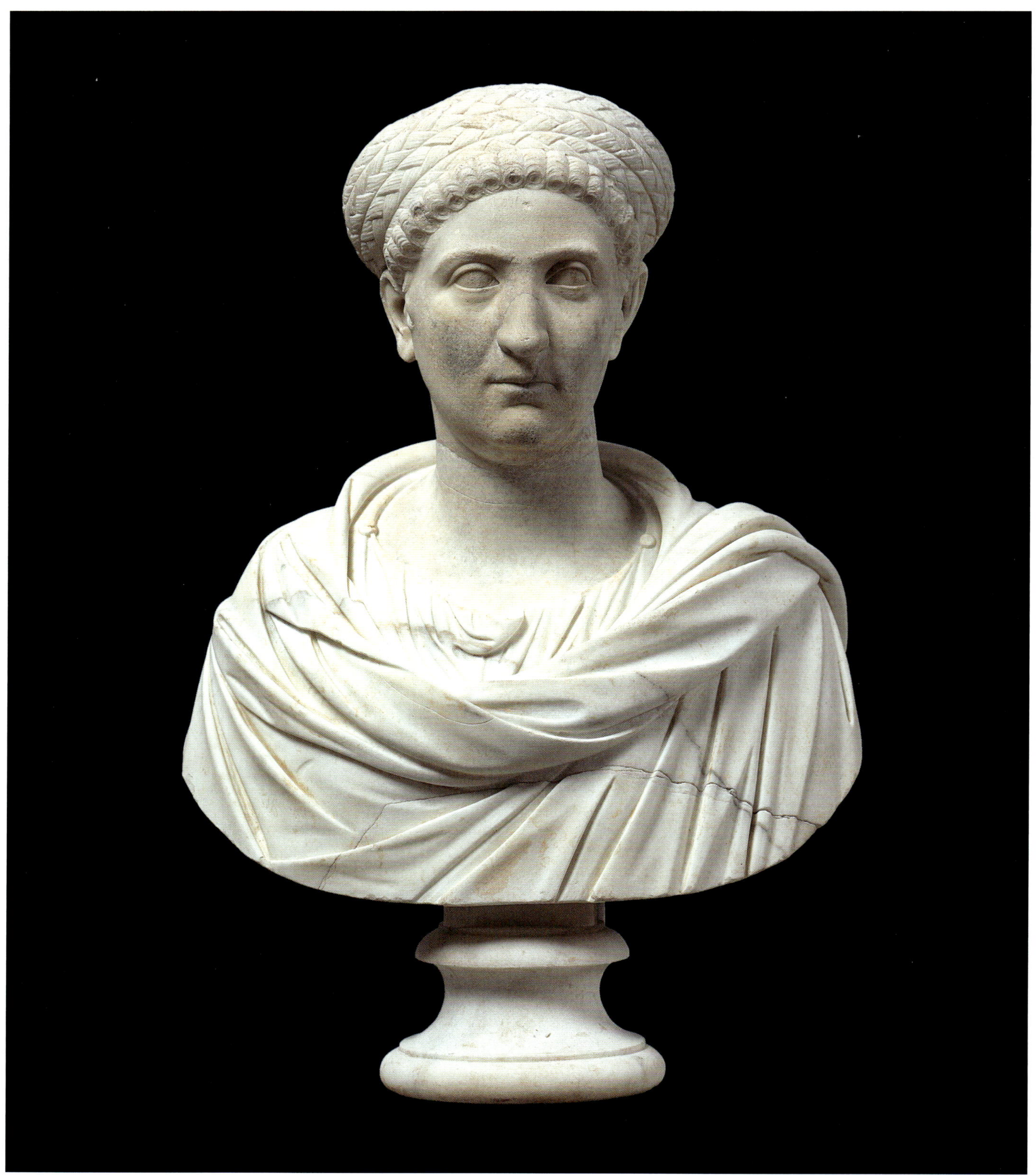

7
Portrait of a Woman, formerly known as Marciana
120–30
Marble; H. 63 cm

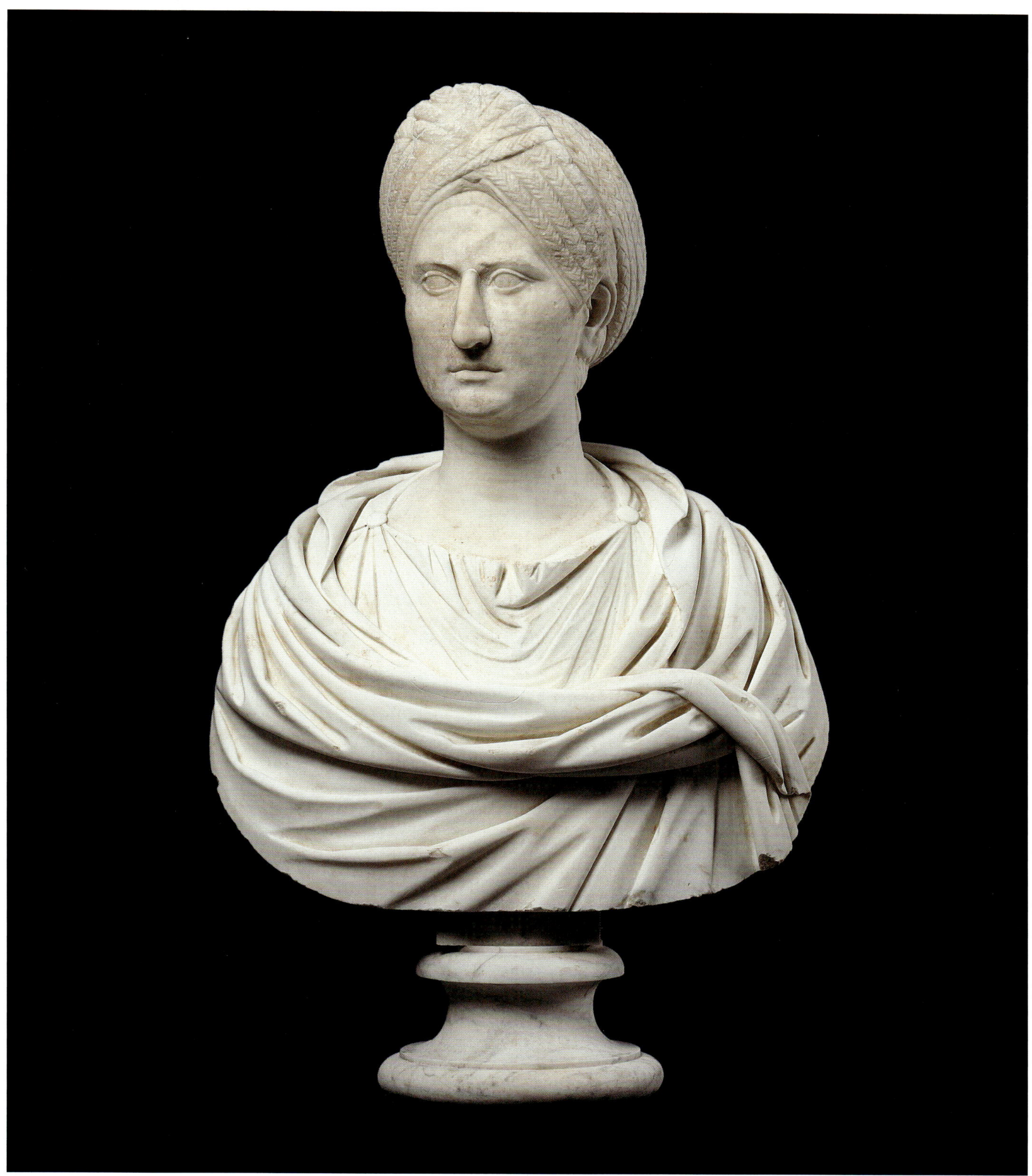

8
Portrait of a Woman, formerly known as Matidia
First half of 2nd century
Marble; H. 80 cm

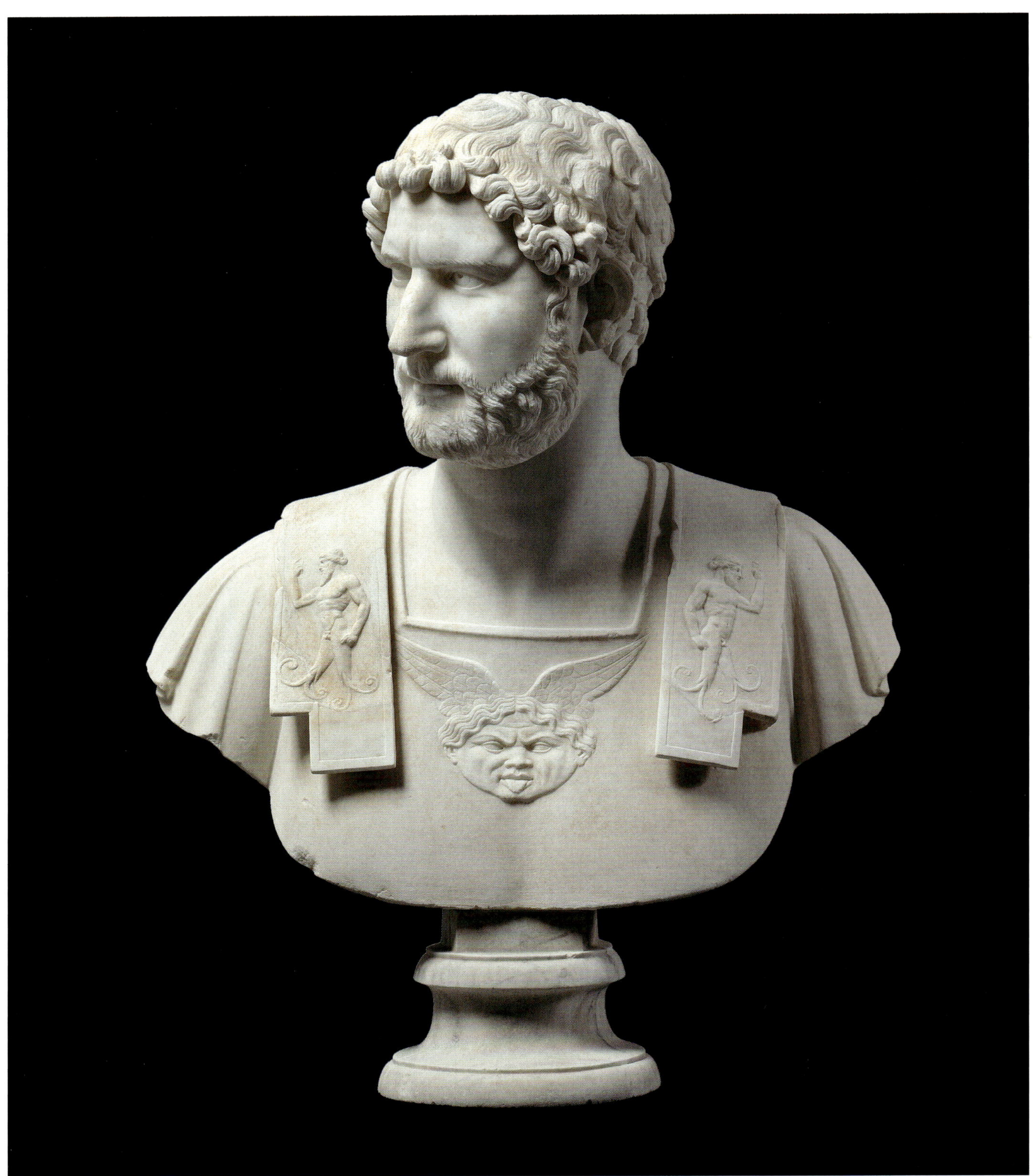

9
Portrait of Hadrian
About 130
Marble; H. 79 cm

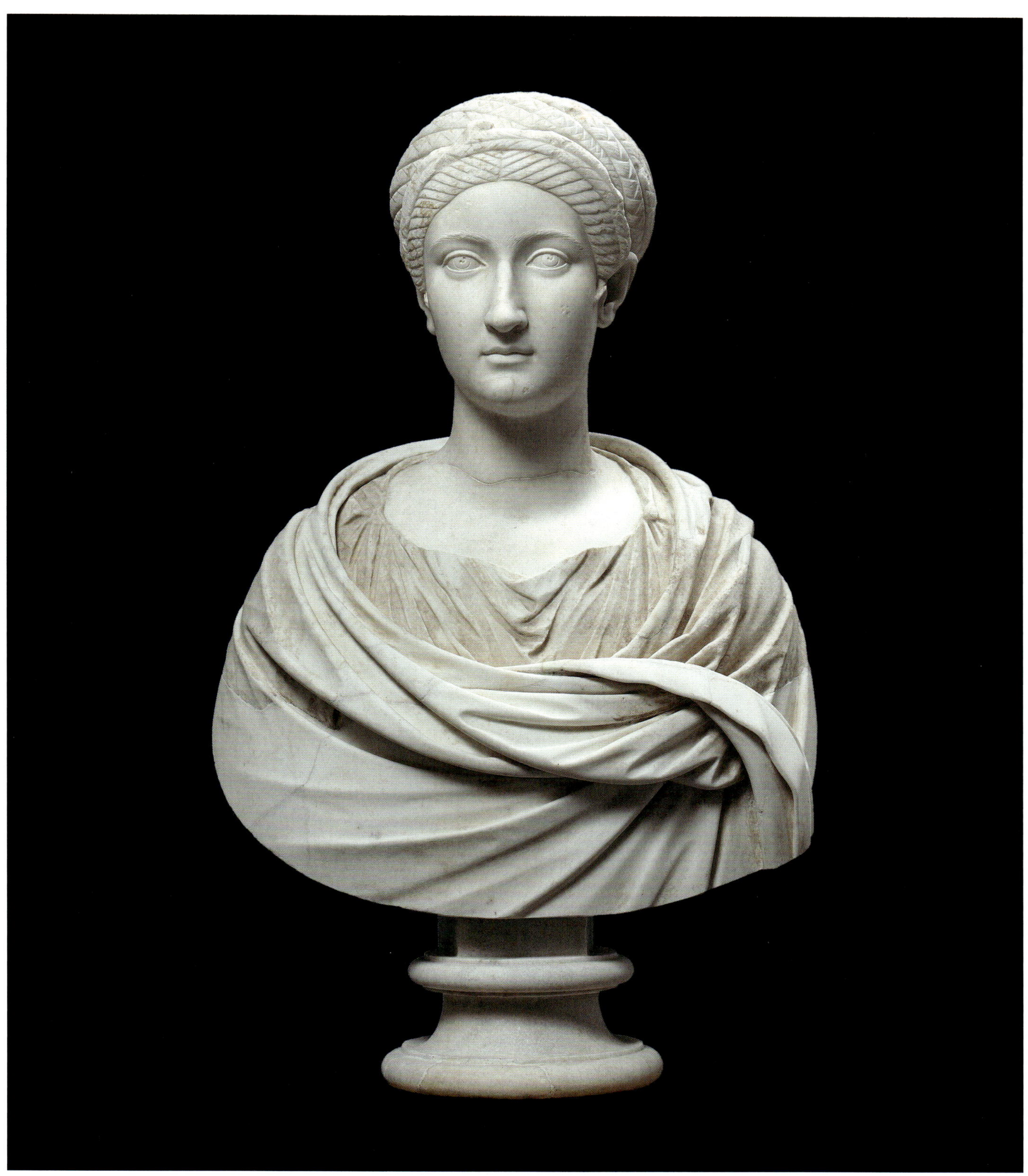

10
Portrait of a Woman, formerly known as Sabina
Second half of 2nd century
Marble; H. 75 cm

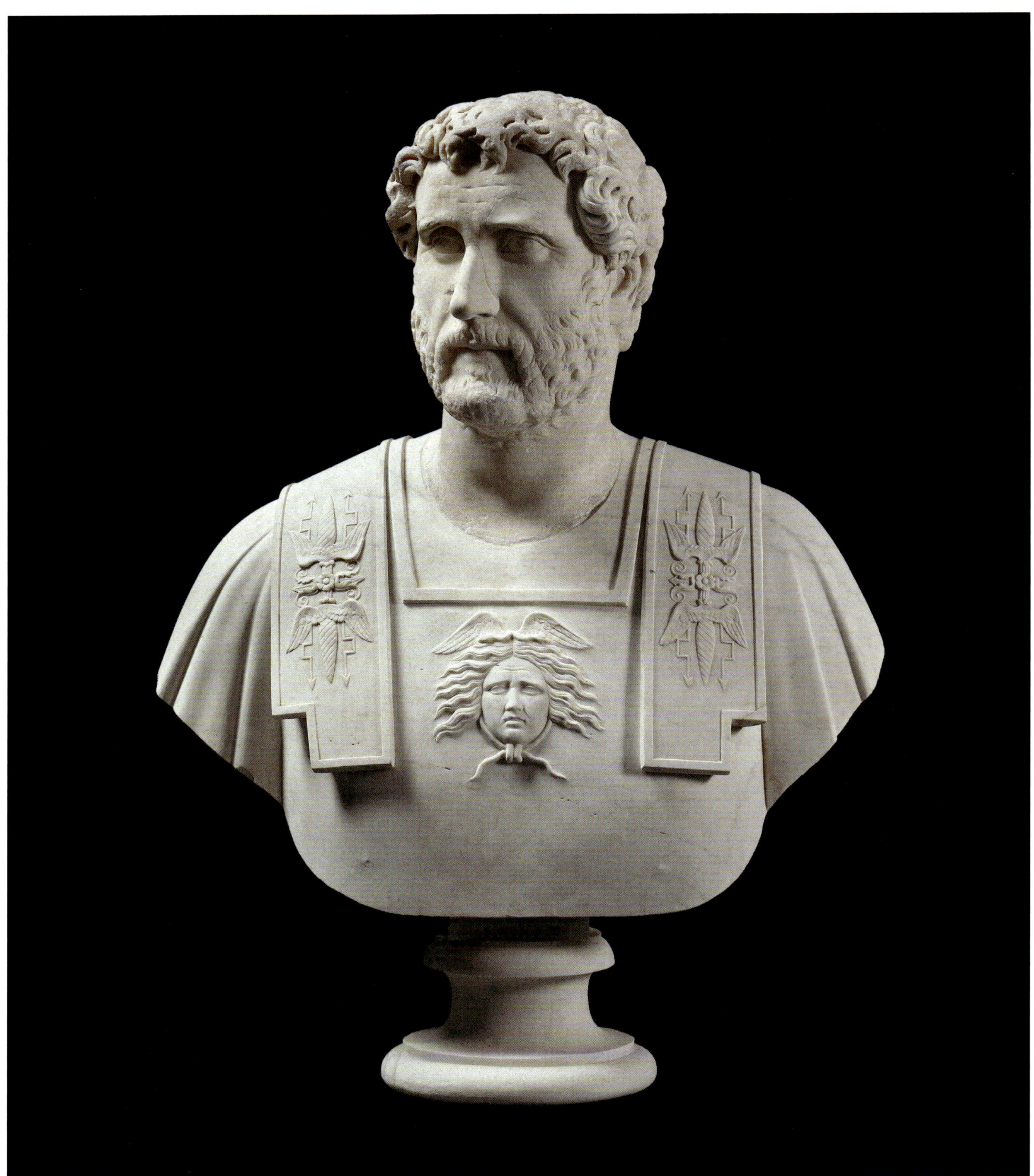

11
Portrait of Antoninus Pius
Mid-2nd century
Marble; H. 81 cm

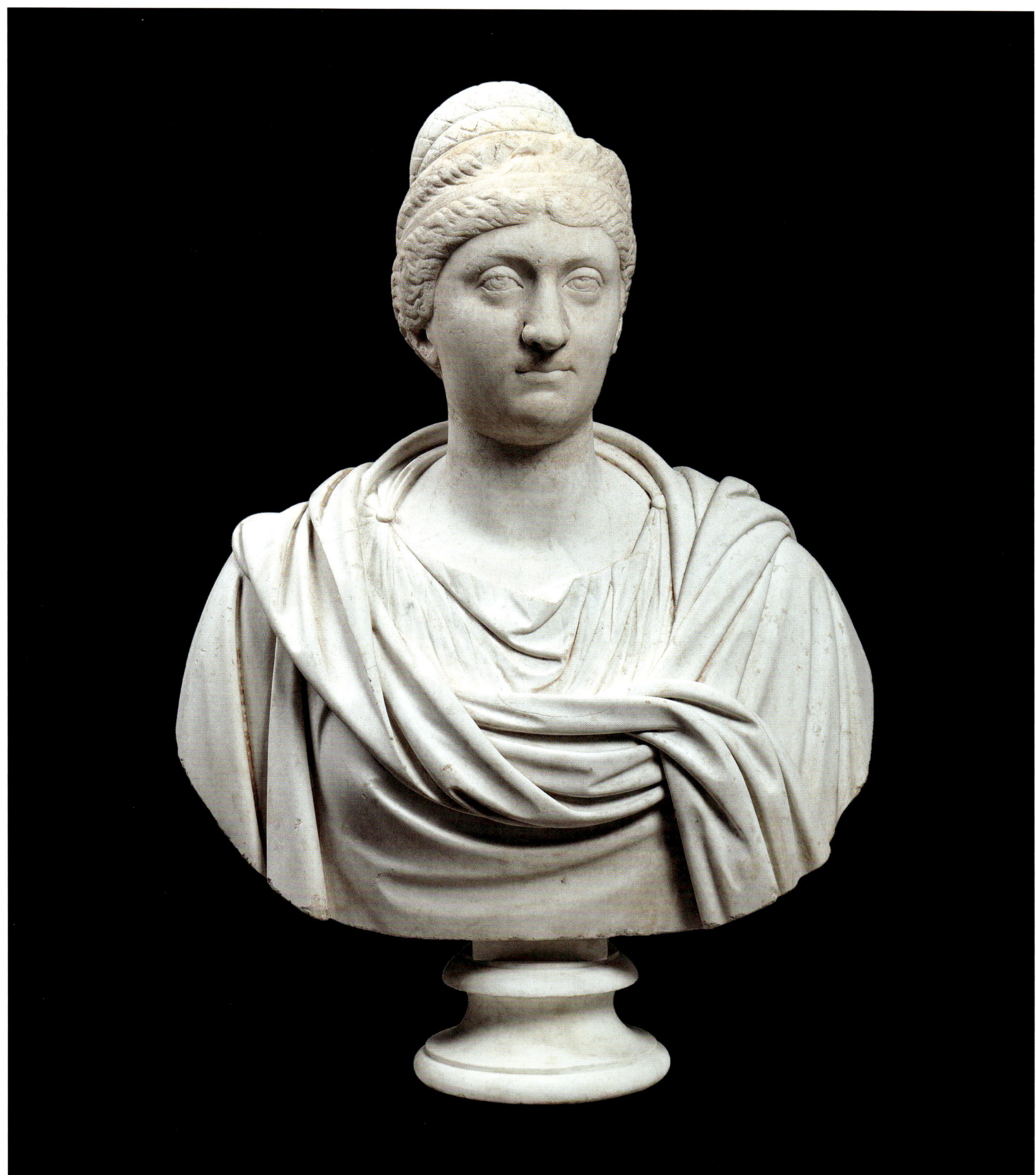

12
Portrait of a Woman,
formerly known as Faustina the Elder
Mid-2nd century
Marble; H. 88 cm

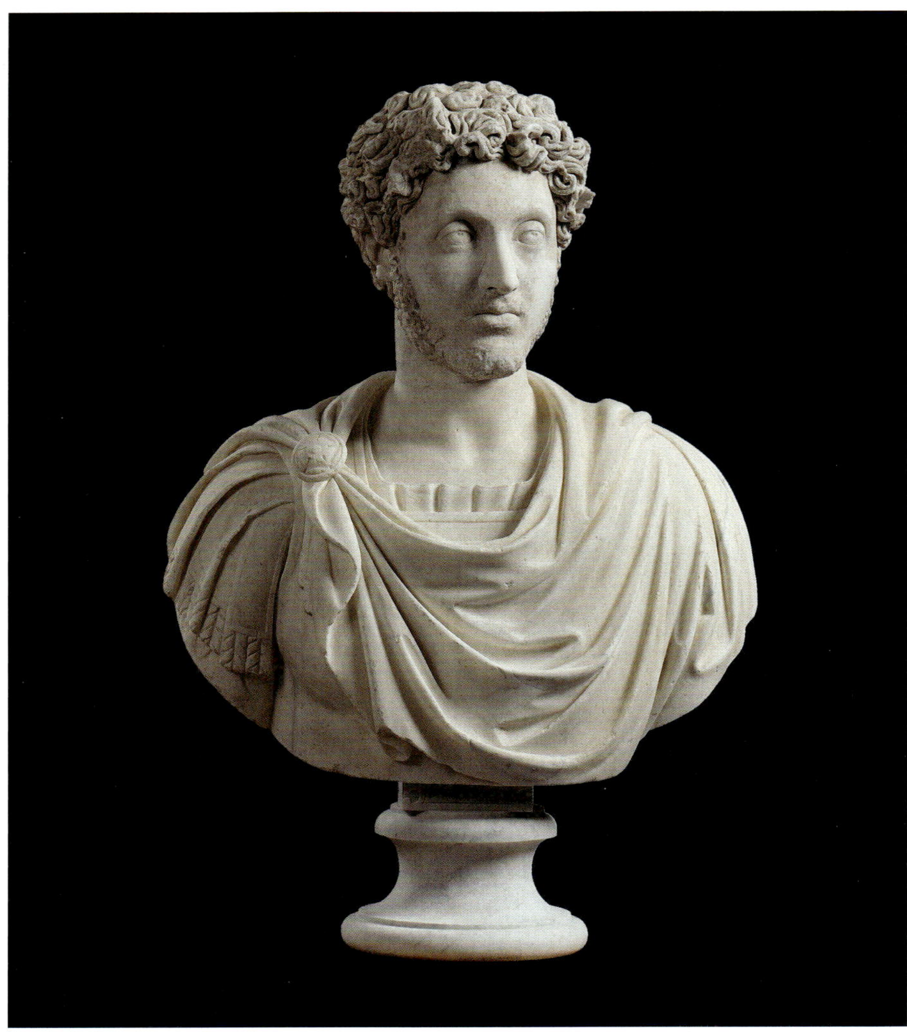

MARCUS AURELIUS knew he was going to be emperor by the age of sixteen, when Antoninus Pius adopted him and singled him out as the primary heir to the empire. Yet Marcus would not ascend to the throne until he was thirty-nine years old. These years spent as the anointed successor resulted in a proliferation of portraits of Marcus as a youth, a phenomenon that sets Marcus and his portraiture apart from his predecessors, who were adopted when they were well into middle age.

In his portraits, Marcus continued the trend started by emperor Hadrian of wearing a beard. But where his predecessors wore short and well-trimmed beards, Marcus opted for a longer, shaggier style, a choice that would have signaled to ancient viewers his devotion to earlier Greek philosophers and their unkempt beards. The beard also alludes to Marcus's many military campaigns, during which personal grooming took a back seat to strategy and battle.

Marcus is the first emperor of the second century for whom we have images dating to both before and after he became emperor. Scholars group Marcus's portraits into four types, two of which are illustrated in this catalogue. The first (cat. 13) shows Marcus as a young man, in his twenties, with full, fleshy cheeks and a closely cropped beard that is very shallowly carved. The second sculpture (cat. 14) represents Marcus after he has become emperor. Contrast his sunken cheeks and slightly furrowed brow with the earlier youthful portrait: now, he bears the weight of the empire on his shoulders.

13
Portrait of Young Marcus Aurelius
144–47
Marble; H. 85 cm

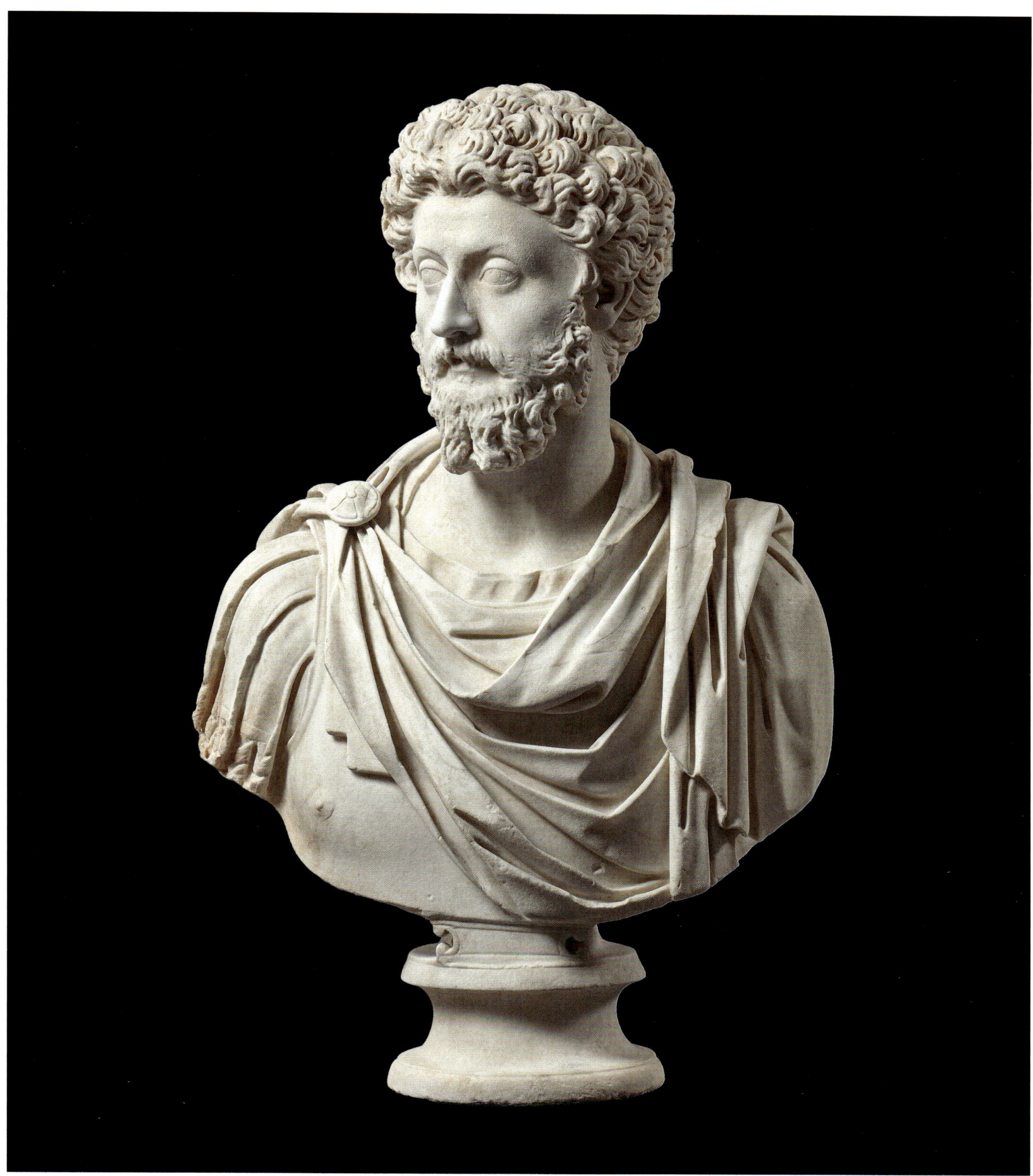

14
Portrait of Marcus Aurelius
Late 2nd century
Marble; H. 92 cm

FAUSTINA THE YOUNGER, the only surviving child of Antoninus Pius and Faustina the Elder, entered the imperial house in 138 around the age of eight. She was raised to be the wife of the future emperor, Marcus Aurelius, with the hope that she would produce suitable heirs to continue the Antonine dynasty—and she succeeded in this respect, giving birth to as many as fourteen children in her lifetime, though only six survived to adulthood.

This portrait was likely created around the time of Marcus's accession to power in 161, possibly to commemorate the birth of one of their children in 162. It depicts Faustina in her early thirties, wearing a simple coiffure of "finger-wave" locks parted over her forehead and pulled back into a loose bun at the back of the neck. With her head turned slightly to her right, she gazes into the distance, exemplifying the dignity and maturity of a Roman matron who has successfully ensured her family's continuation.

Because Faustina spent the majority of her life in the imperial court, she was depicted in at least ten portrait types over the course of three decades, more than any other imperial woman. Her earliest portraits show her around the age of fifteen to seventeen, perhaps at the time of her marriage to Marcus in 145, and her portraits continued to be produced until her death in 175 or 176. These types can be distinguished based on minor variations in her hairstyle, which was typically parted at the center and arranged in a bun at the back. Sculptors usually depicted Faustina with an oval face, round cheeks, and heavy-lidded, almond-shaped eyes. This eye shape in particular featured prominently in Antonine portraiture: sculptors used it frequently to visually connect portraits of members of the imperial family to one another.

15
Portrait of Faustina the Younger
About 160
Marble; H. 73 cm

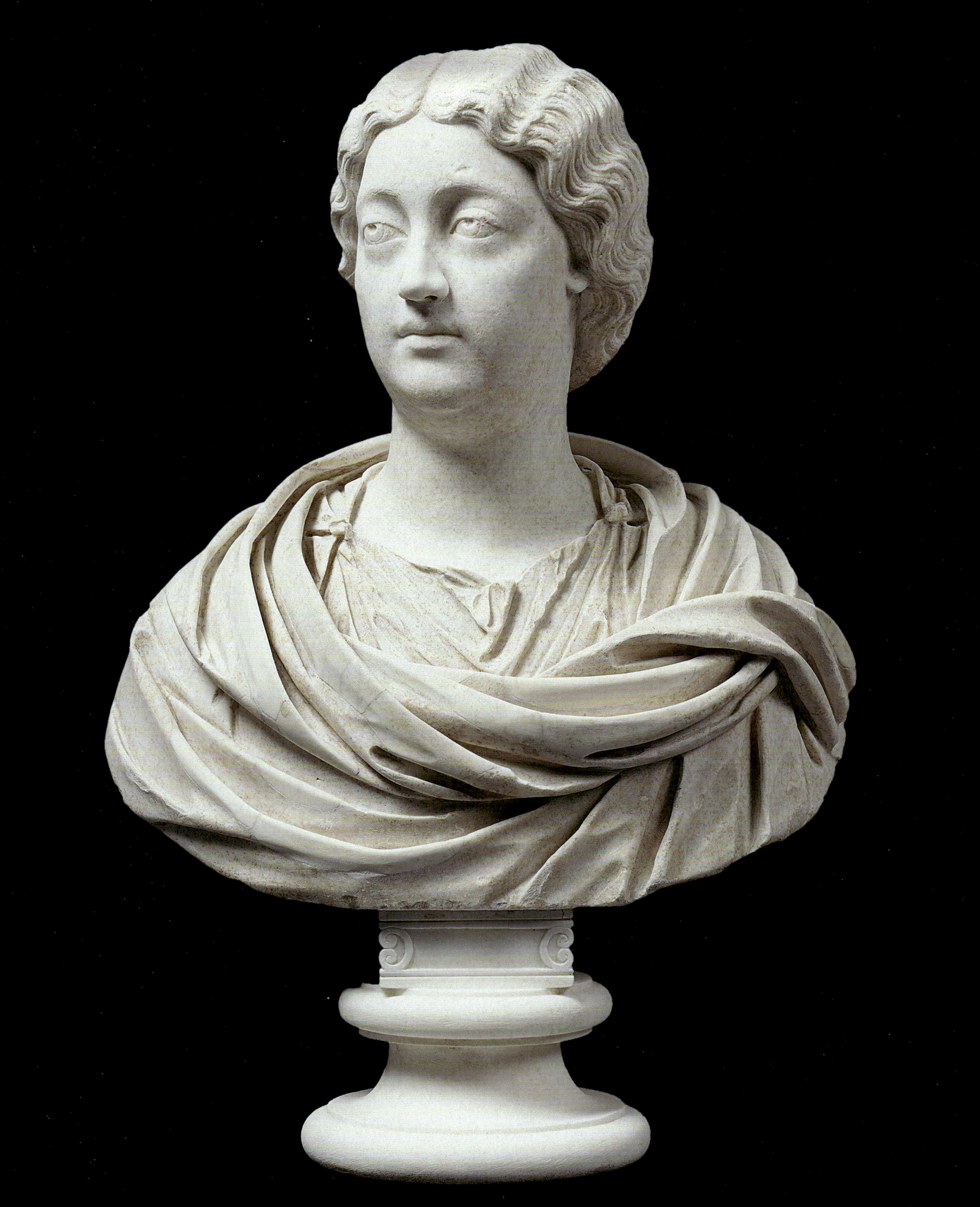

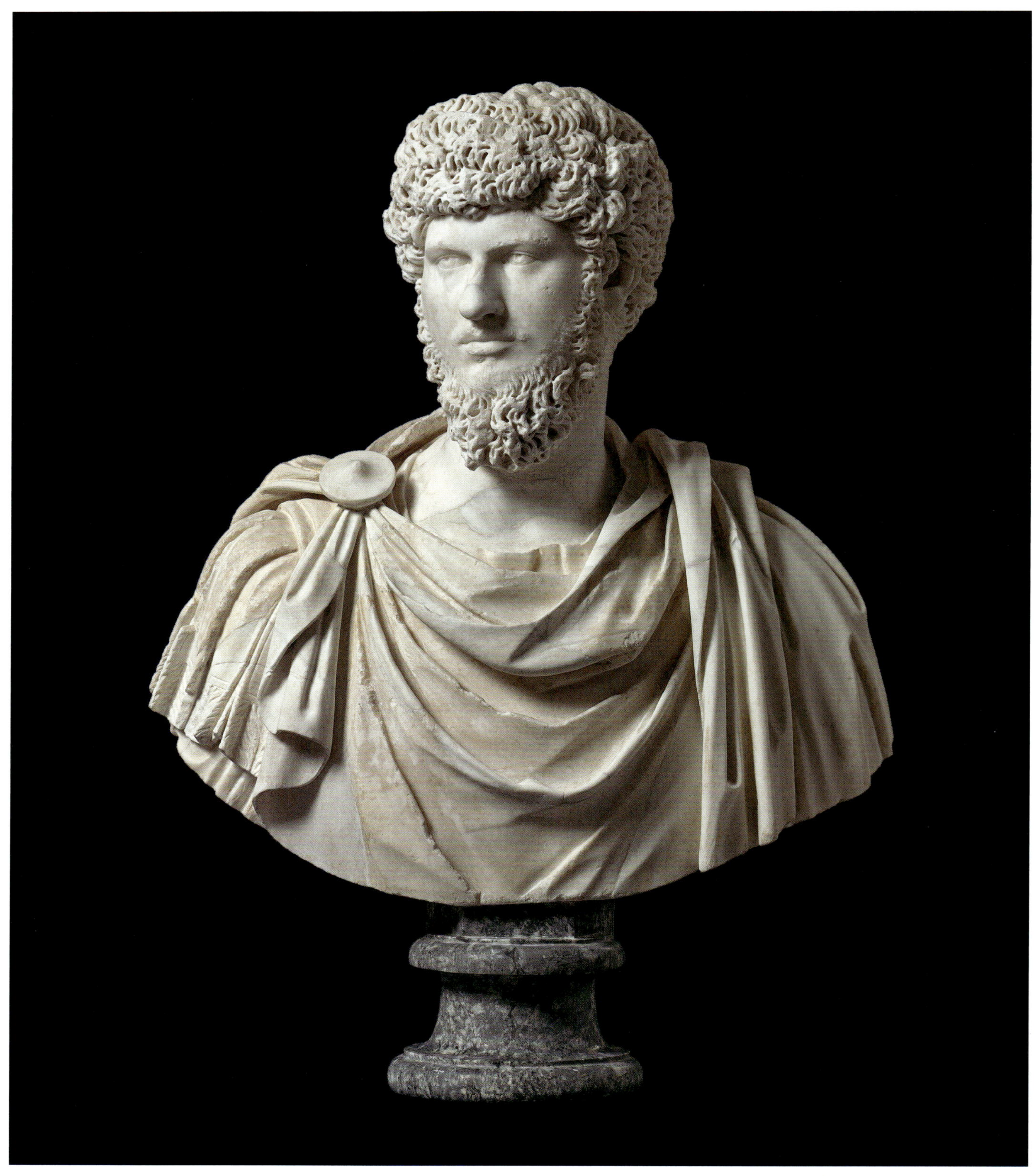

16
Portrait of Lucius Verus
Second half of 2nd century
Marble; H. 93 cm

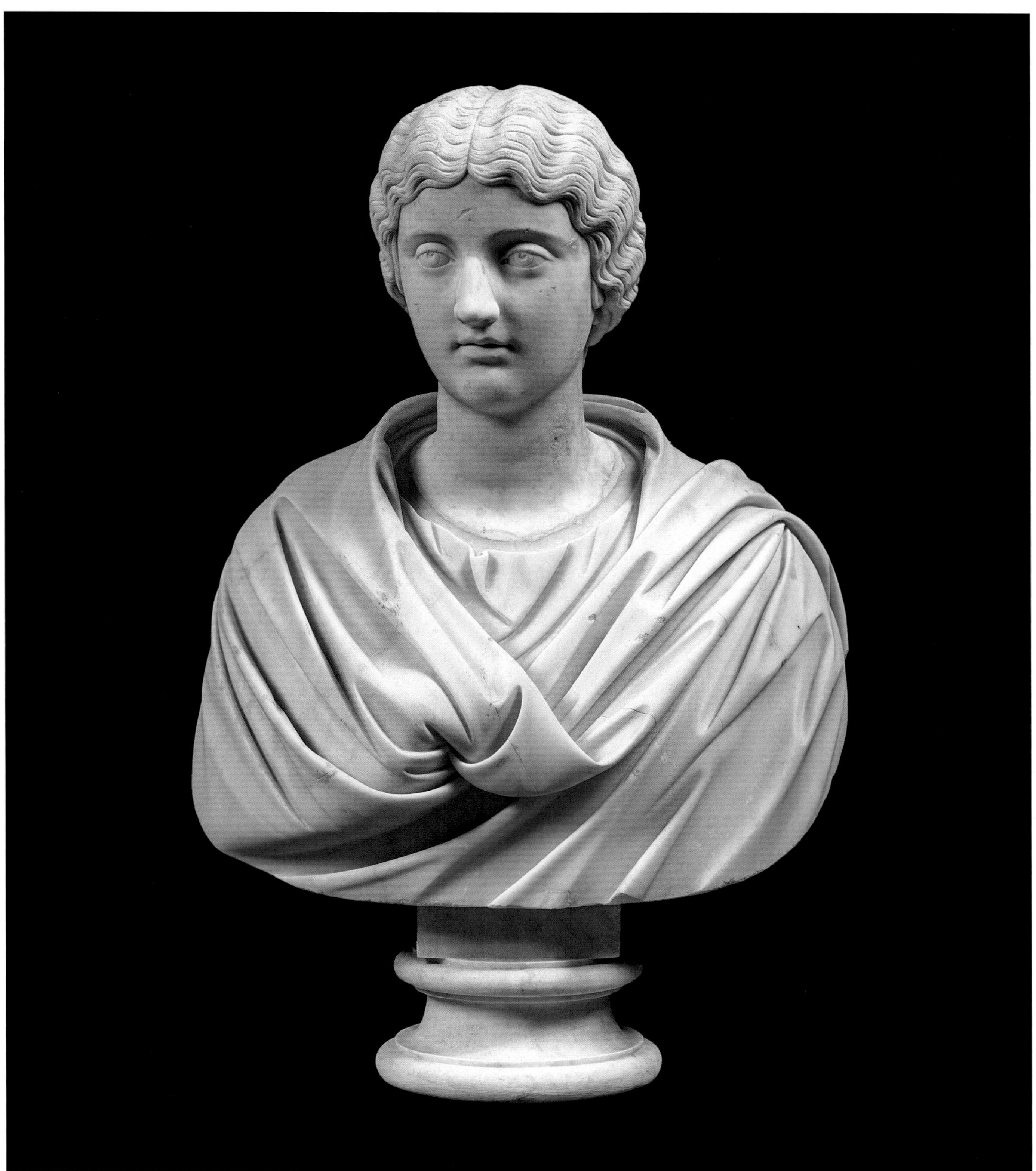

17
Portrait of a Woman, formerly known as Lucilla
150–80
Marble; H. 76 cm

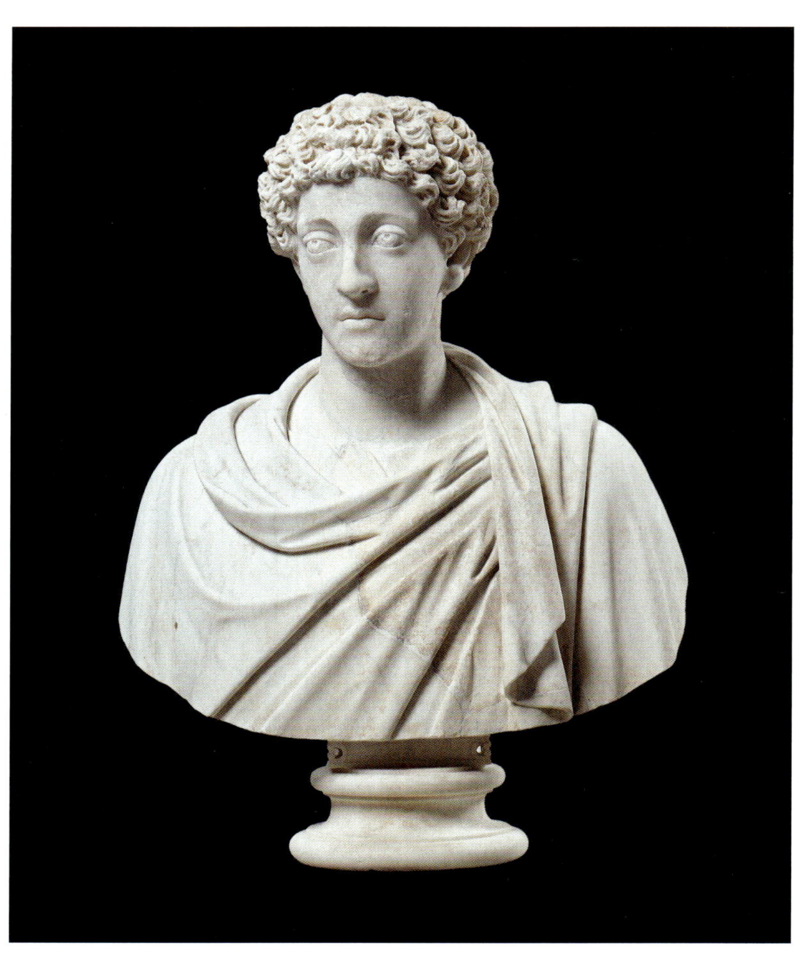

18
Portrait of Young Commodus
170–80
Marble; H. 76 cm

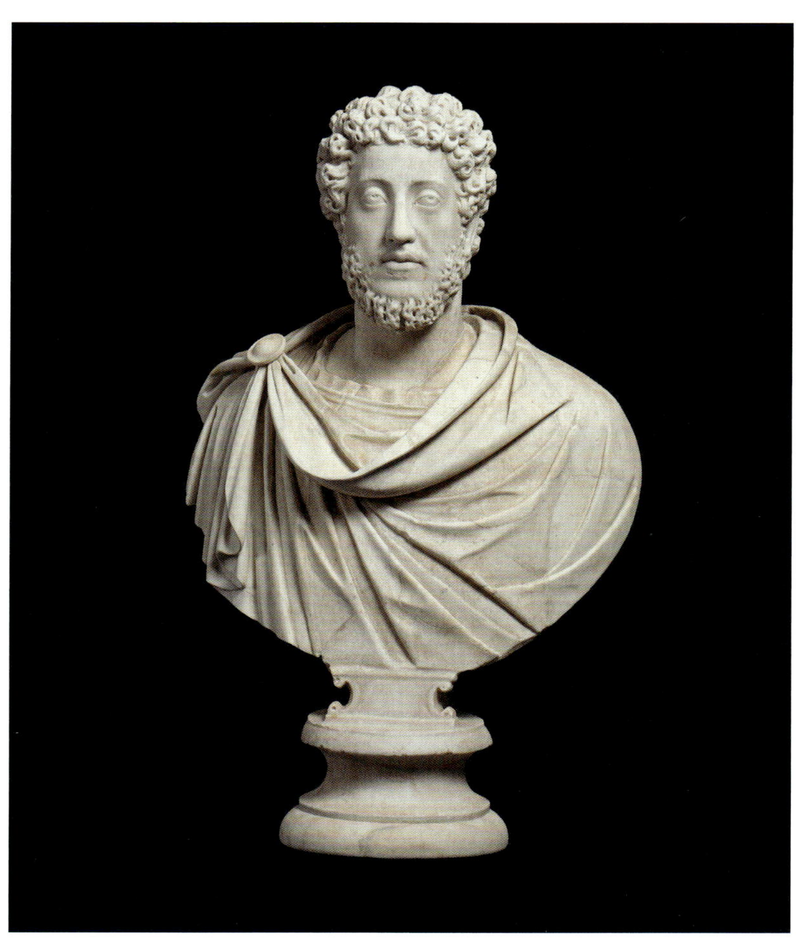

19
Portrait of Commodus
Late 2nd century
Marble; H. 93 cm

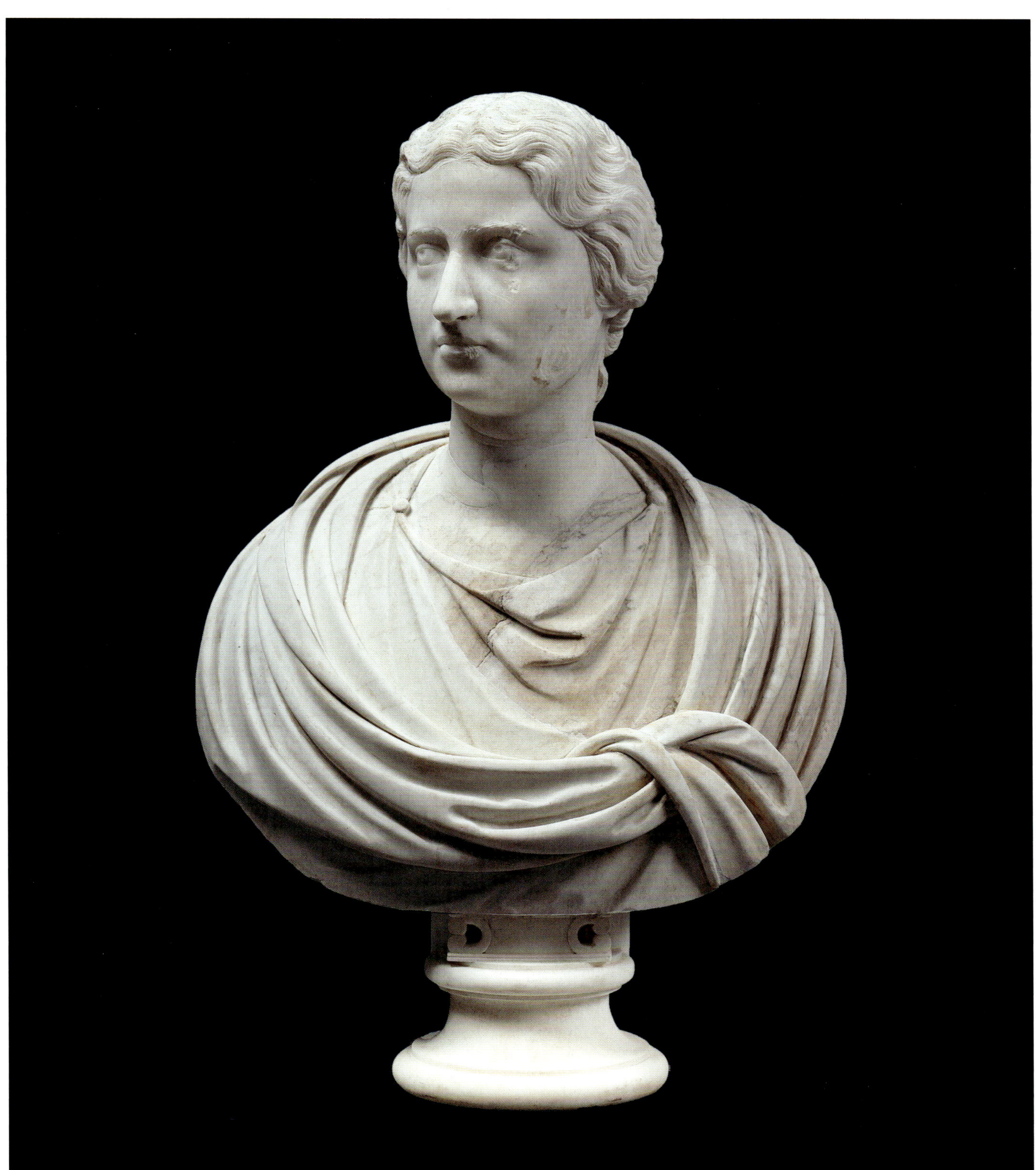

20
Portrait of a Woman, formerly known as Crispina
Second half of 2nd century
Marble; H. 75 cm

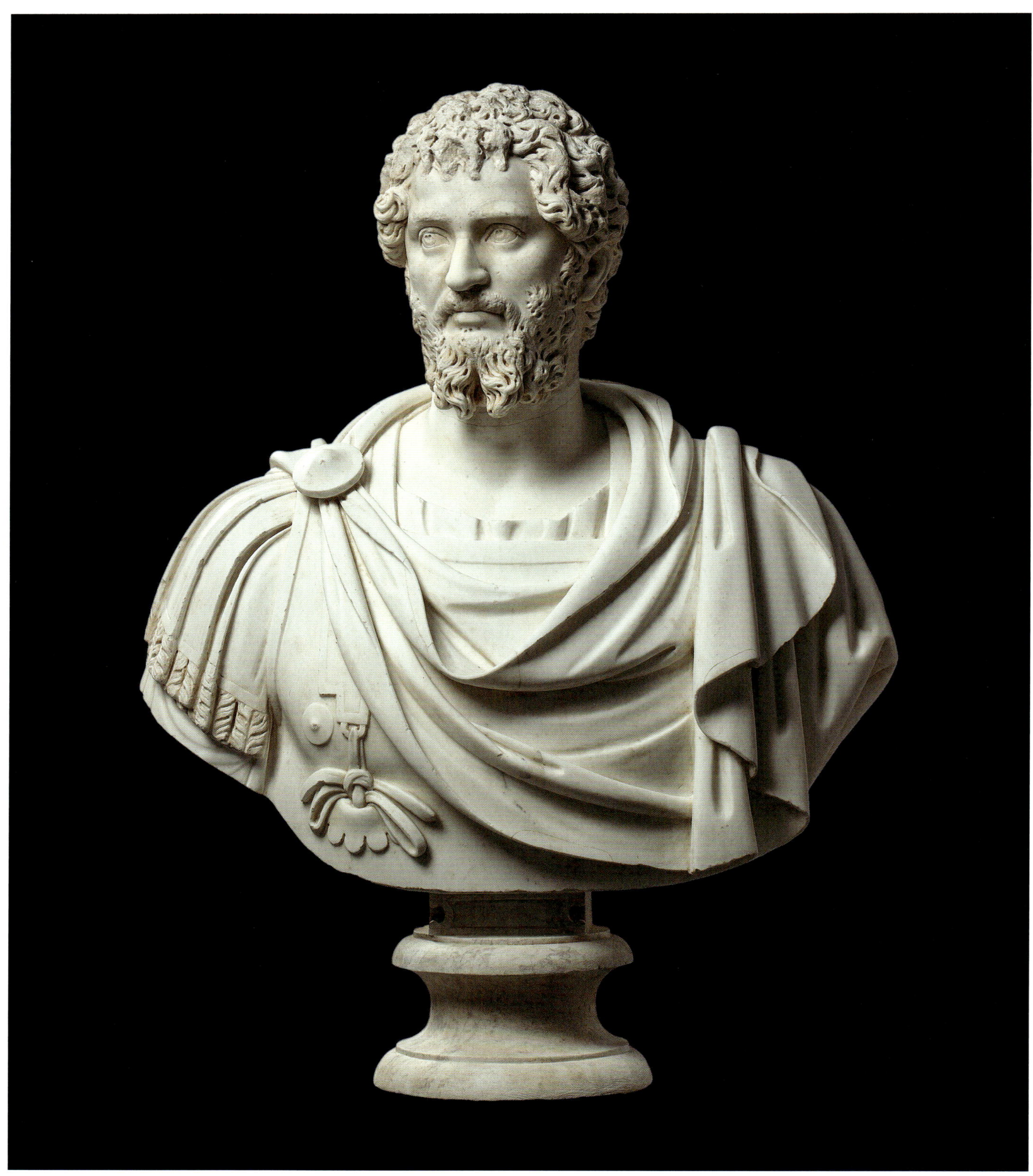

21
Portrait of Septimius Severus
Early 3rd century
Marble; H. 92 cm

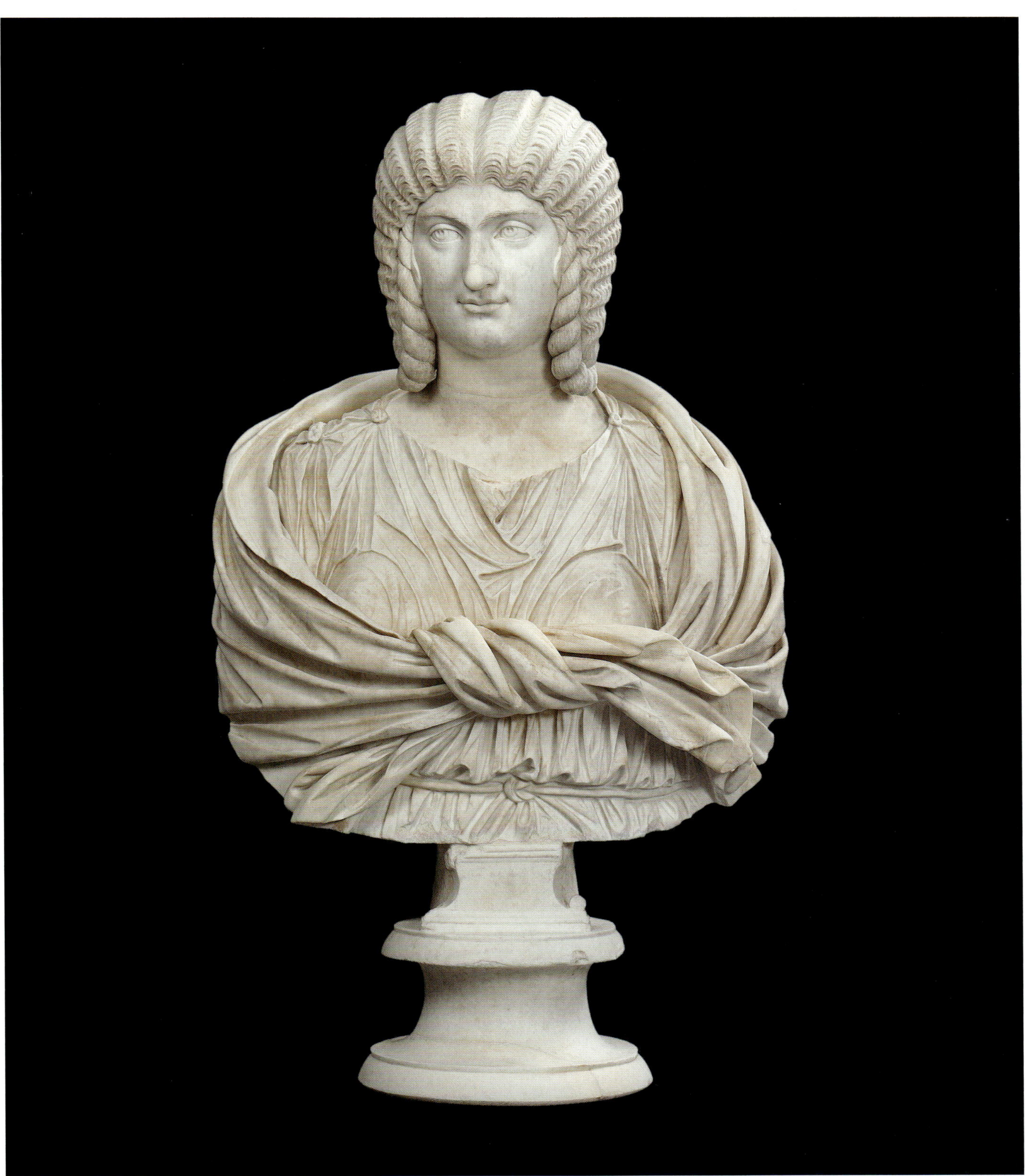

22
Portrait of Julia Domna
Early 3rd century
Marble; H. 93 cm

FUNERARY ART

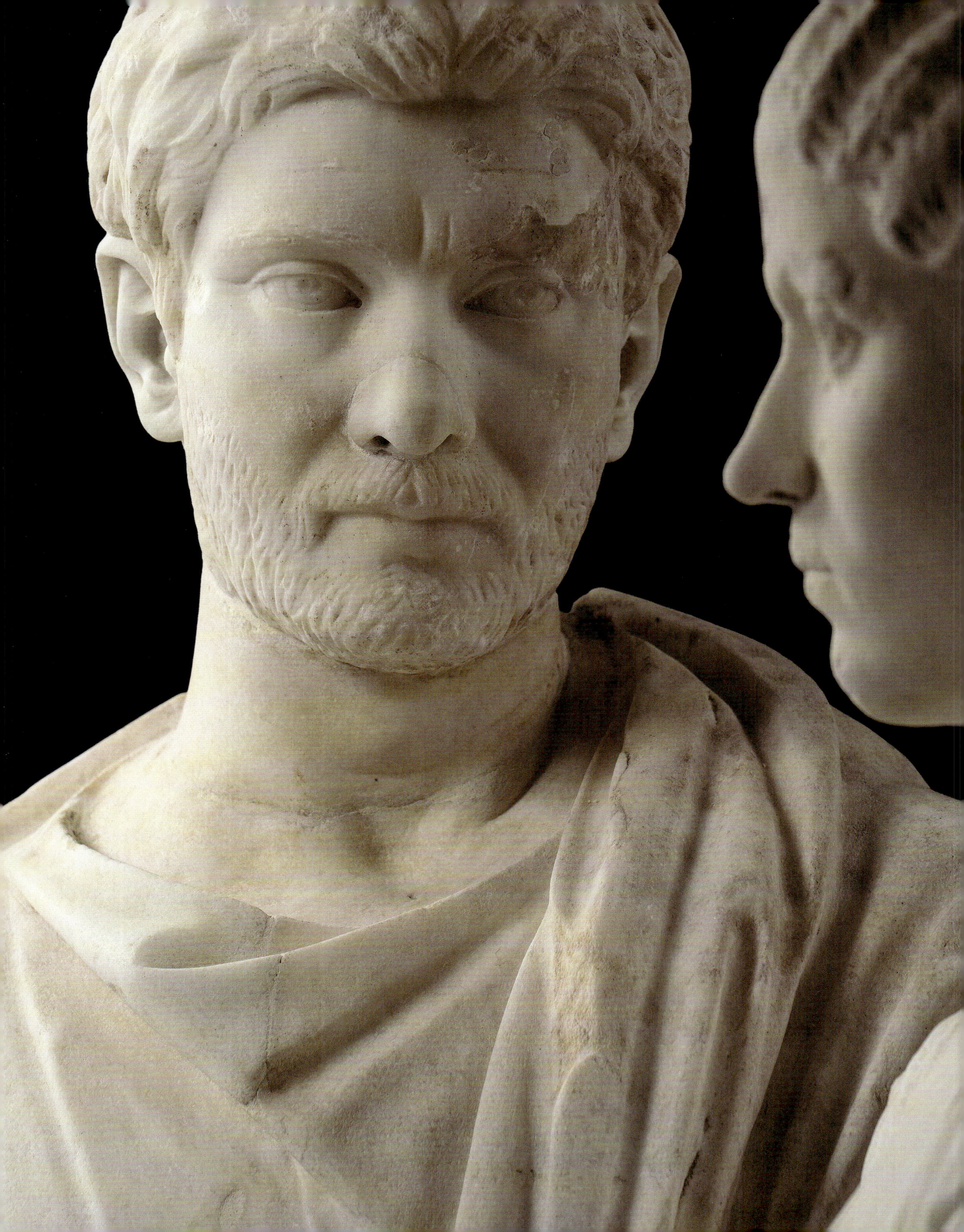

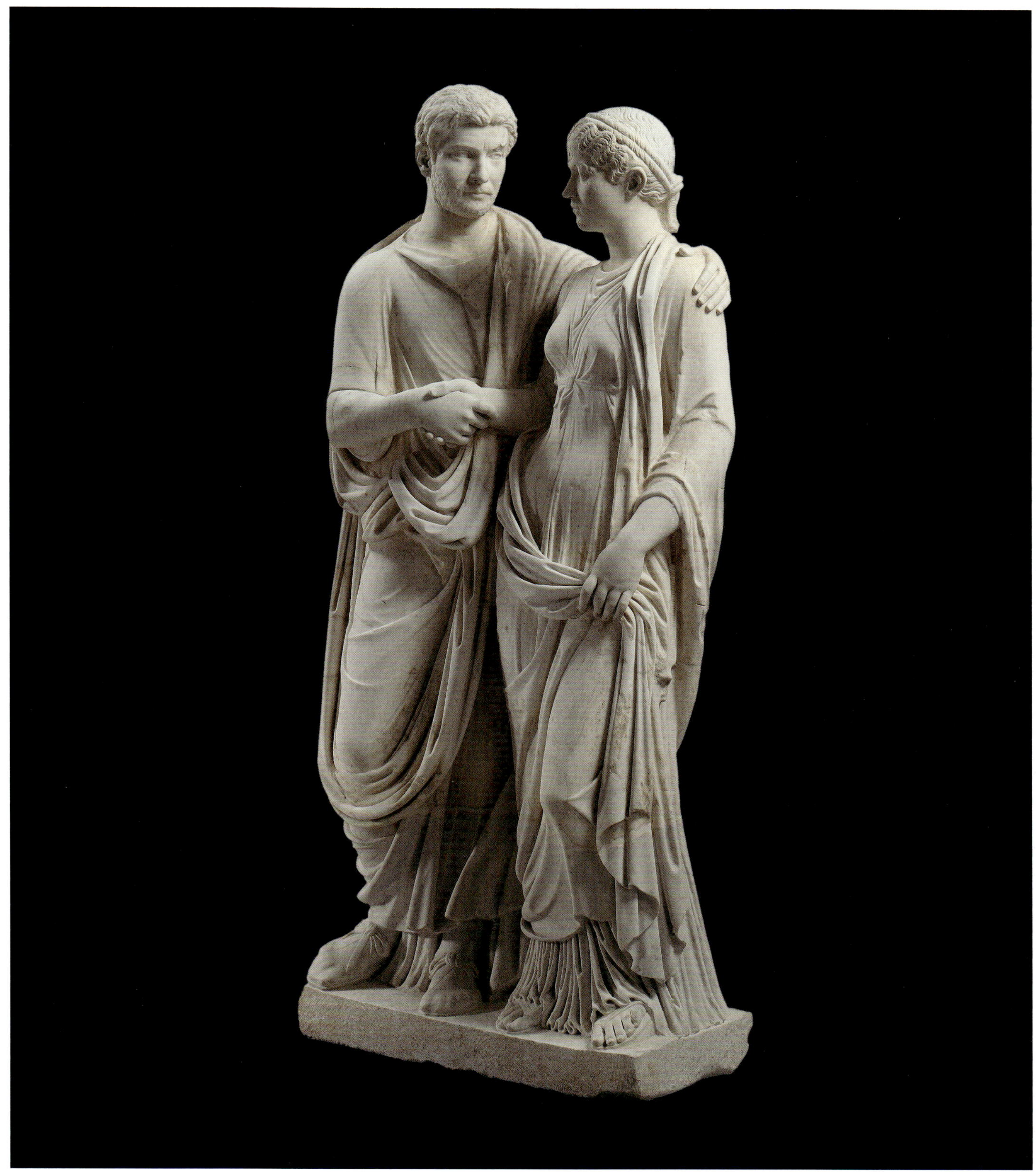

23
Portrait Group of Husband and Wife
2nd century
Marble; 182 × 81 × 38 cm

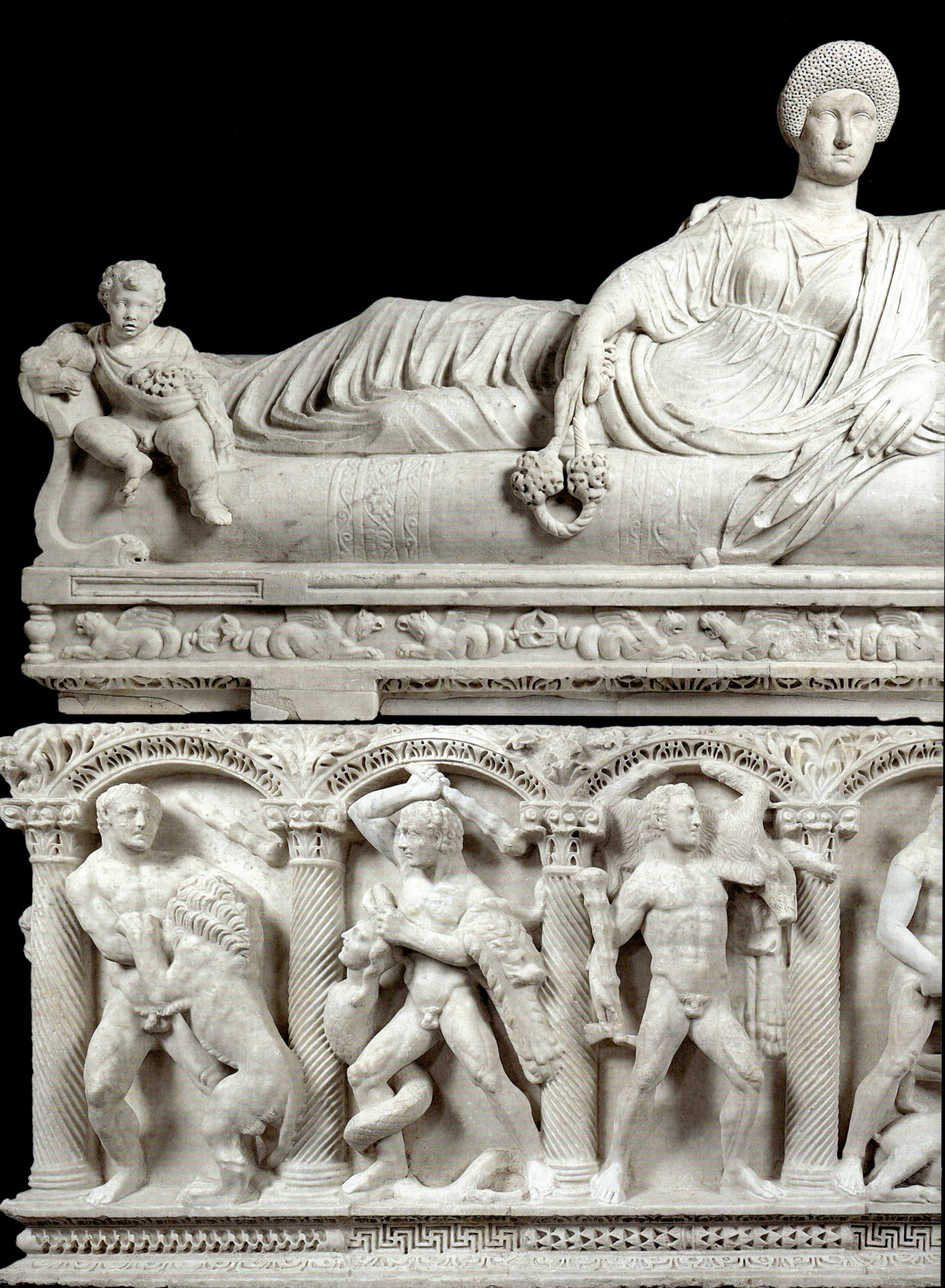

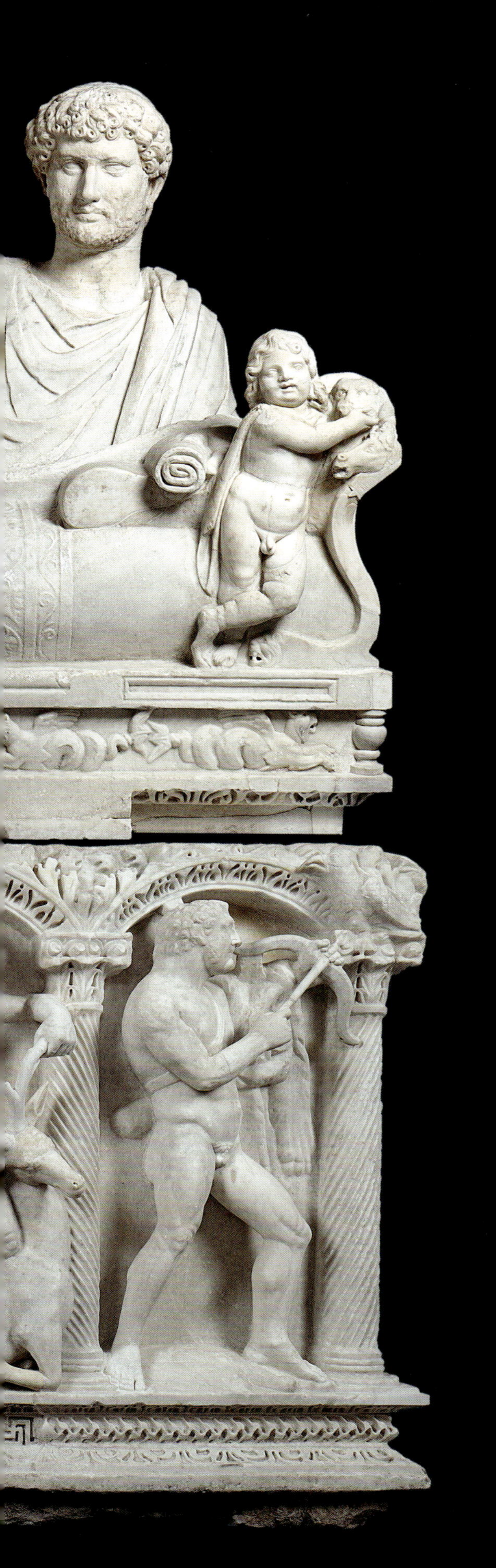

A WEALTHY COUPLE CHOSE THIS SARCOPHAGUS as their final resting place. Standing nearly eight feet tall when assembled, it towers over most viewers. The style of the sarcophagus, which separates the scenes carved on its sides into small compositions framed by columns, is most closely associated with workshops in Asia Minor (present-day Turkey). It is largely intact and therefore one of the most impressive examples of its kind. It likely would have been shipped in an unfinished state and the final touches would have been completed in Rome. This allowed the clients to customize some elements, such as the portrait heads, which were made separately and inserted into the bodies at the neck; the ancient heads now affixed to these figures were added in the modern era and are not original to the work.

The public nature of Roman tombs meant that families could display their wealth and status through the size, design, and placement of their funerary monuments even after death. The pose of the deceased couple may allude to the Roman practice of reclining during banquets and formal meals. Roman tombs were regularly visited by family and loved ones, and some were even outfitted with banquet couches so that the living could dine with or in honor of the deceased.

The sarcophagus's decoration might hint at the couple's hopes for the afterlife. The scenes carved on its sides tell the story of Hercules and the Twelve Labors, a popular theme on many Roman sarcophagi. After killing his wife and children, Hercules uses his strength and cleverness to complete twelve nearly impossible tasks and atone for his crimes, so that when he dies, he becomes immortal.

24
Sarcophagus Depicting the Labors of Hercules and Lid with Reclining Couple
Second half of 2nd century
Marble; lid: 128 × 239 × 119 cm;
sarcophagus: 98 × 242 × 119 cm

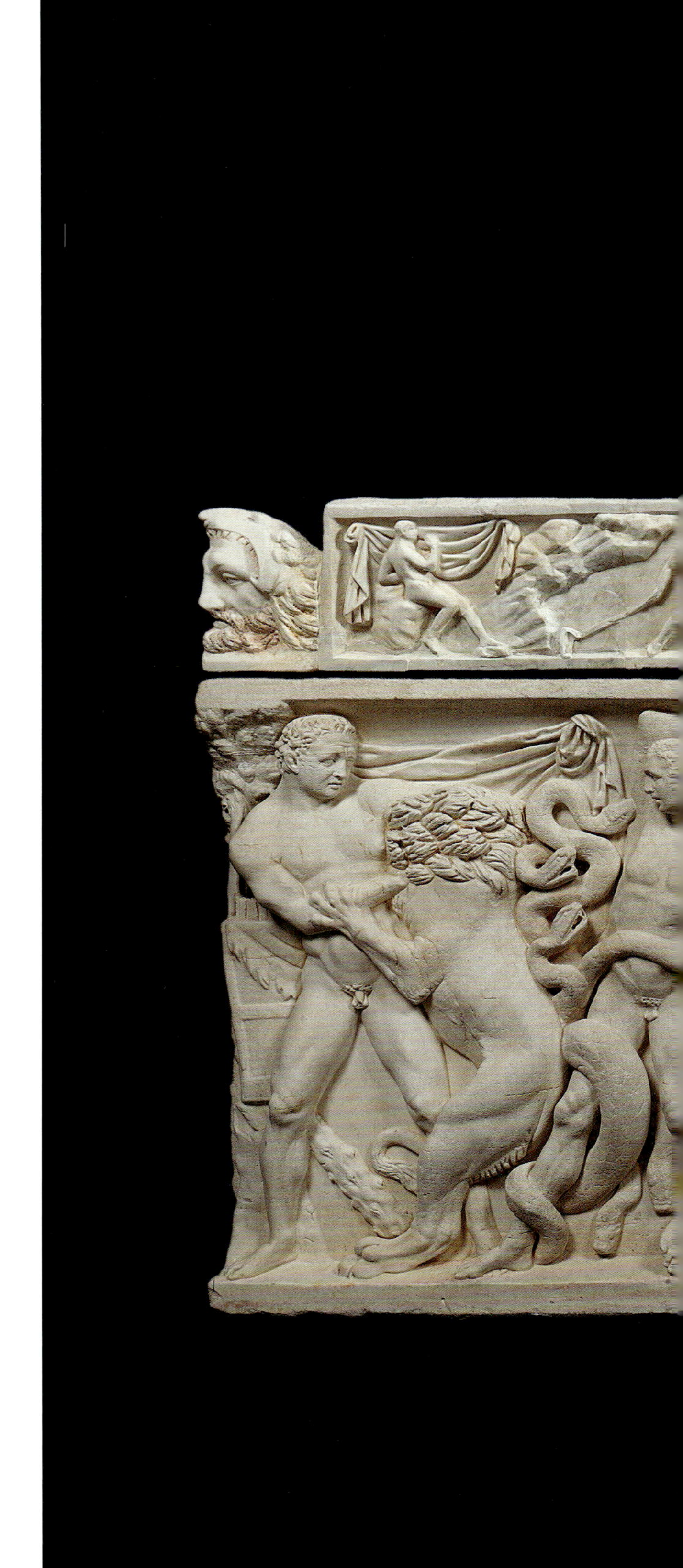

25
Sarcophagus Depicting the Labors of Hercules
About 160–70
Marble; lid: 22 × 241 × 96 cm; sarcophagus: 80 × 239 × 98 cm

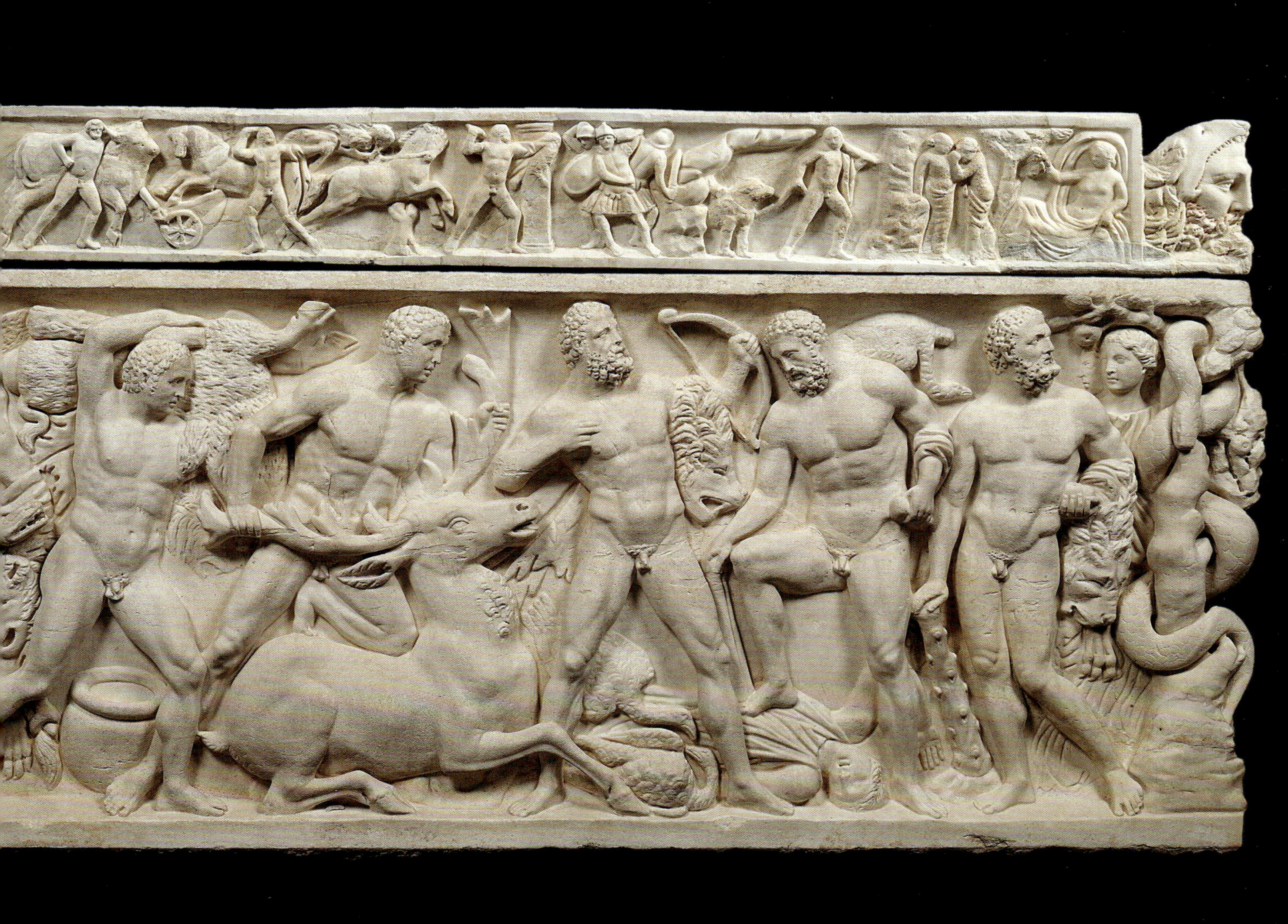

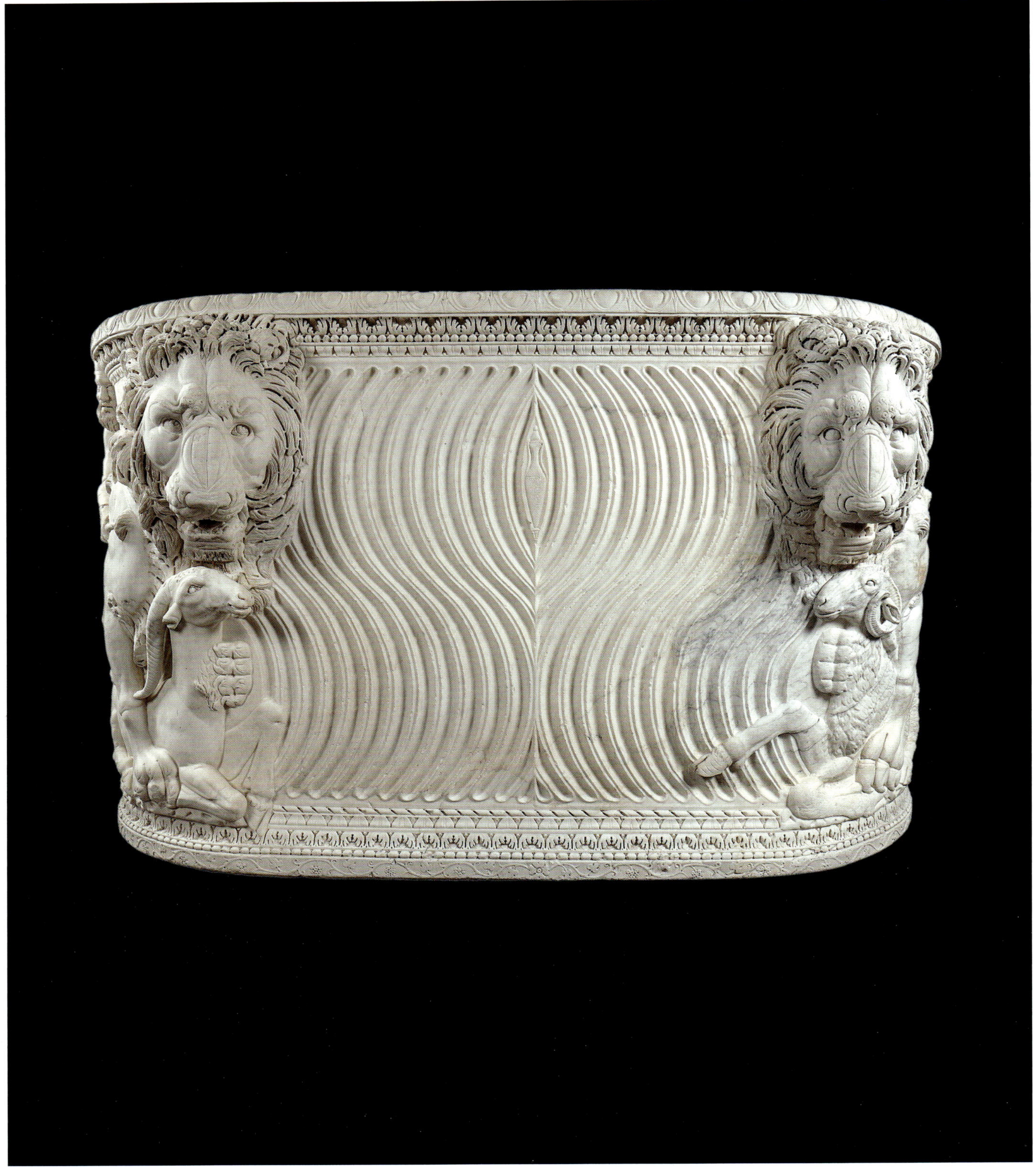

26
Strigilated Sarcophagus with Lions
About 260–70
Marble; 146 × 266 × 160 cm

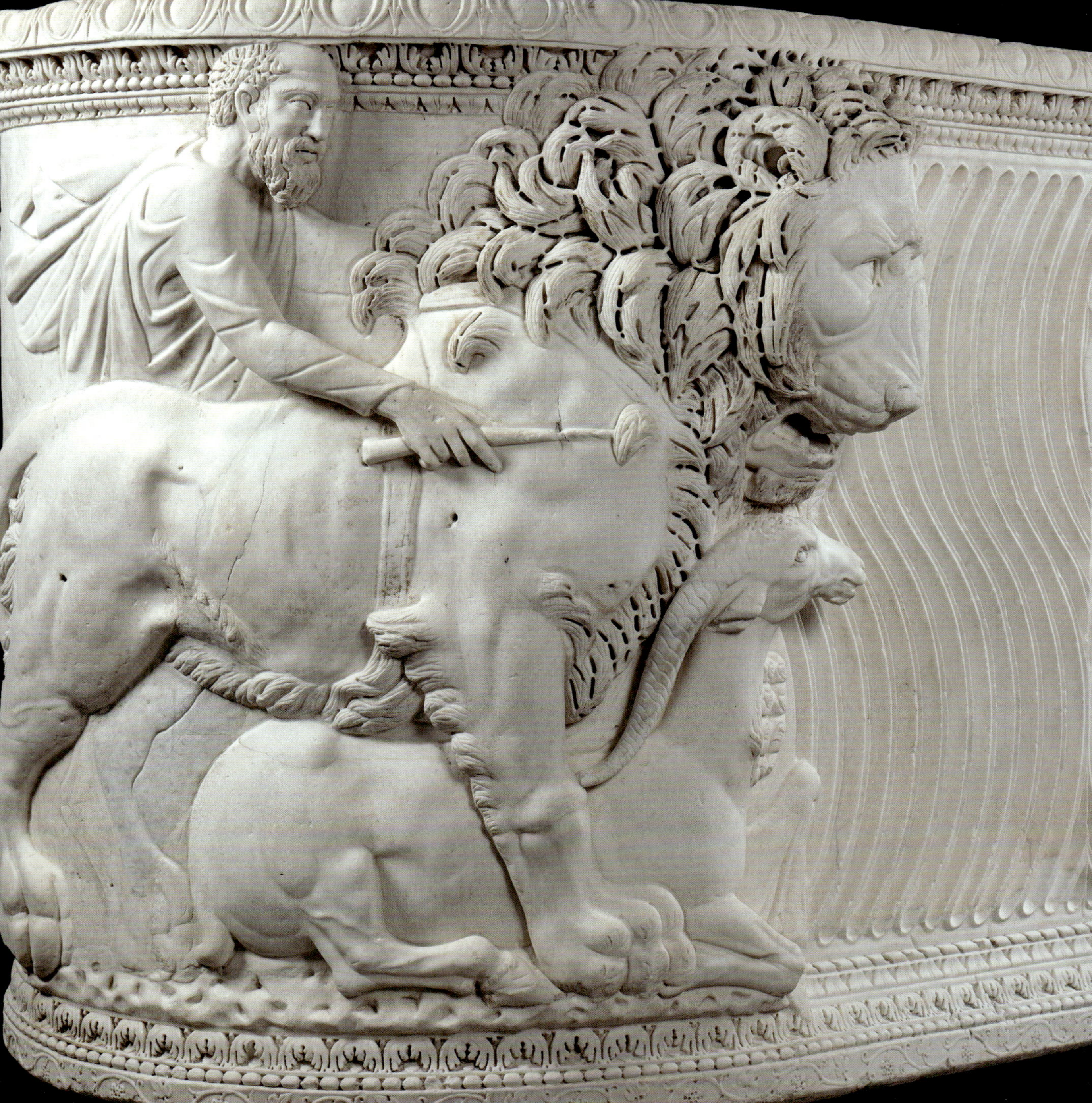

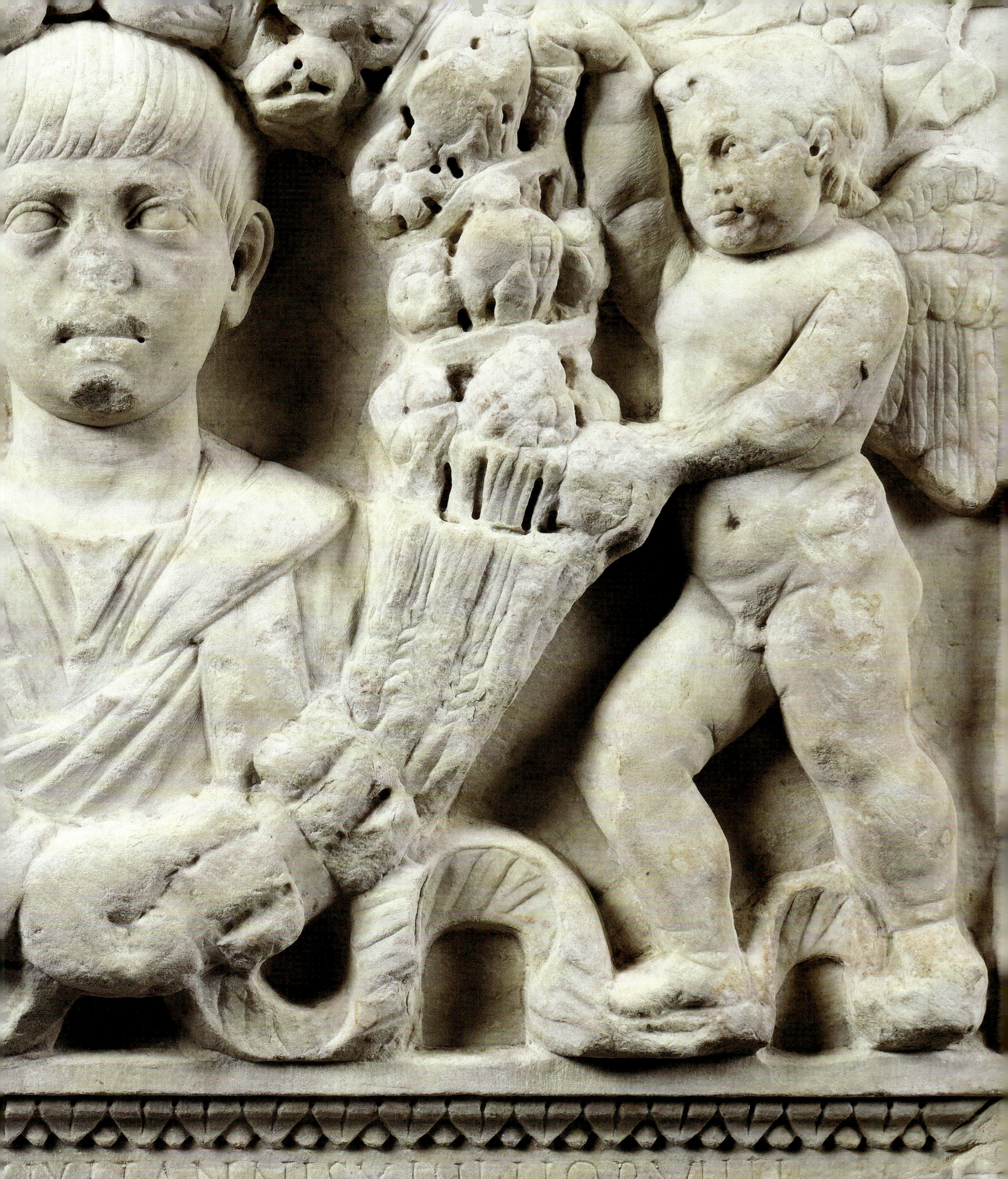
IXII ANNIS XIIII HOR VIII
ARCIVS THREPTVS ET MARCIA

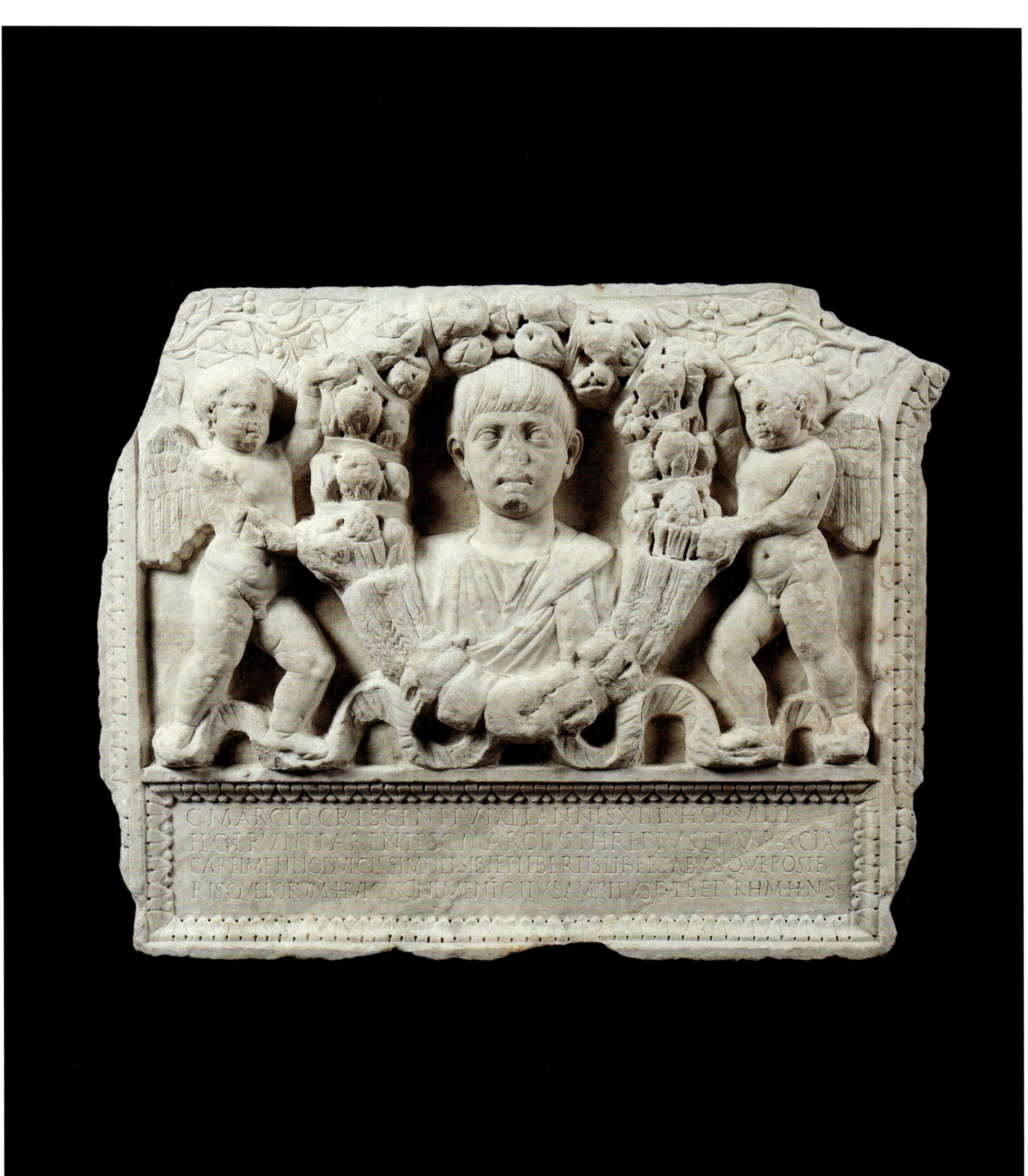

27
Funerary Monument of a Boy,
Gaius Marcius Crescens
2nd century
Marble; 74 × 94 × 16 cm

GODS & GODDESSES

THIS GODDESS would have looked old-fashioned to ancient Roman viewers. A sculptor created the work by copying a then-five-hundred-year-old Greek sculpture. The figure's garment, an ancient Greek *peplos*, hangs in folds that resemble vertical columns. This type of drapery commonly appeared in Greek bronzes, more so than in marbles, which indicates that the now-lost original statue may have been a bronze.

Both the figure's garment and style—how the drapery is rendered, the subject's unsmiling facial expression, and her front-facing pose—are hallmarks of the Greek "Severe" style dating to about 470 to 460 BCE. Sculptors produced copies and variants of Severe-style sculptures during the Hellenistic and Roman periods, possibly as a sober and dignified antidote to the often-extravagant artistic styles of their own eras. The Greek original that inspired this work likely represented one of the major female Olympian goddesses: Hera, the goddess of marriage and family, or Demeter, the goddess of agriculture.

The statue's appellation "Hestia Giustiniani" dates to the years before it entered the Torlonia Collection, when it was held in the collection of Vincenzo Giustiniani, an Italian banker who assembled a massive art collection in the late sixteenth and early seventeenth centuries. Inventories of the Giustiniani Collection described this statue either as the Roman goddess Vesta (or Hestia, to Greeks), the goddess of the hearth and home, or more often as a priestess of Vesta, known as a Vestal Virgin. The latter is an unlikely identification given that the figure does not wear the distinctive headdress of the Vestals. The use of the goddess's Greek name *Hestia* was introduced in the nineteenth century and has persisted. Hestia's role was to tend the sacred fire on Mount Olympus; as a result, she did not feature in many mythological stories, and representations of Hestia rarely appear in Greek art.

28
Statue of a Goddess, known as the Hestia Giustiniani
First half of 2nd century
Marble; 200 × 78 × 53 cm

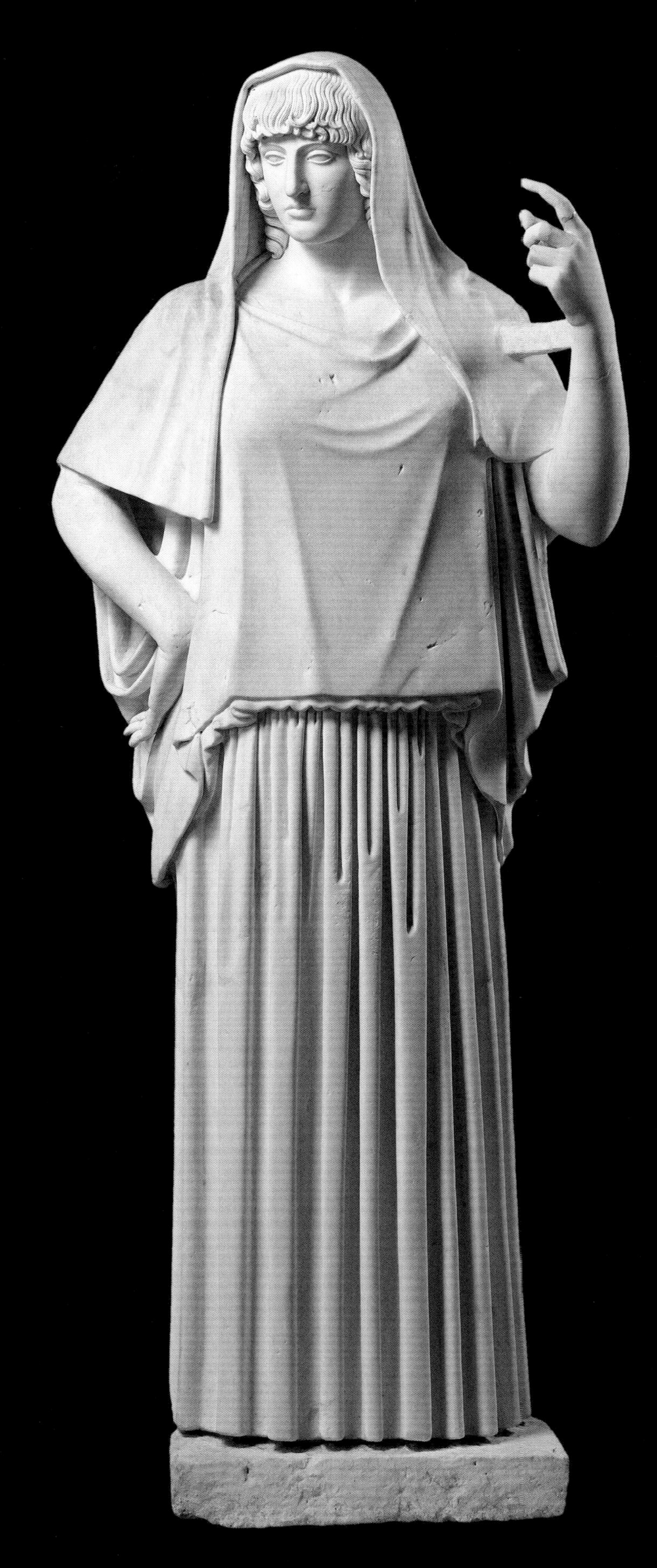

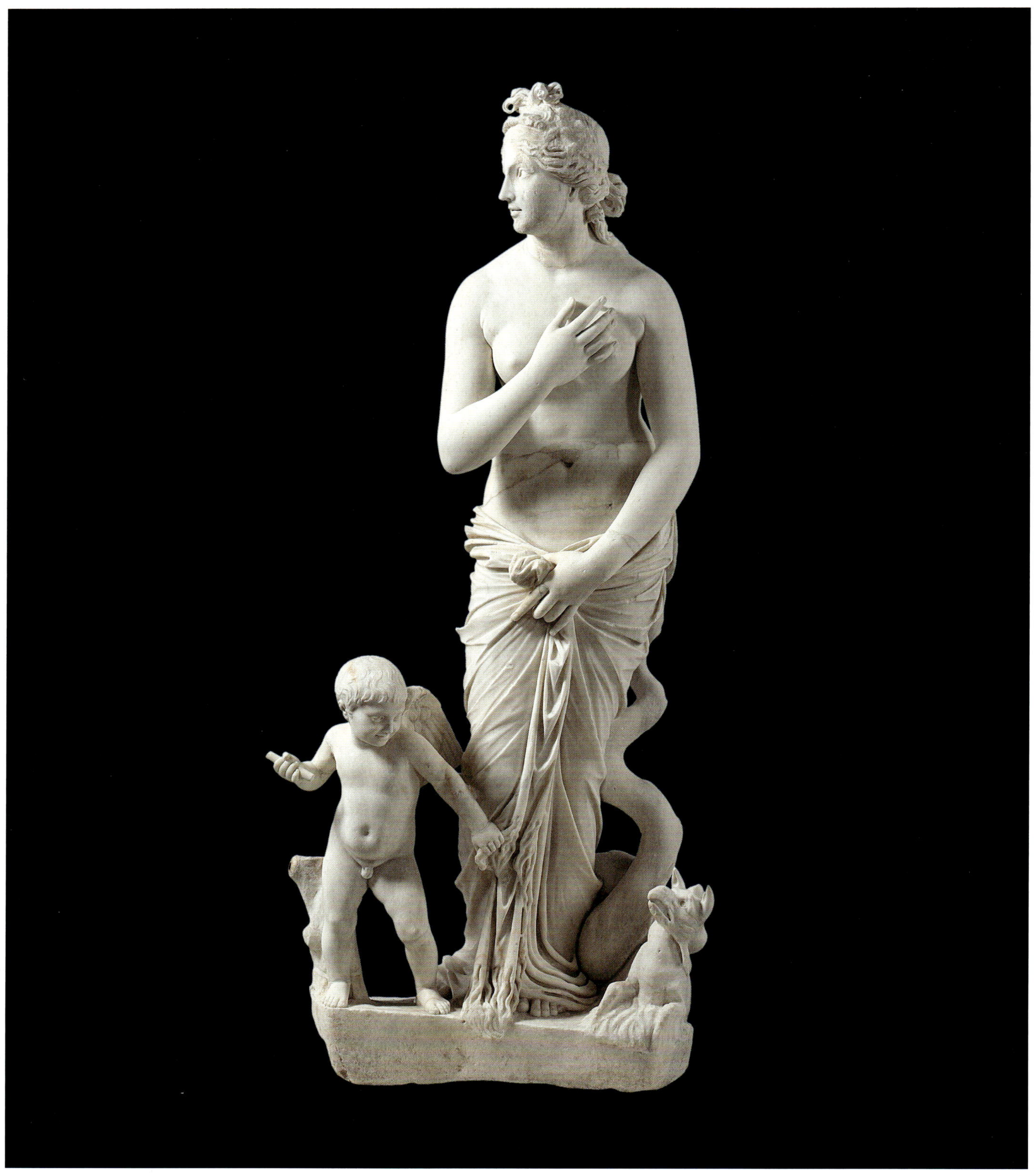

29
Statue of Aphrodite with Eros and Ketos
First half of 2nd century
Marble; 191 × 87 × 50 cm

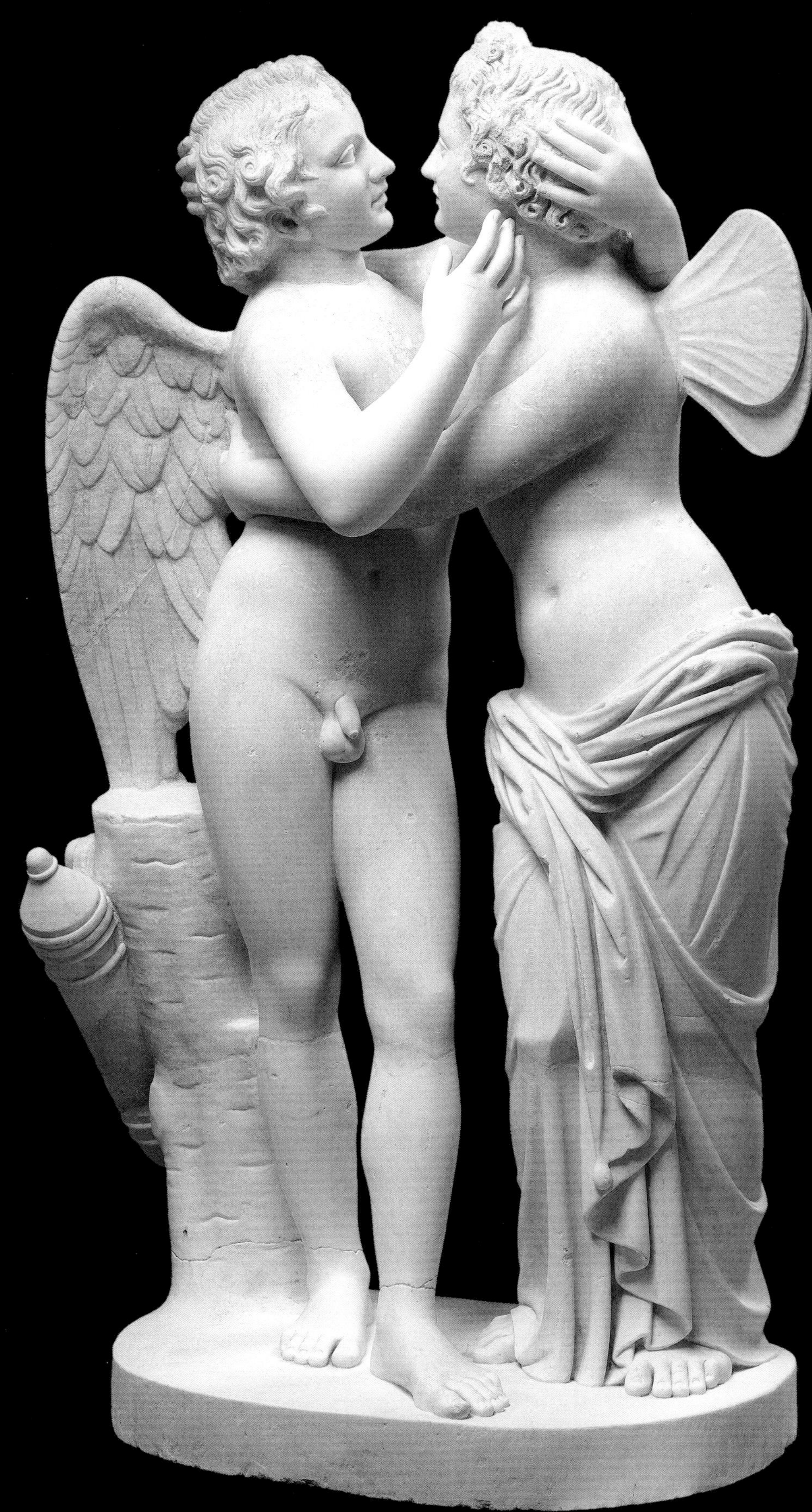

30
Statue of Cupid and Psyche
Second half of 2nd century
Marble; 130 × 81 × 54 cm

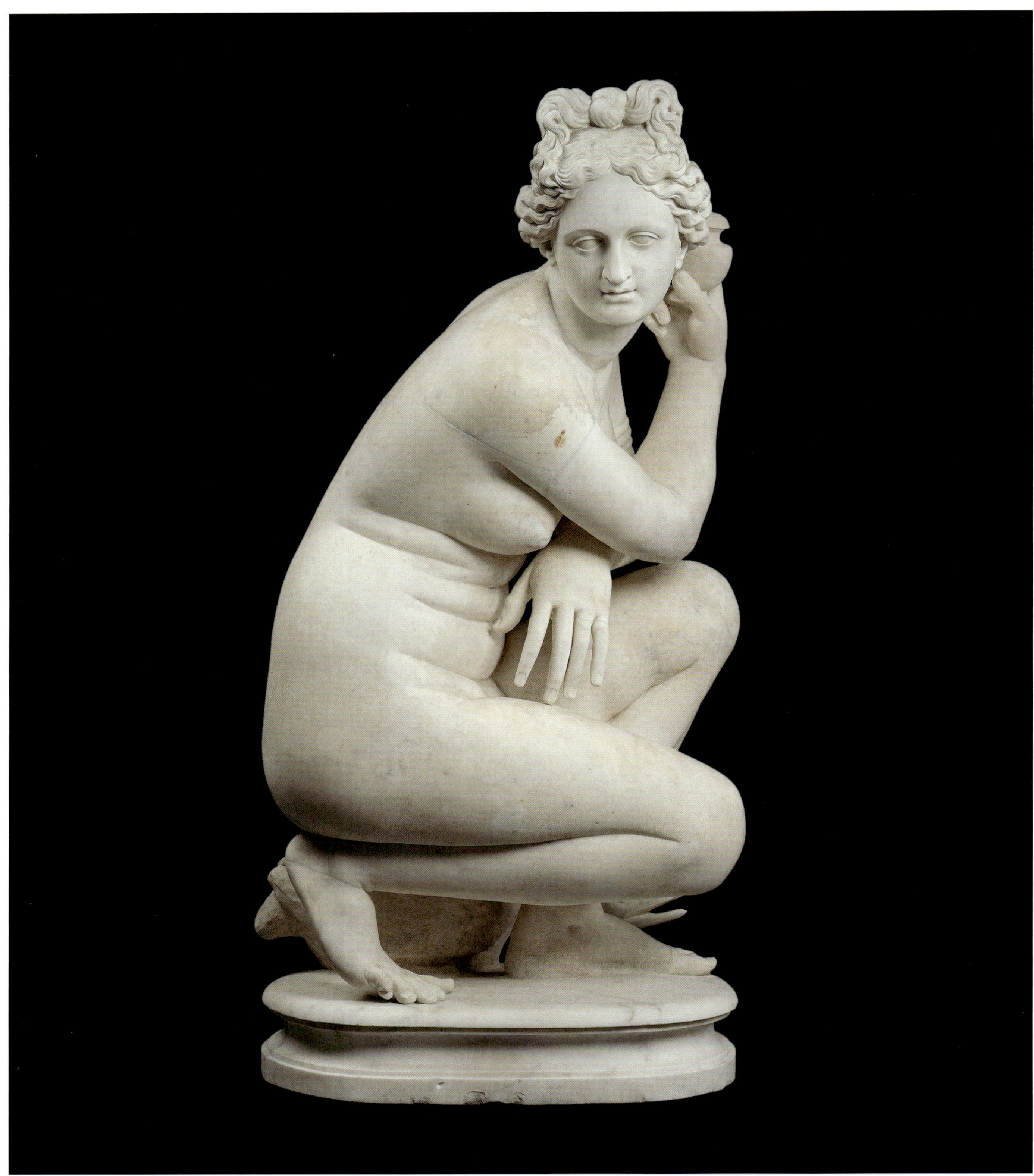

31
Statue of Crouching Aphrodite
1st century
Marble; 128 × 45 × 64 cm

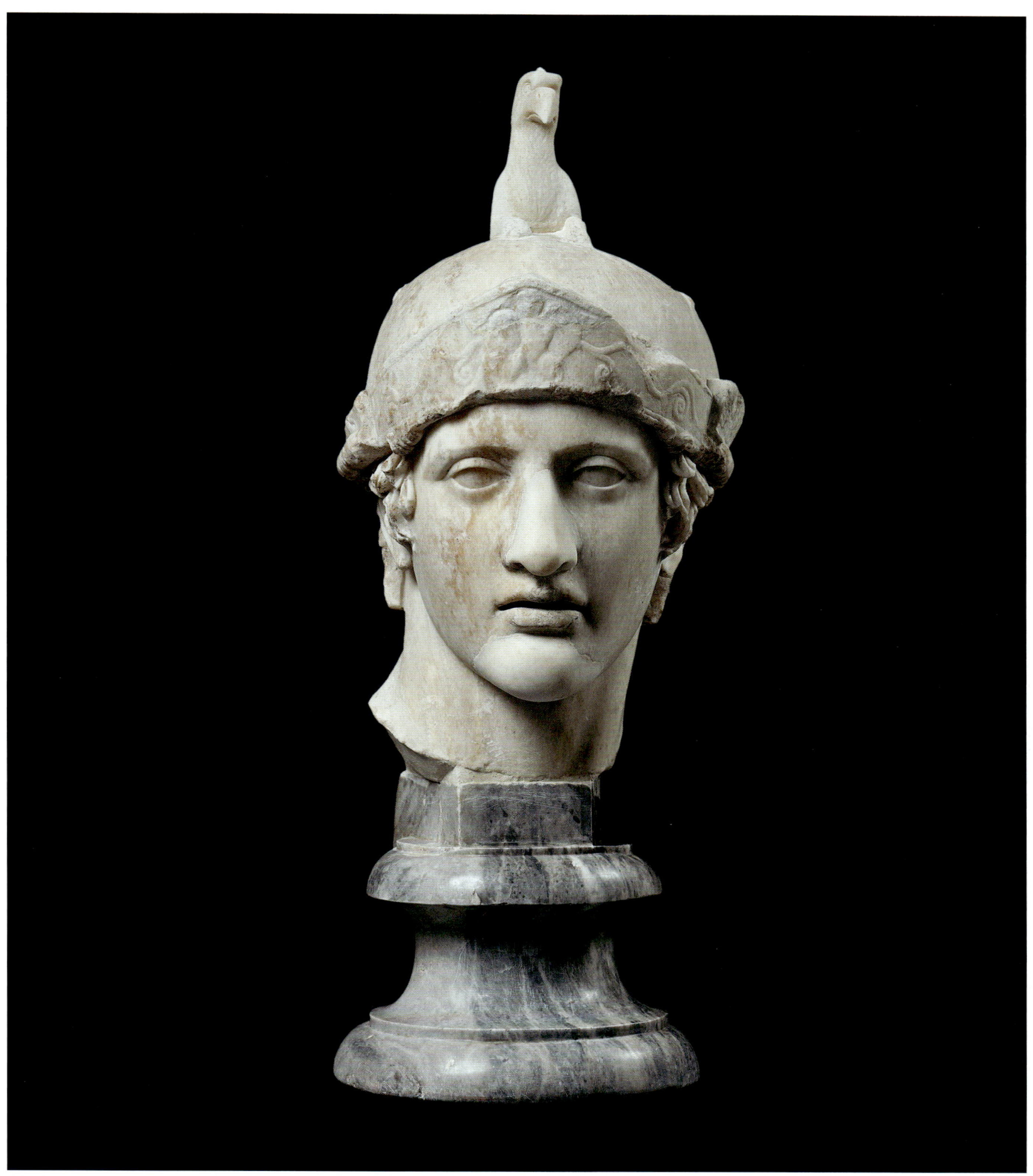

32
Head of Mars
First half of 2nd century
Marble; 63 × 24 × 26 cm

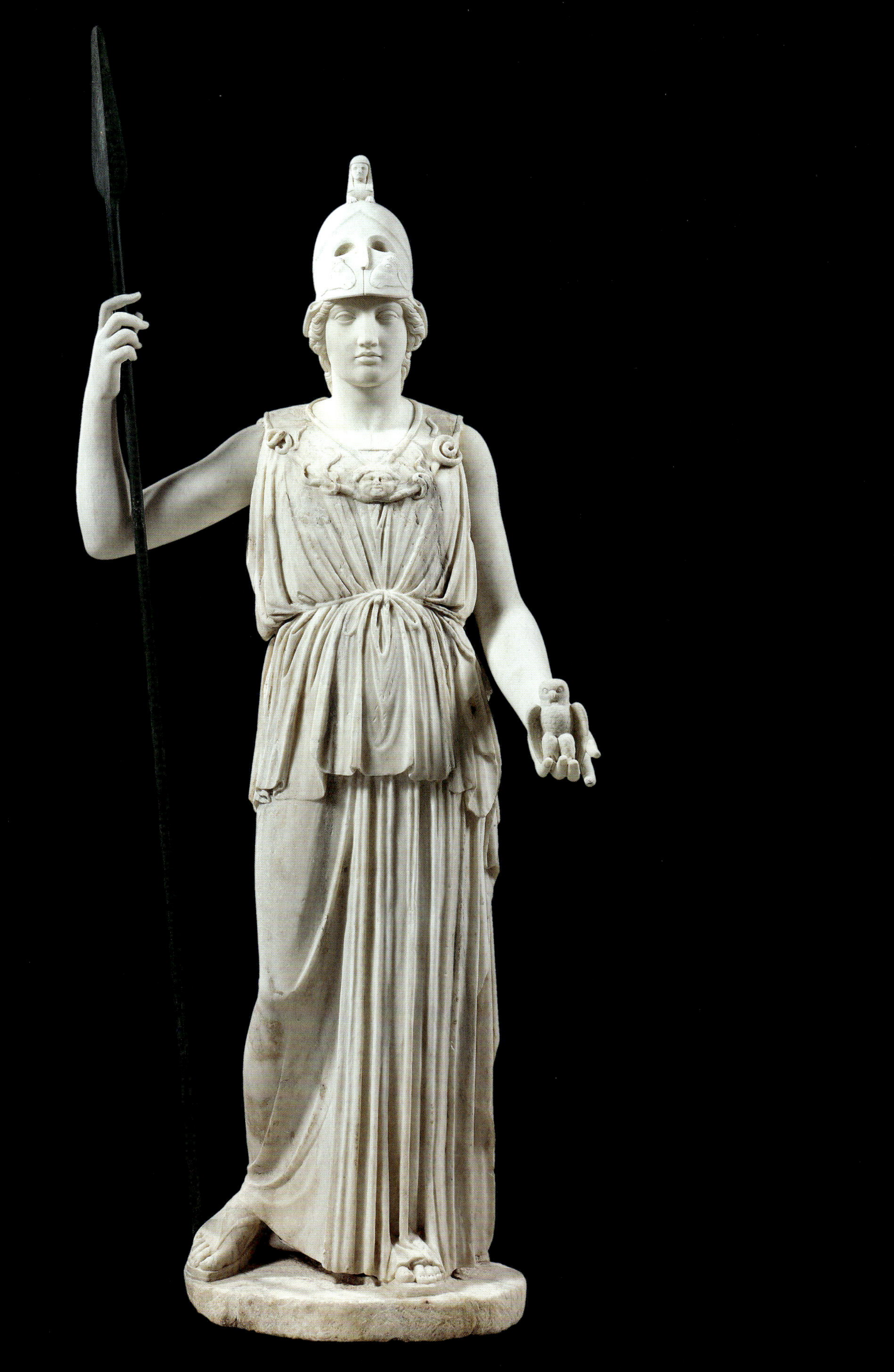

ATHENA, as she was known to Greeks, or Minerva to Romans, was the goddess of wisdom. A Roman sculptor based this statue on one of the most famous sculptures from ancient Greece: the Athena Parthenos, the monumental statue of the goddess housed in the Parthenon on the Athenian Acropolis. The original, made in the fifth century BCE, was lost long ago, but the Greek author Pausanias's writings give us some idea of what it looked like. He described the Athena Parthenos as wearing a long tunic, a helmet, and an armored breastplate, holding a statue of Nike (Victory) in one hand and a spear in the other, with her shield propped against her leg. This statue, made several centuries later, preserves Athena Parthenos's most iconic feature: the breastplate covered in snakes and adorned with the face of the gorgon Medusa, a figure from Greek mythology who has writhing, living serpents for hair.

Once part of the famed Giustiniani Collection, this Athena has undergone significant physical changes over the centuries. At some point in its history, its gray-streaked Pentelic marble was covered with a coating of gypsum to achieve a more uniform surface. The sculpture is also now on its third head: the first is long gone; the second wore a simple helmet, as seen in artists' drawings made when the statue was in the Giustiniani Collection; and this head, the third, was attached at some point after the statue entered the Torlonia Collection. The modification probably took place at the same time that the left arm holding a small owl was added—the owl being the symbol of both the city of Athens and the Torlonia Family.

33
Statue of Athena
Late 1st century BCE–early 1st century CE
Marble; 181 × 70 × 46 cm

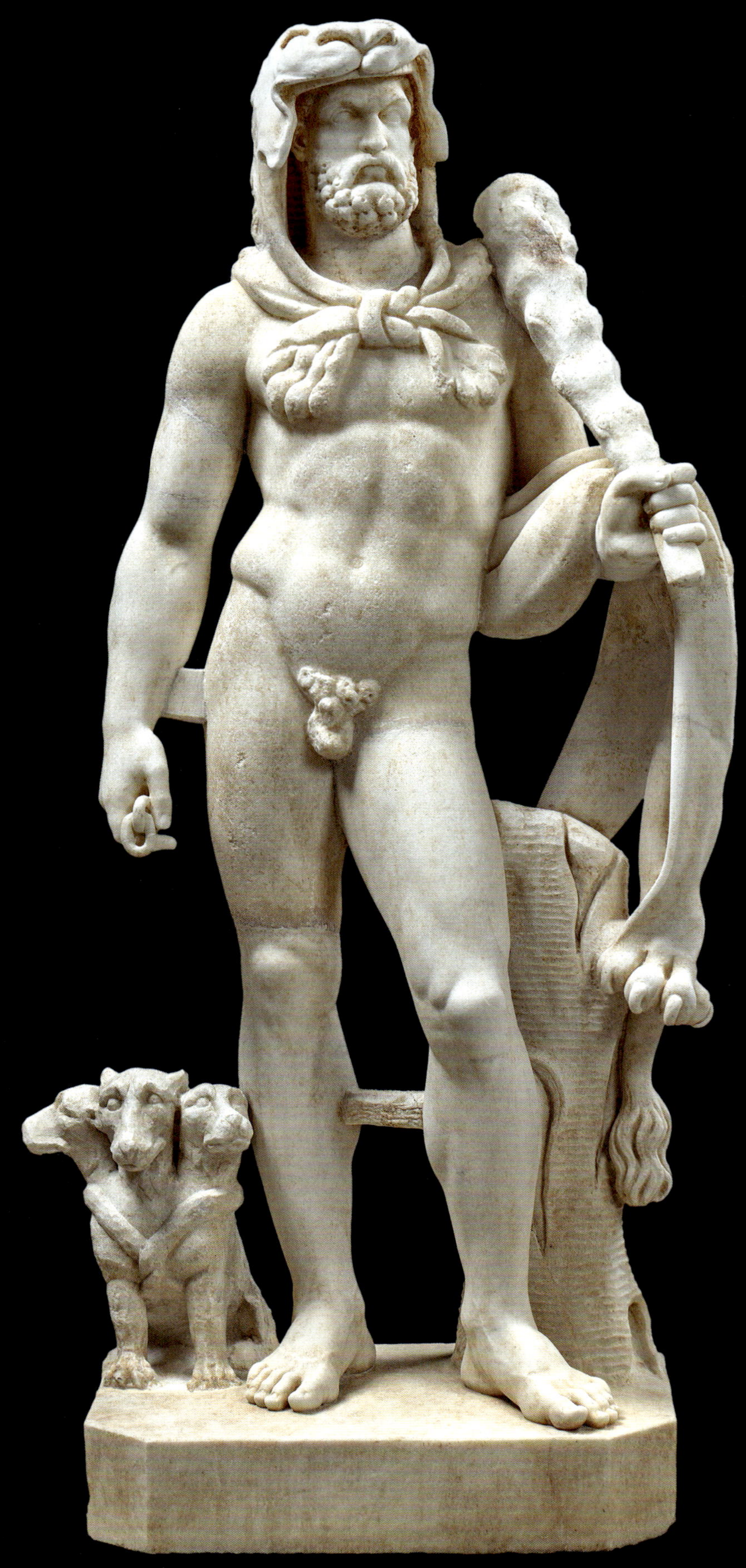

34
Statue of Hercules
Late 2nd century
Marble; 100 × 51 × 30 cm

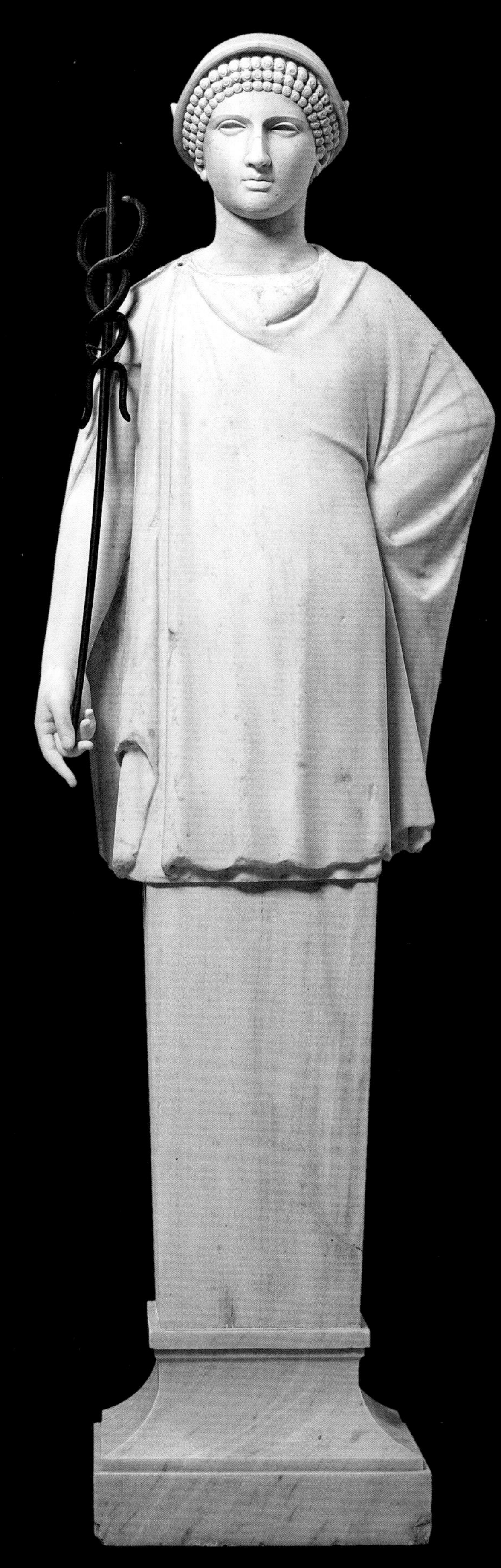

35
Statue of Mercury in the Form of a Herm
2nd century
Marble; 182 × 61 × 30 cm

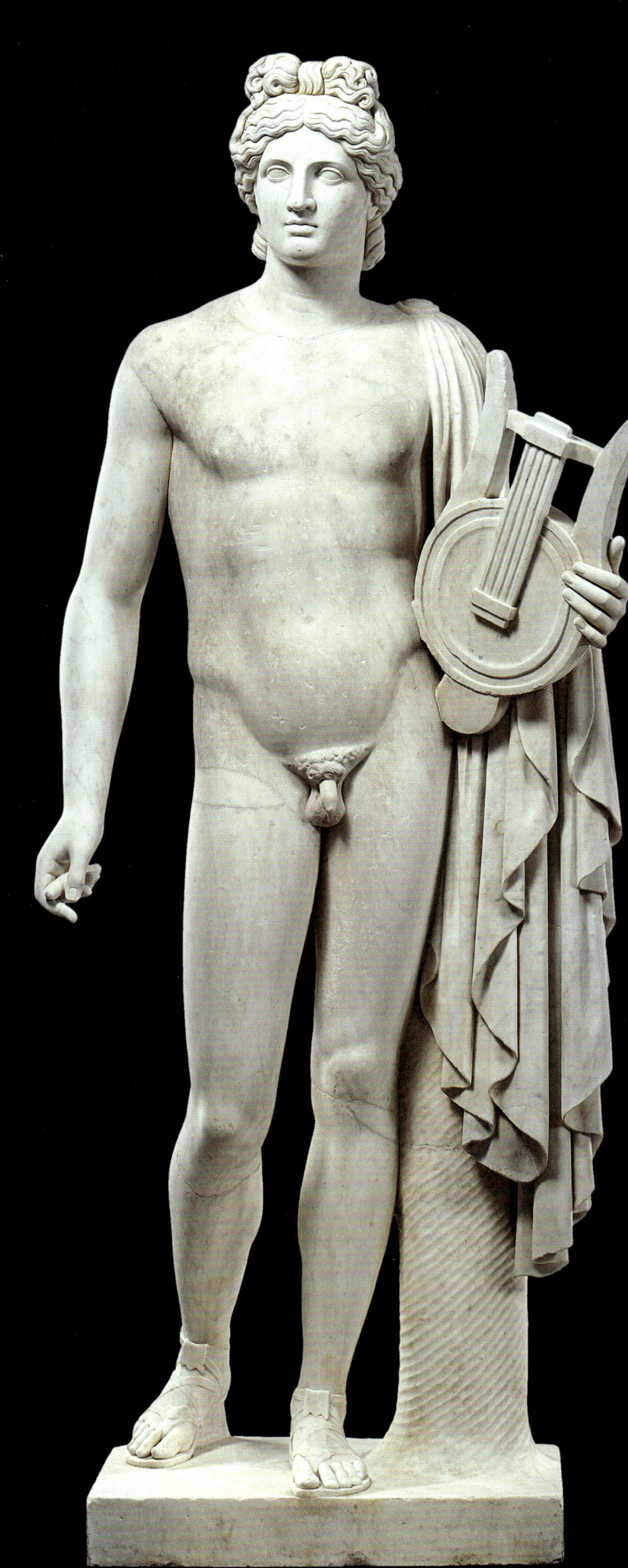

36
Statue of Apollo
2nd century
Marble; 187 × 75 × 56 cm

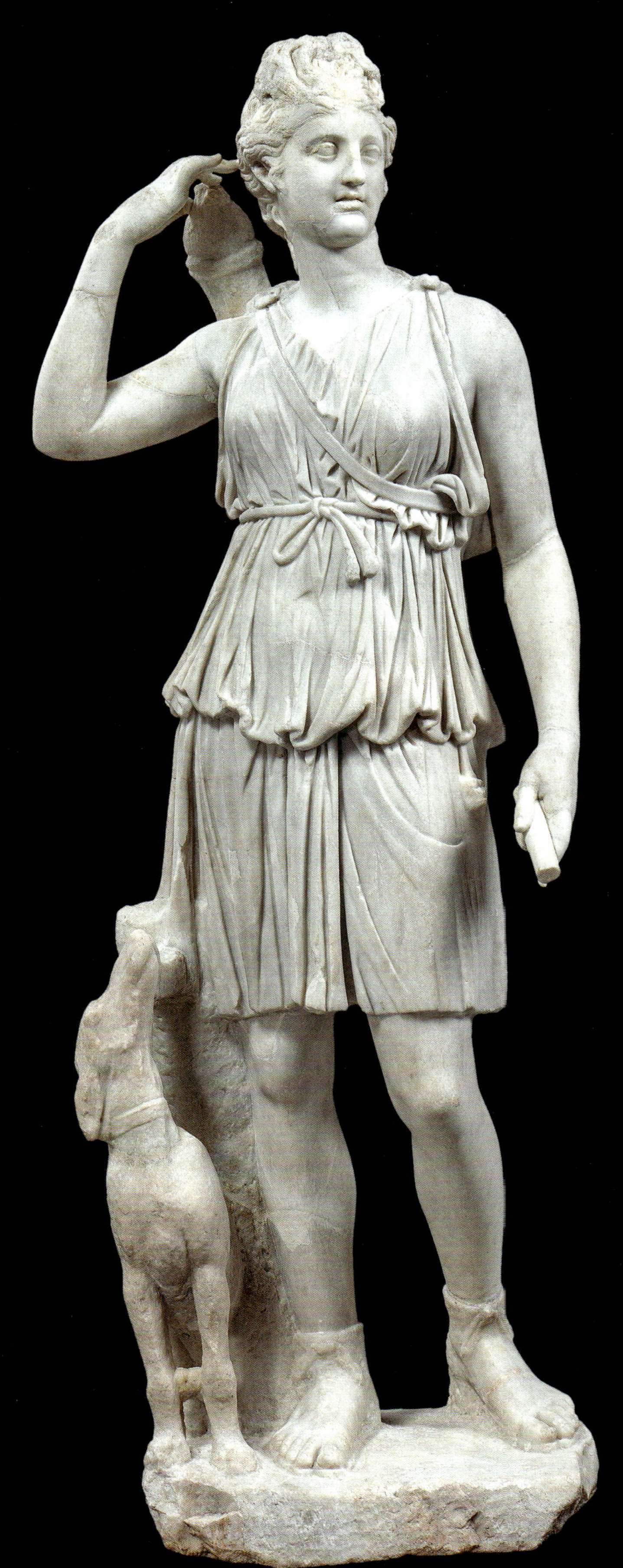

37
Statue of Artemis
Second half of 2nd century
Marble; 164 × 65 × 52 cm

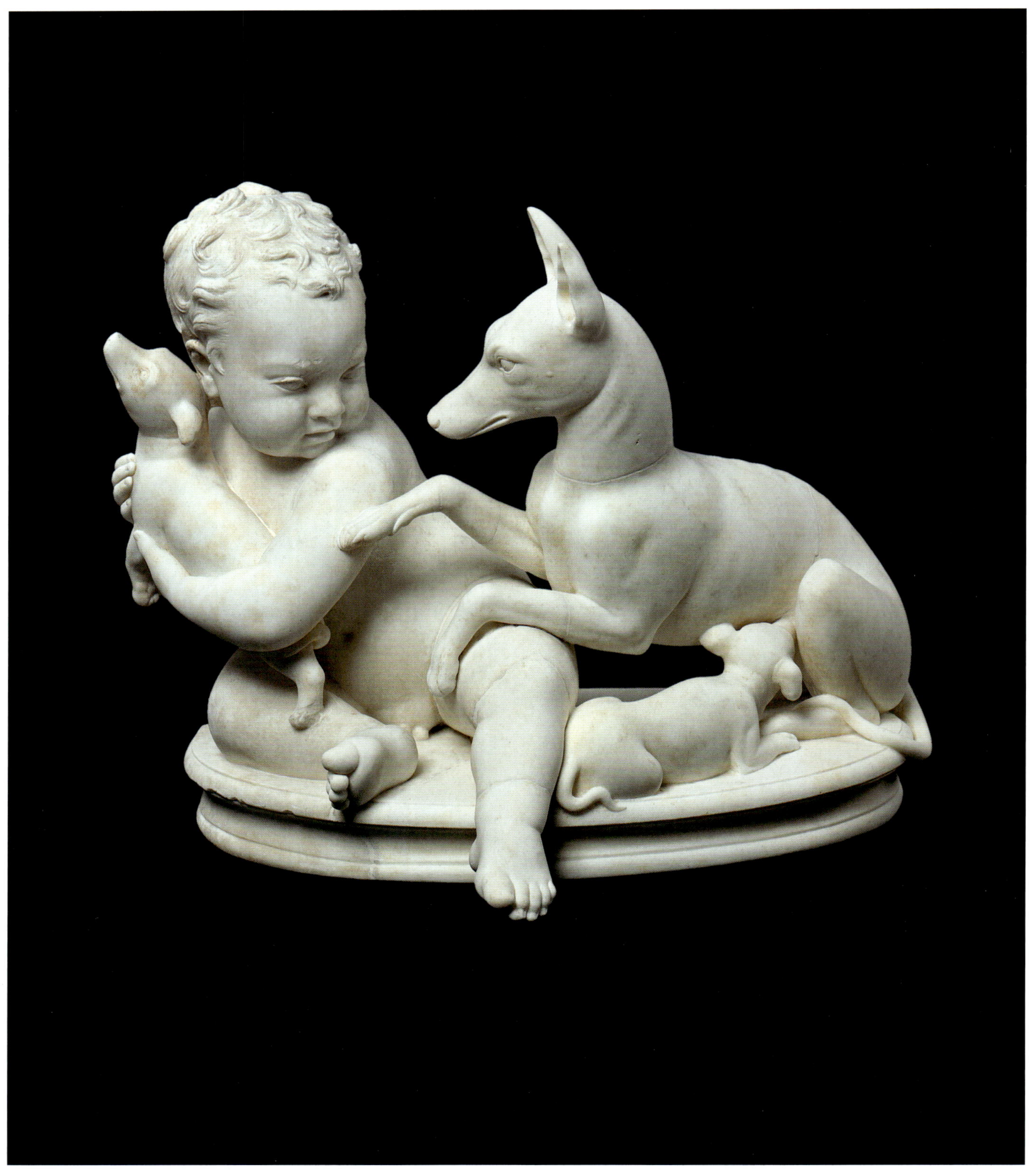

38
Statue of a Boy with Dogs
2nd century
Marble; 48 × 59 × 41 cm

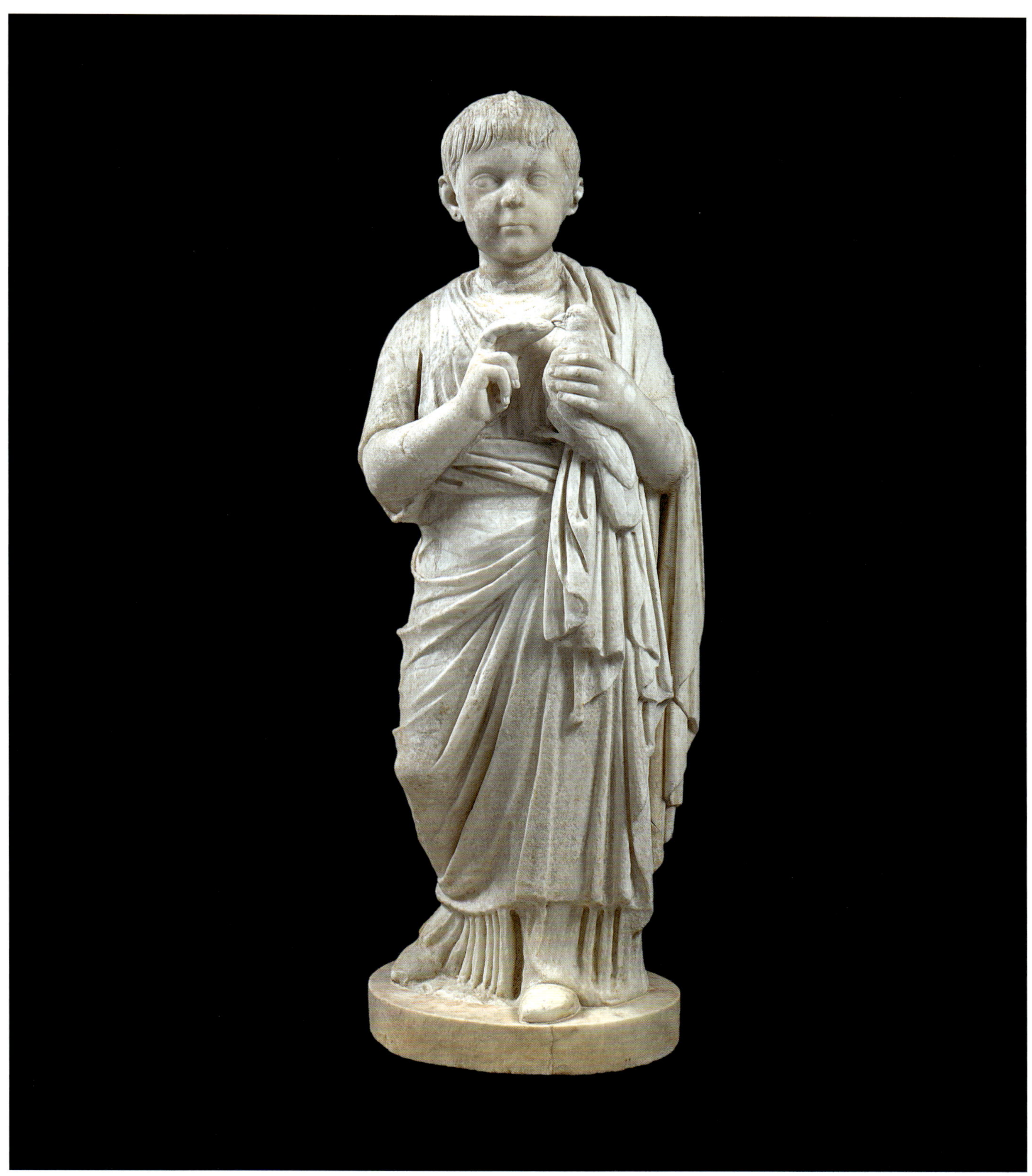

39
Statue of a Girl Holding a Bird
First half of 2nd century
Marble; 96 × 36 × 33 cm

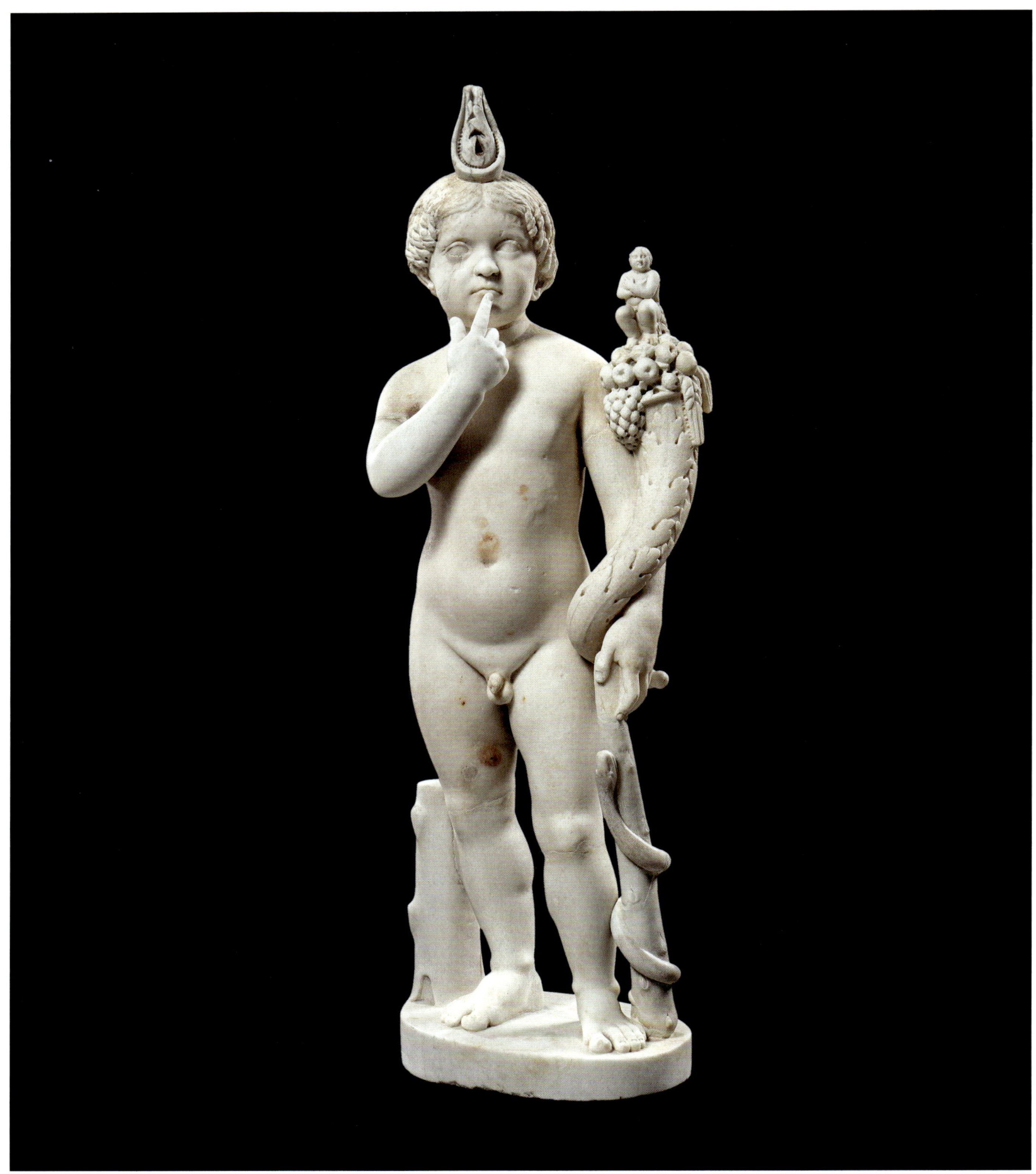

40
Statue of a Boy, restored as Harpocrates
1st–2nd century
Marble; 88 × 33 × 28 cm

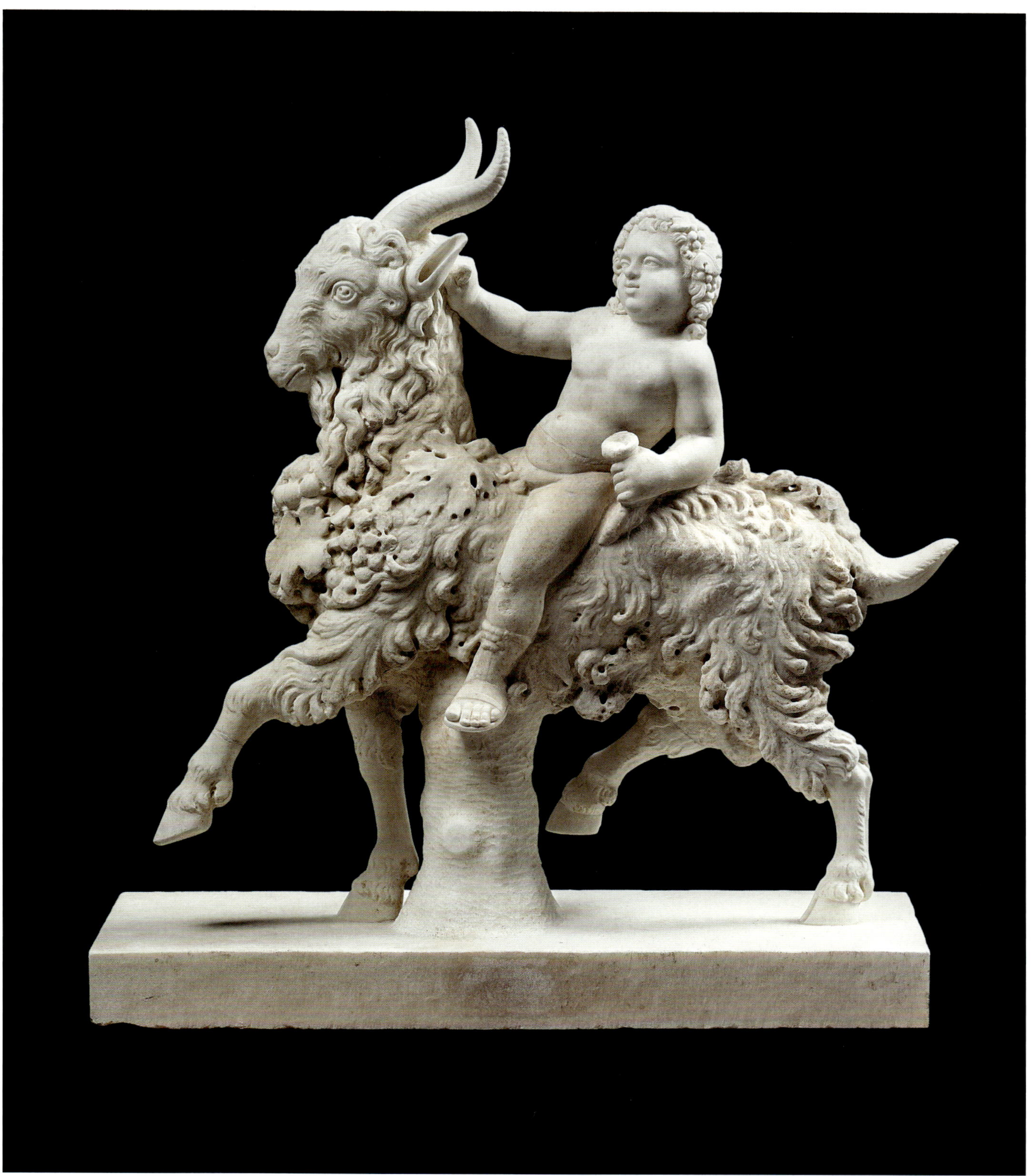

41
Statue of the Infant Bacchus on a Ram
1st–2nd century
Marble; 60 × 60 × 21 cm

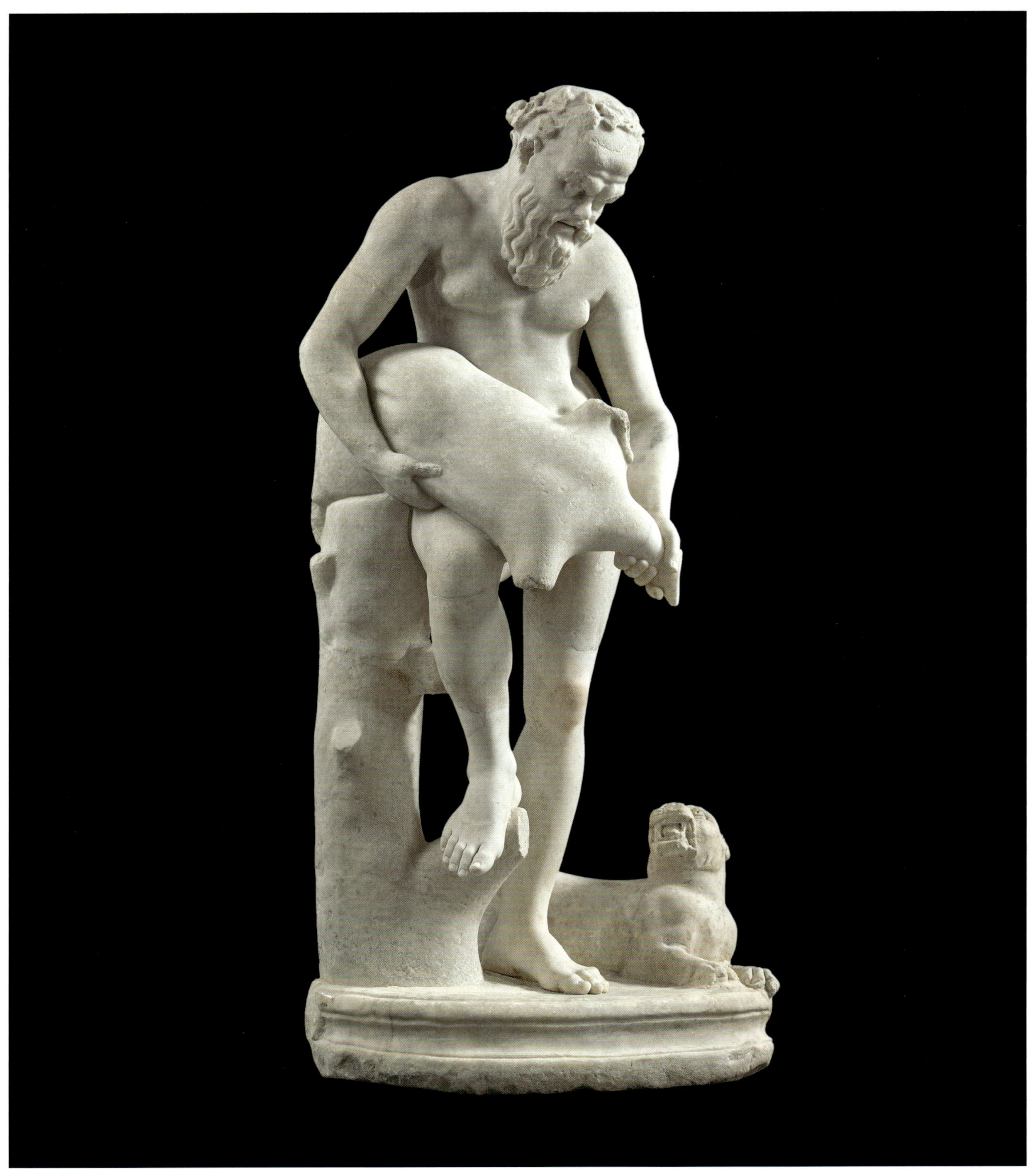

42
Statue of the Cesi-Type Silenus (Old Satyr)
1st century
Marble; 125 × 63 × 56 cm

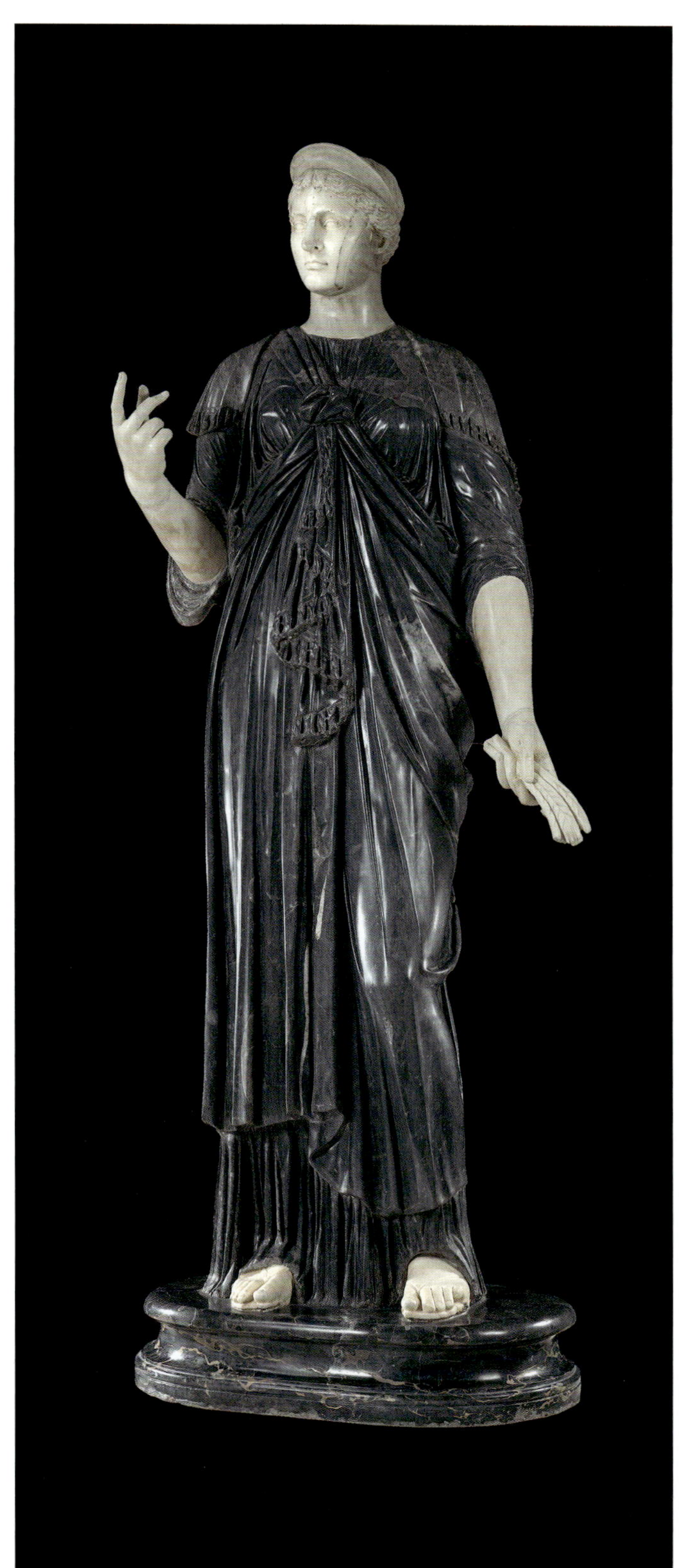

43
Statue of Isis, restored as Ceres
2nd–early 3rd century
Marble; 198 × 89 × 66 cm

44
Statue of Isis
2nd century
Marble; 151 × 49 × 49 cm

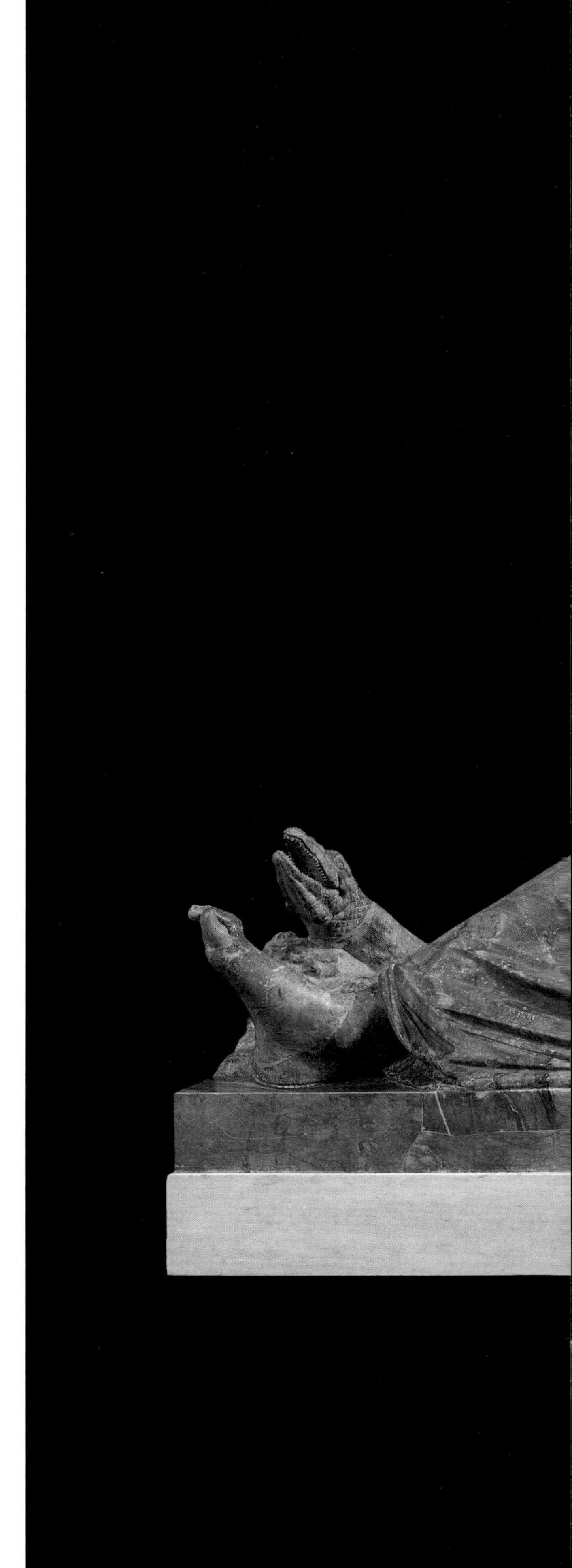

45
The Torlonia Nile, formerly the Barberini-Albani Nile
Late 1st century
Marble; 148 × 230 × 80 cm

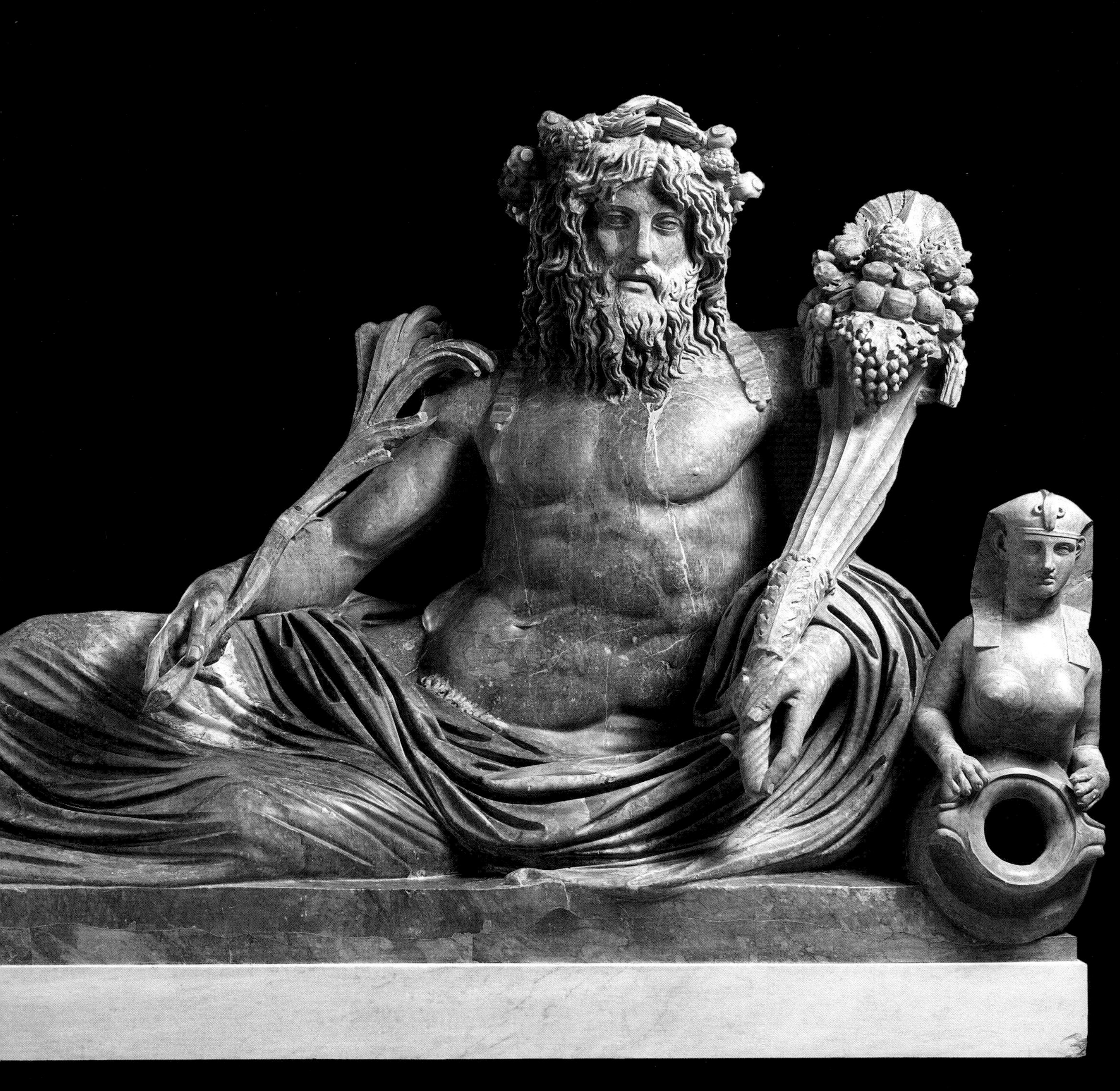

ARTEMIS, THE VIRGIN HUNTRESS, wears a costume that refers to the realms over which she has domain: the animals projecting from her dress, including dogs, deer, cattle, and griffins, allude to her role as overseer of wild beasts both real and imagined; the zodiac symbols of Cancer, Scorpio, and Aries on her chest represent her lunar nature; and the thick beribboned garland draped around her neck may refer to her role as a goddess of nature concerned with vegetation and the fertility of the earth. Artemis's most striking feature, however, is the rows of pendulous "breasts"—a typical feature of Ephesian images of Artemis that was not often used in Roman imagery. Different interpretations have been offered for the bulbous forms: they may represent breasts, bull testicles, or large amber or resinous beads. If they do signify breasts, we can interpret them as a sign of Artemis's role as nurturer and protector.

The Torlonia work reproduces a cult statue of the goddess that once stood in the largest temple to Artemis in antiquity, located in the city of Ephesus on the west coast of Asia Minor (present-day Turkey). The original cult statue, which functioned as an embodiment of the goddess and an object of veneration, was likely a *xoanon*, a wooden statue or trunk with arms and a head crafted from different materials, upon which clothing and garlands were draped. The statue was probably destroyed by a fire in the fourth century BCE and replaced with a marble statue. By the second century CE, when this work was made, marble versions of Ephesian Artemis had spread across the Roman Empire, suggesting that her protective nature had become generalized and less closely tied to the city where this type was born.

46
Statue of Artemis Ephesia
2nd century
Marble; 117 × 33 × 37 cm

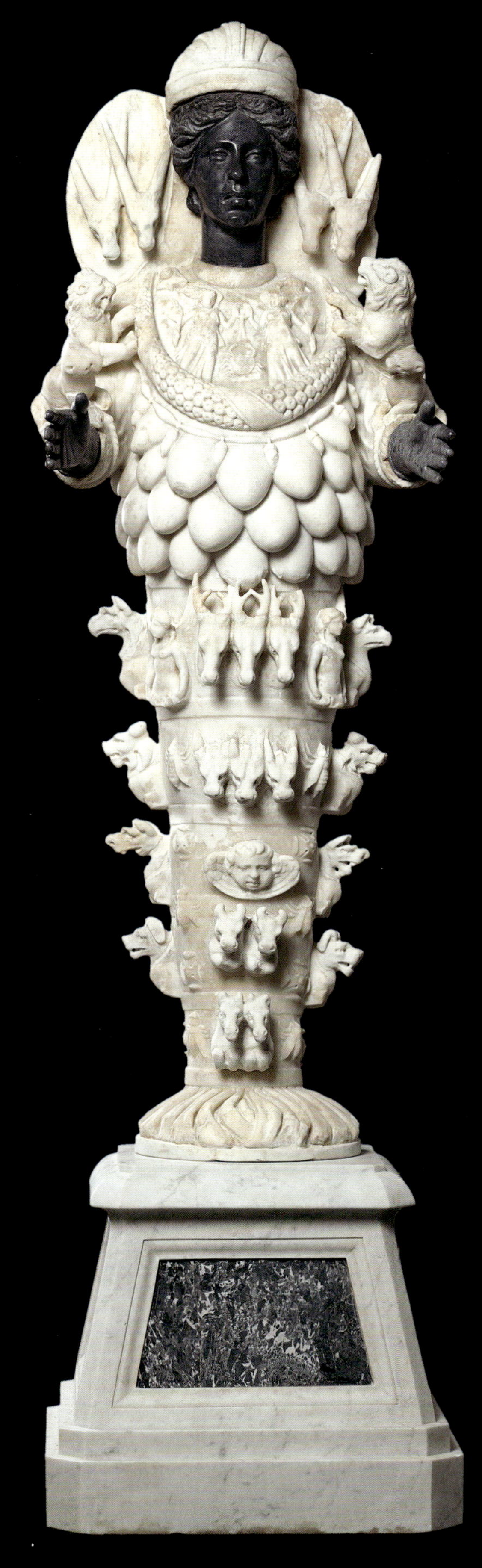

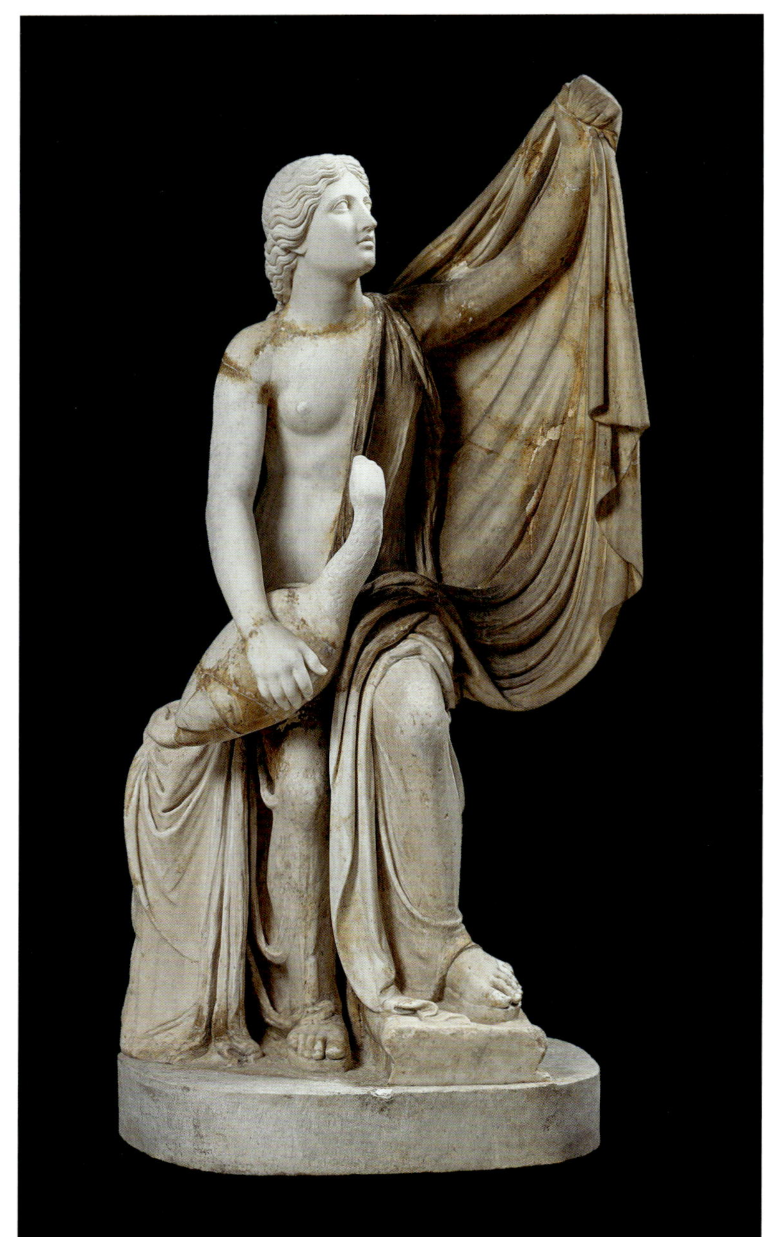

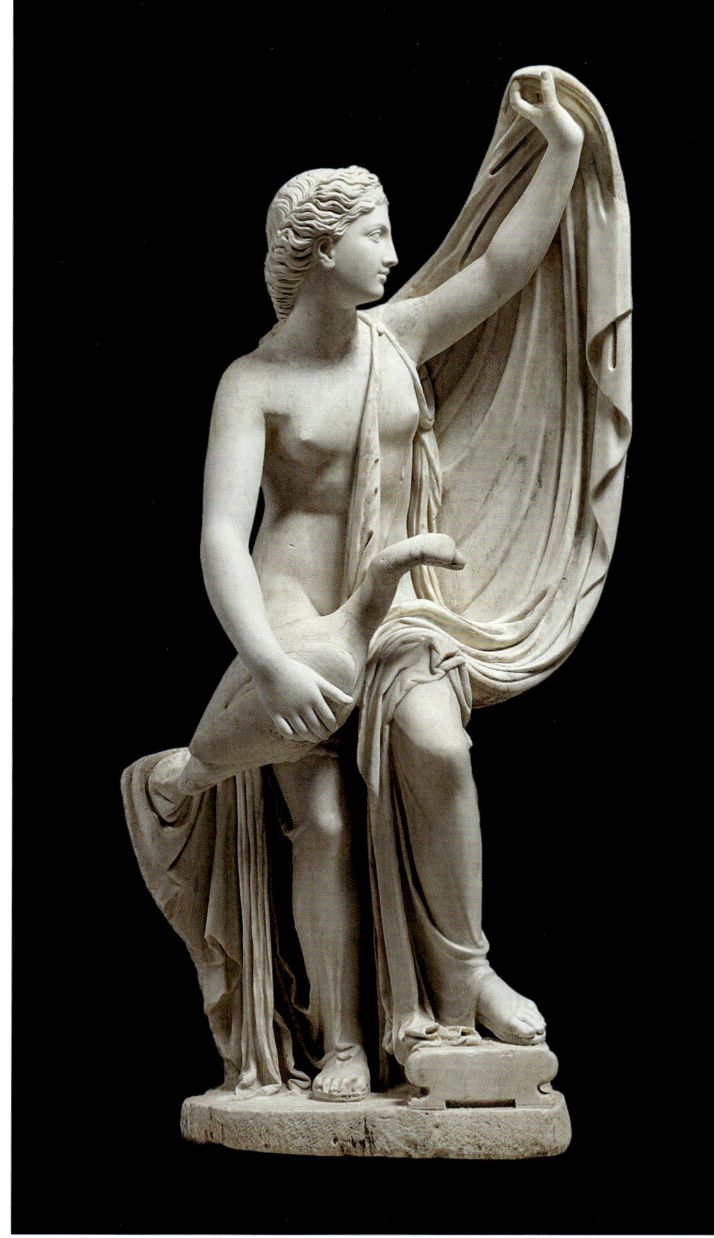

47
Statue of Leda and the Swan
Late 2nd century
Marble; 143 × 69 × 49 cm

48
Statue of Leda and the Swan
First half of 2nd century
Marble; 141 × 68 × 43 cm

LEDA, THE QUEEN OF SPARTA, HOLDS A SWAN in her lap. In both of these strikingly similar sculptures, she gently supports the bird with her right hand. But the swan is no mere animal: it is the supreme god Zeus (or Jupiter, to Romans), who transformed himself in order to seduce the mortal woman. Both sculptors expertly rendered the sheer, diaphanous tunic clinging to Leda's left breast and the thicker, voluminous cloak she raises with her left hand.

The two Torlonia statues of Leda and the swan number among more than twenty known surviving examples of this subject, which modern scholars believe is based on a work created by the Greek sculptor Timotheus in the fourth century BCE. This sculptural type demonstrates a remarkable level of formal and stylistic consistency across the different replicas, a feature that is best appreciated when the works are displayed side by side. For Roman audiences, this level of standardization and seriality in sculptural production was not viewed as inferior or rote imitation. Rather, Roman versions of earlier sculptures by renowned Greek artists were considered valuable, and an ancient person might purchase one as a demonstration of their cultural sophistication—just as a person today might purchase a print of a favorite artwork. Some Roman sculptures of Greek works are even signed by their artists, a clear indication that the objects were valued in their own right and not just for what they evoked.

Note a major difference between these works: the sculpture on the right (cat. 48) has been fully cleaned by Torlonia Laboratories' conservators, but parts of the one on the left (cat. 47) were intentionally left uncleaned to demonstrate how the surface of the marble has changed over time. Interventions from the early modern era, such as Greek pitch used as an adhesive and filler, as well as organic substances applied to help the modern additions blend with the ancient stone, are visible. Atmospheric pollutants have settled on and interacted with the marble, darkening the uncleaned areas on Leda's cloak and parts of her body and the swan. In select areas, Torlonia conservators aimed to remove surface alterations without interfering with the marble's natural patina, restoring these parts to resemble what they looked like when the work was exhibited in the nineteenth century.

RELIEFS

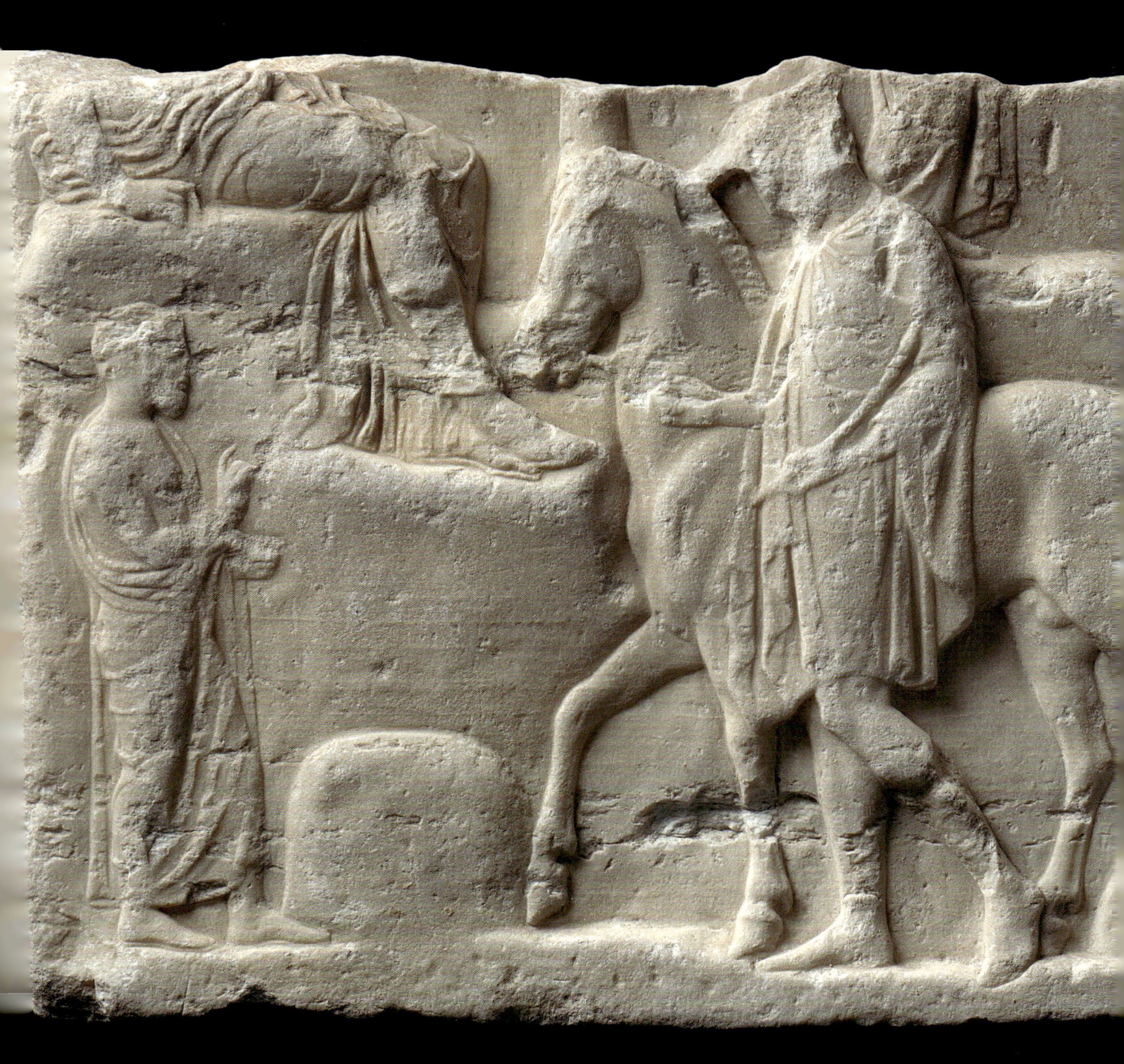

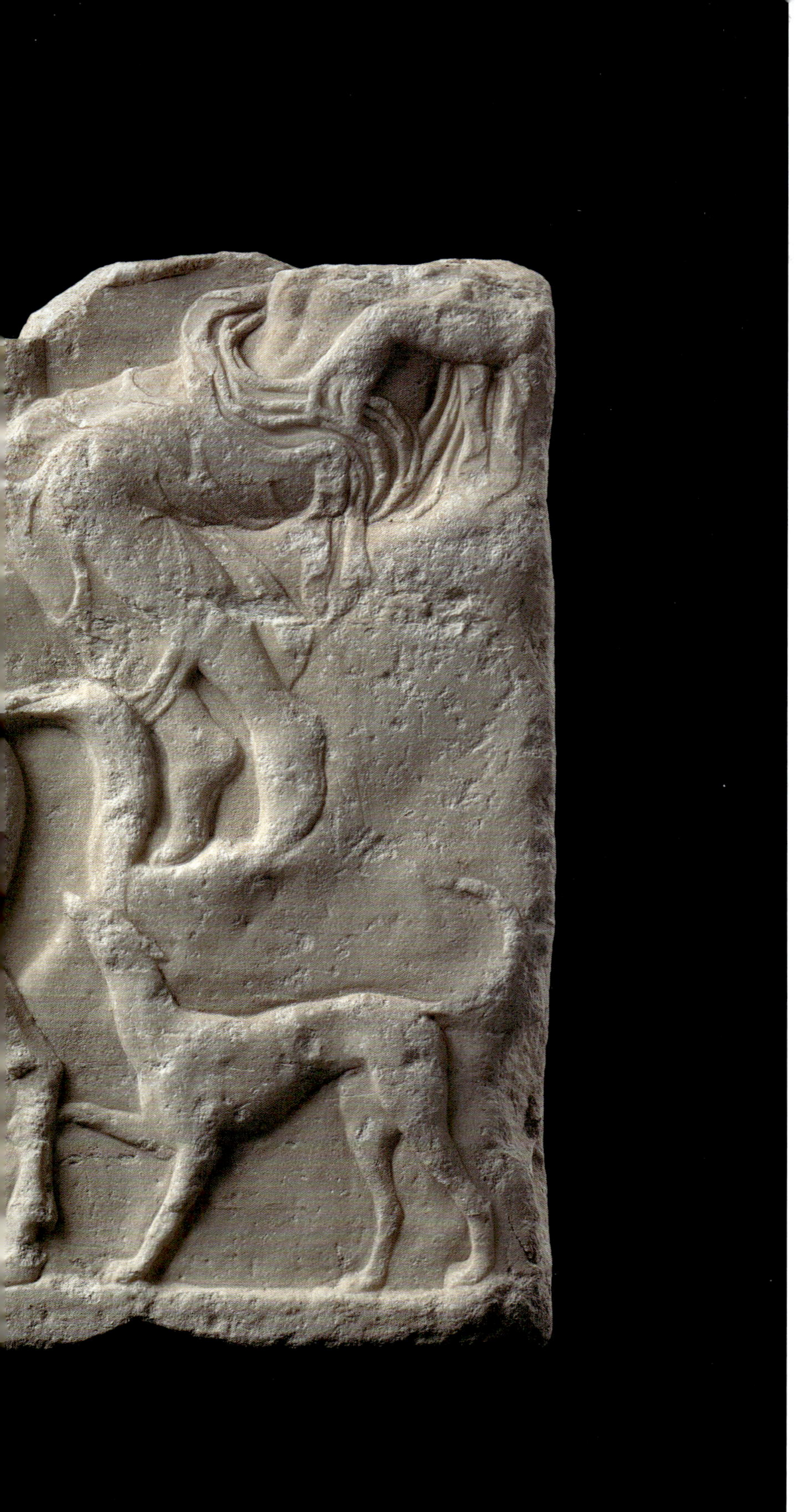

49
Attic Votive Relief
Late 5th century BCE
Marble; 41 × 67 × 11 cm

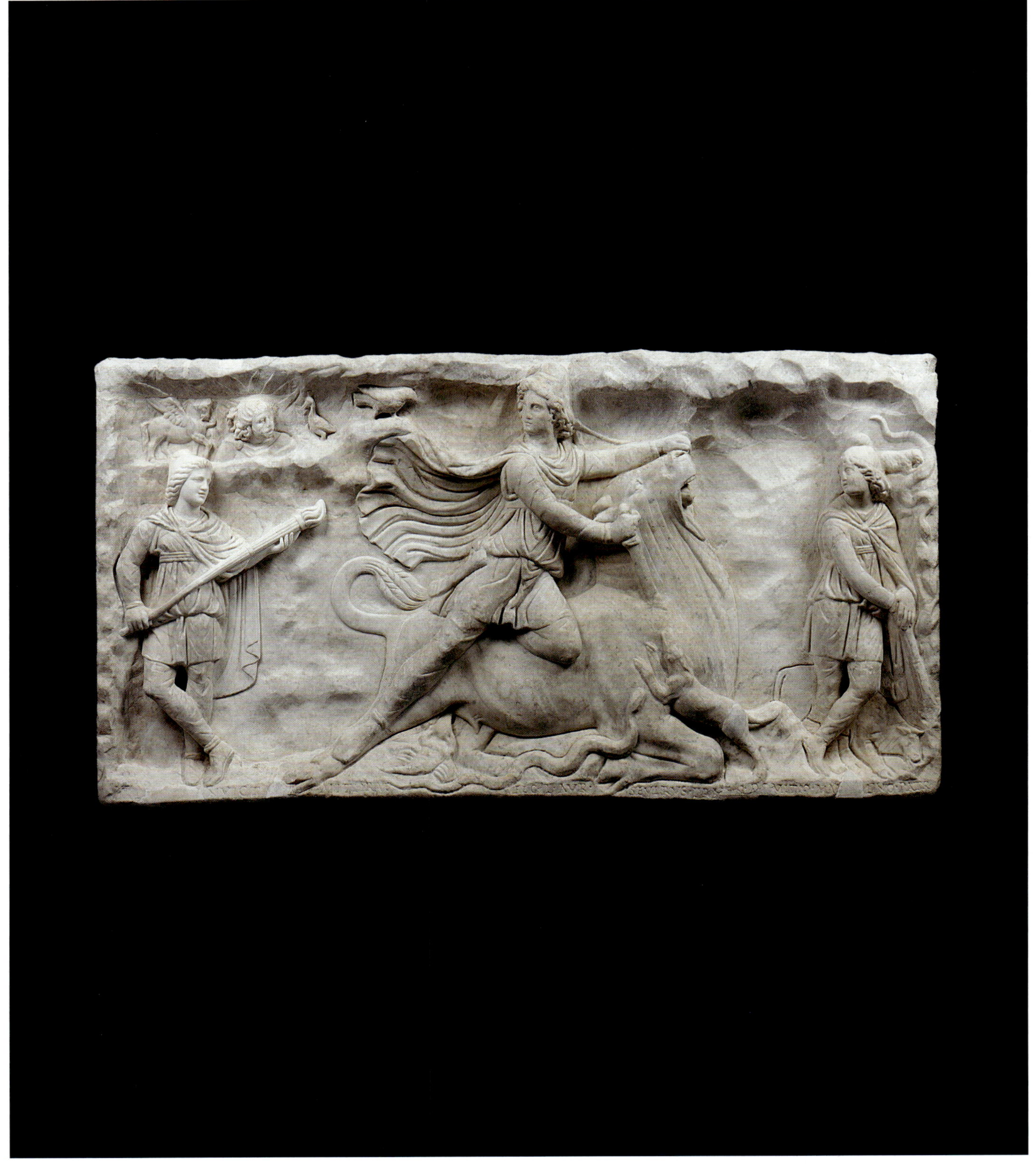

50
Relief of Mithraic Sacrifice
2nd century
Marble; 88 × 165 × 18 cm

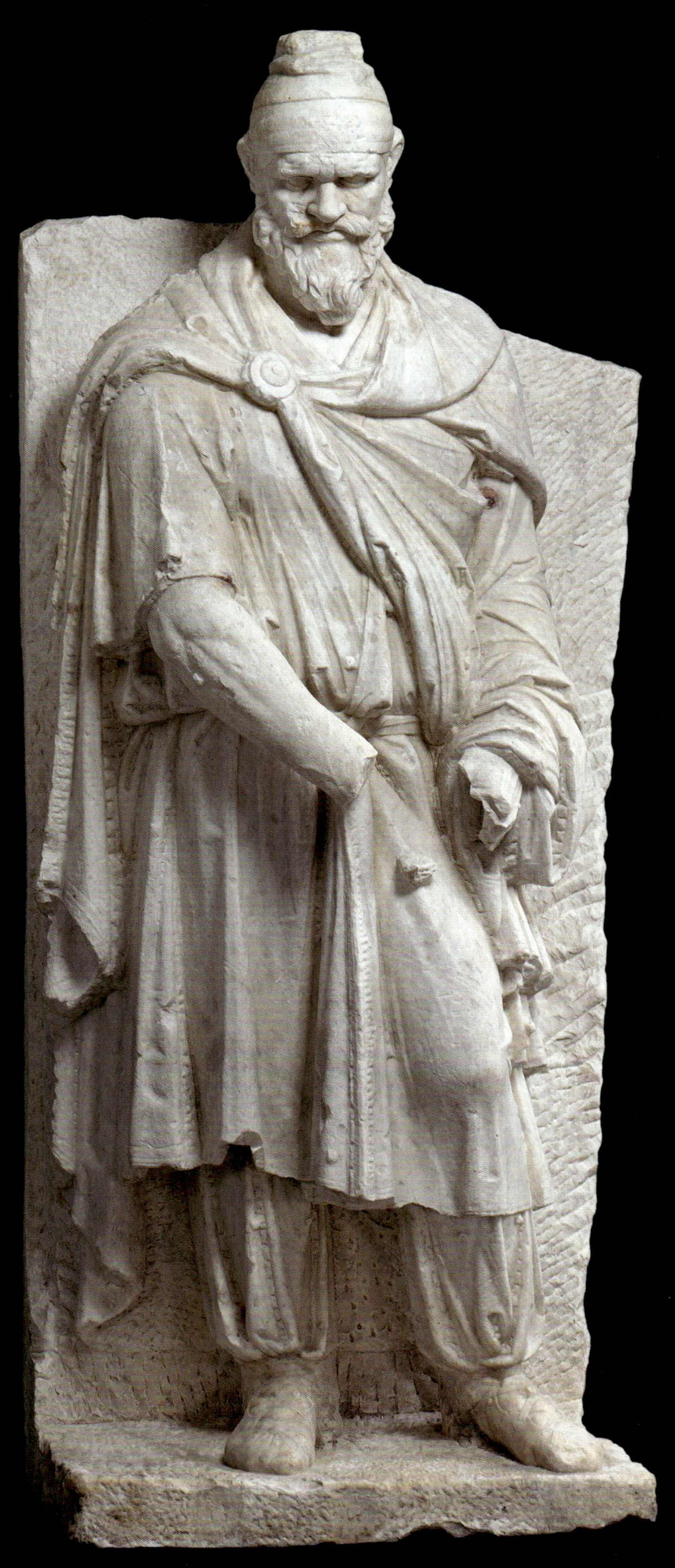

51
Unfinished Statue of a Dacian Prisoner
Early 2nd century
Marble; 245 × 111 × 70 cm

PORTUS was the primary port of imperial Rome. This large relief, excavated on the Torlonia estate at the site of the ancient city in 1864, offers a rare representation of the place where it was found. The dizzying array of worldly and divine images in this scene, both real and imagined, can help contemporary viewers imagine the sights and stimuli that ancient people might have experienced when they sailed or stepped into the port.

Ships, people, and sculptures crowd this bustling, dynamic harbor. Atop the leftmost merchant ship, three people make a sacrifice over an altar, likely in thanks for a safe journey. On a small boat at the rear of the ship, a single nude seafarer—perhaps an individual of African descent based on his hairstyle and facial features—steers the massive oar. The ship's sail bears images of the Capitoline she-wolf suckling the twins Romulus and Remus, the legendary founders of Rome. The smaller vessel at the right is already docked, and its crew members are unloading their cargo. A single, large eye—a symbol to ward off evil—floats in the space beneath the smaller ship's sail, while a lighthouse peeks out from between the ships, evoking the actual monument that once welcomed ancient sailors. Behind the smaller ship we can see another monument that no longer exists: a triumphal arch topped with a statue of a man driving a chariot led by four elephants.

Two statues of male figures flank the lighthouse: one with a lighthouse-shaped headdress represents the city of Portus, while the other, holding a cornucopia, may represent the Roman people. In the center stands a nude, bearded figure of Neptune, the Roman god of the sea; perhaps the sculptor included him to evoke his good favor. Depictions of Bacchus, the god of wine and revelry, appear in the upper right corner and on the ships' prows, perhaps also functioning as an auspicious figure. The inscription "V. L." on the left ship's sail could stand for *Votum Libero* or "dedicated to Liber," which suggests that this relief once functioned as a votive offering to Liber Pater ("Free Father"), the native Italian counterpart to Bacchus.

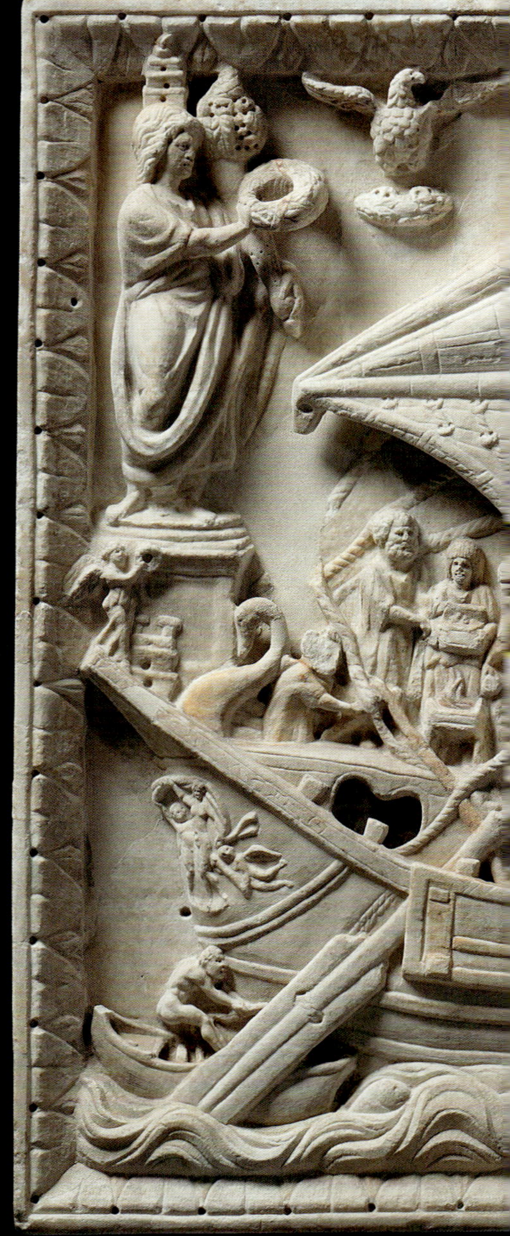

52
Portus Relief
Late 2nd–early 3rd century
Marble; 74 × 123 × 15 cm

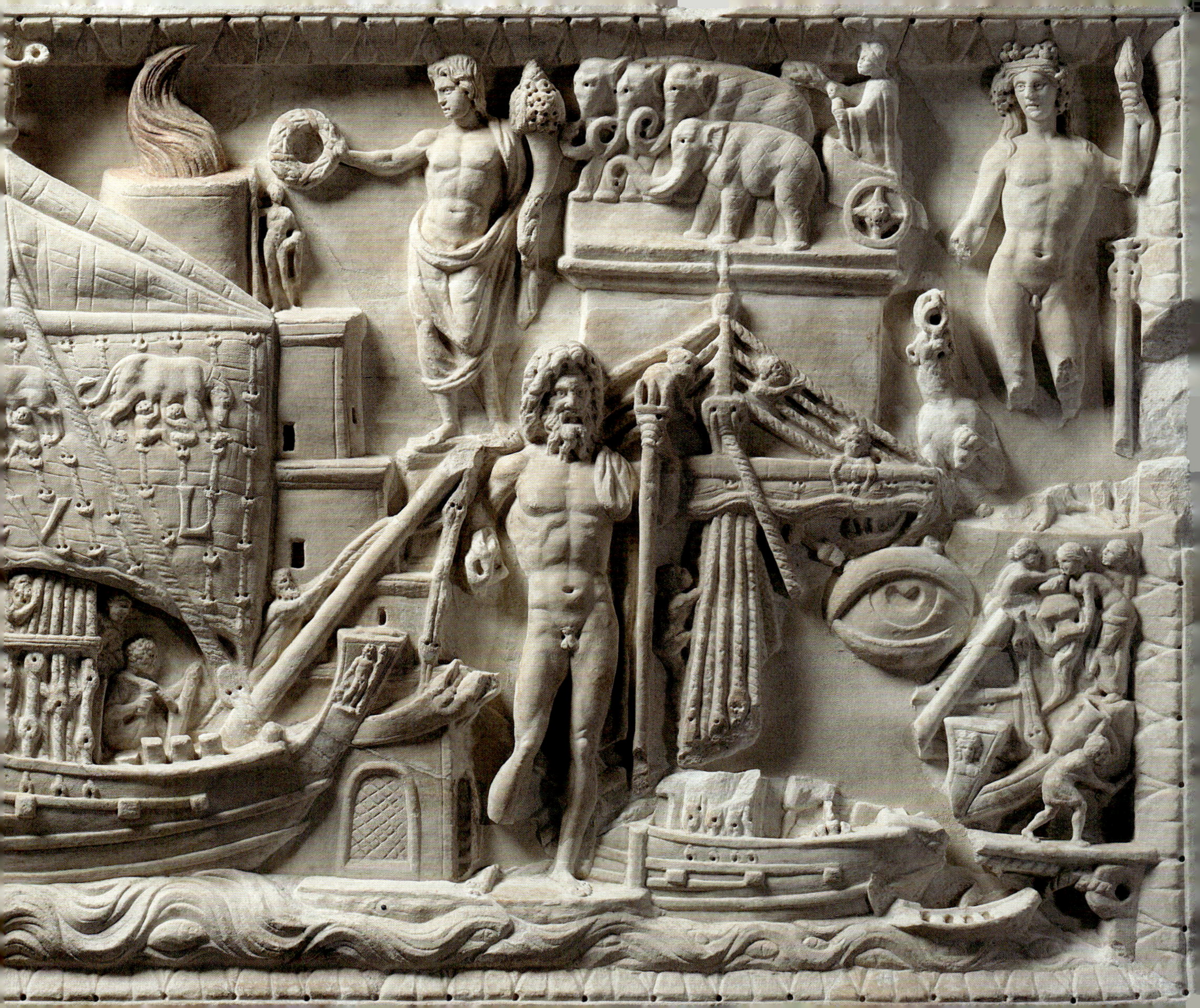
V L

IDEAL FORMS

KNOWN AS GERMANICUS, this idealized, nude young man is the lone bronze in the Torlonia Collection. The work was found in 1874 during excavations at a Torlonia estate in present-day Sabina, Italy (ancient Cures). As with many ancient works, it has both ancient and modern components that require some close looking to parse. In this case, the key is the draped stump affixed to the statue's right leg. Such supports are common for marble sculptures because the stone is vulnerable to fractures, especially at points where the marble narrows or projects out. Bronze sculptures, however, do not need extra struts and supports because of the material's inherent strength.

The draped stump is therefore a telltale giveaway: the right leg and stump were added by a modern restorer using plaster, not bronze. The nineteenth-century restorer may have misunderstood the aesthetic and functional characteristics of ancient Roman marble sculpture; they may have looked at comparable marble sculptures, abundant in collections around Rome, and assumed that a draped stump was essential or original to this type of design. Alternatively, the restorer may have recognized a need for additional support because the new leg was made of a weaker material than bronze. Whatever the reason, this bronze figure would not have needed any supports to stay upright when it was first created.

This work has historically been interpreted as Germanicus, a general and politician born into the powerful Julio-Claudian family, to which the first five Roman emperors belonged. This identification was based on the presence of several ancient fragments found buried near the statue when it was excavated in the nineteenth century. It remains unclear how these small, fragmentary pieces led restorers to reconstruct the head as that of Germanicus.

53
Statue of Germanicus
1st century
Bronze; 219 × 111 × 79 cm

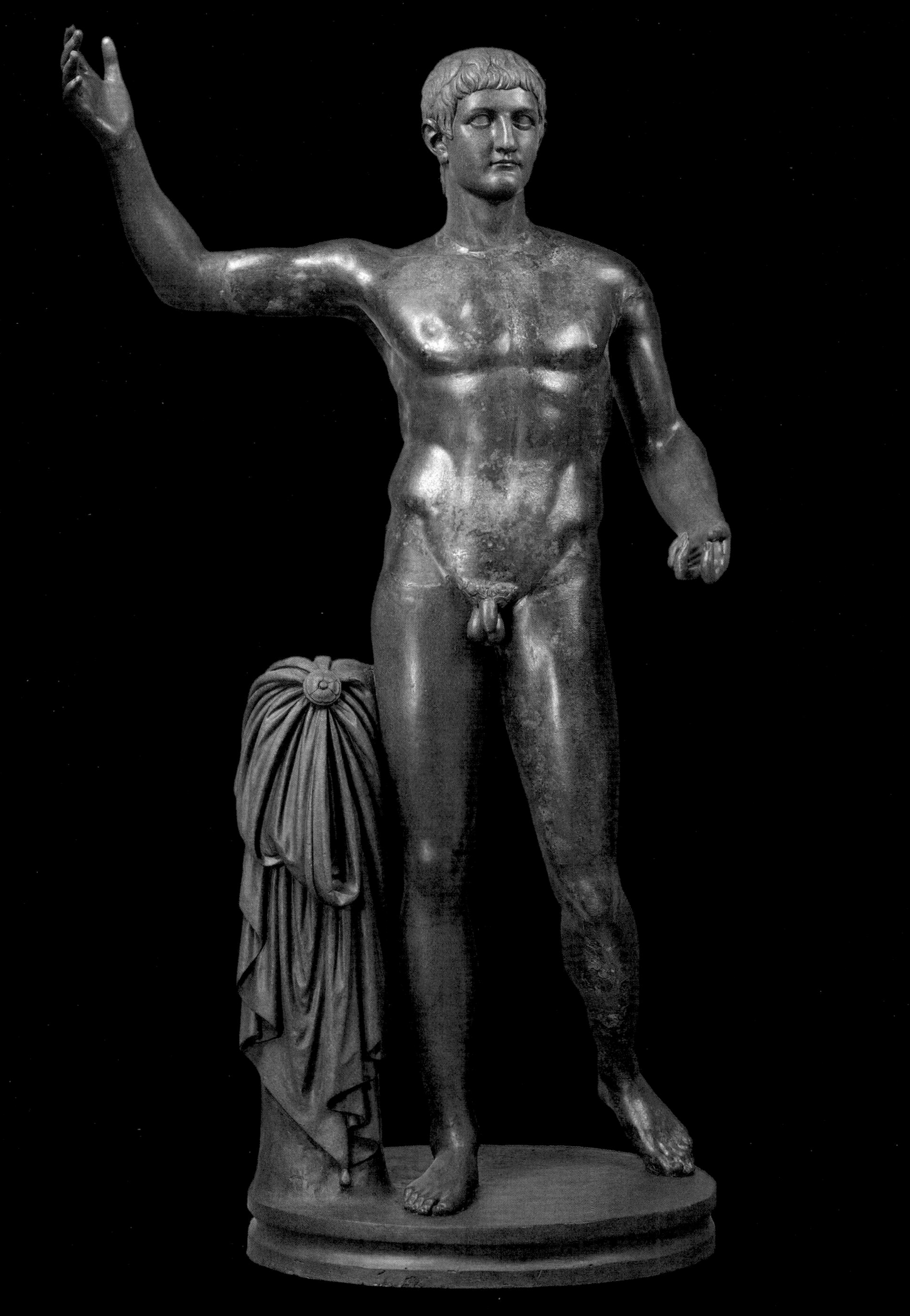

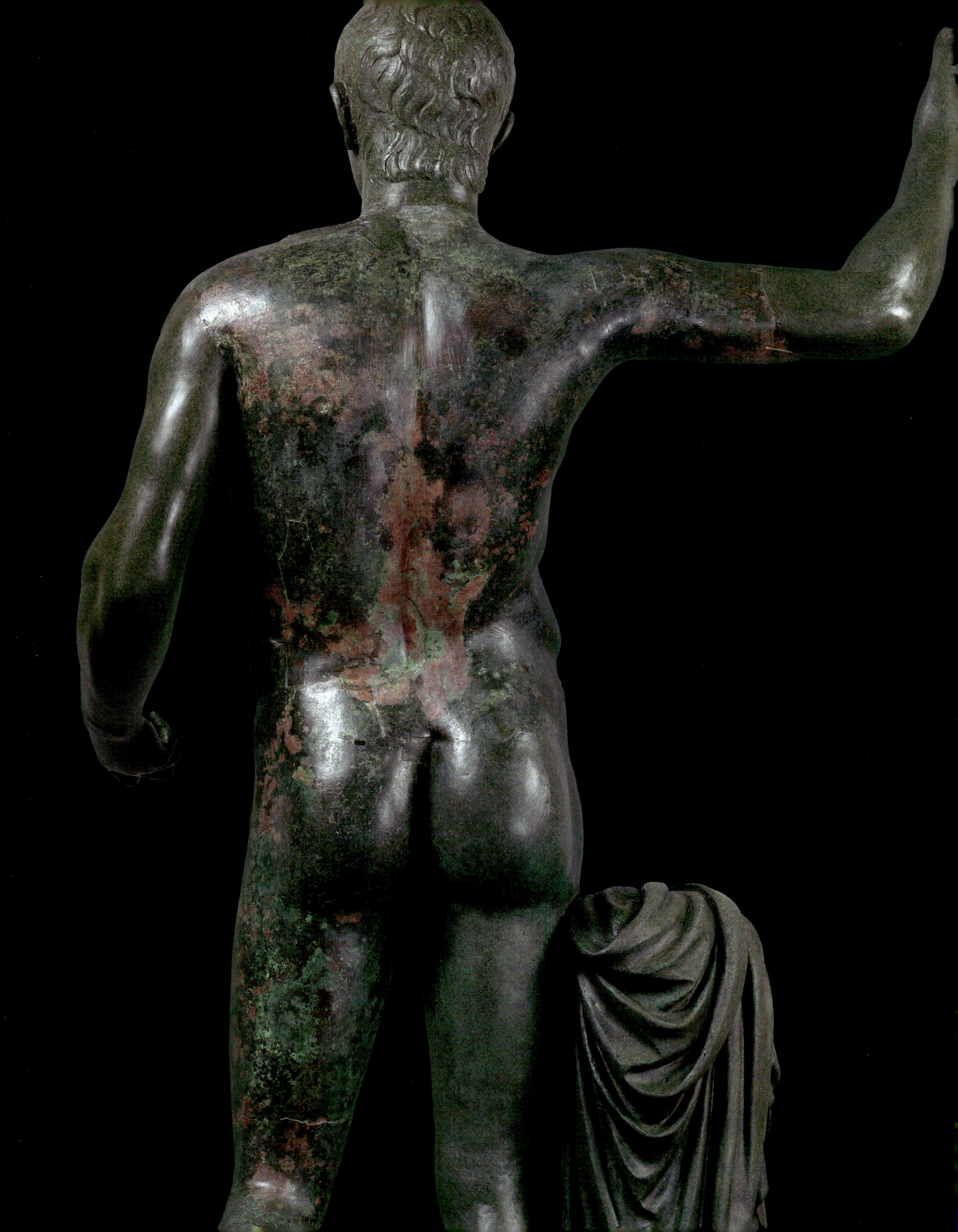

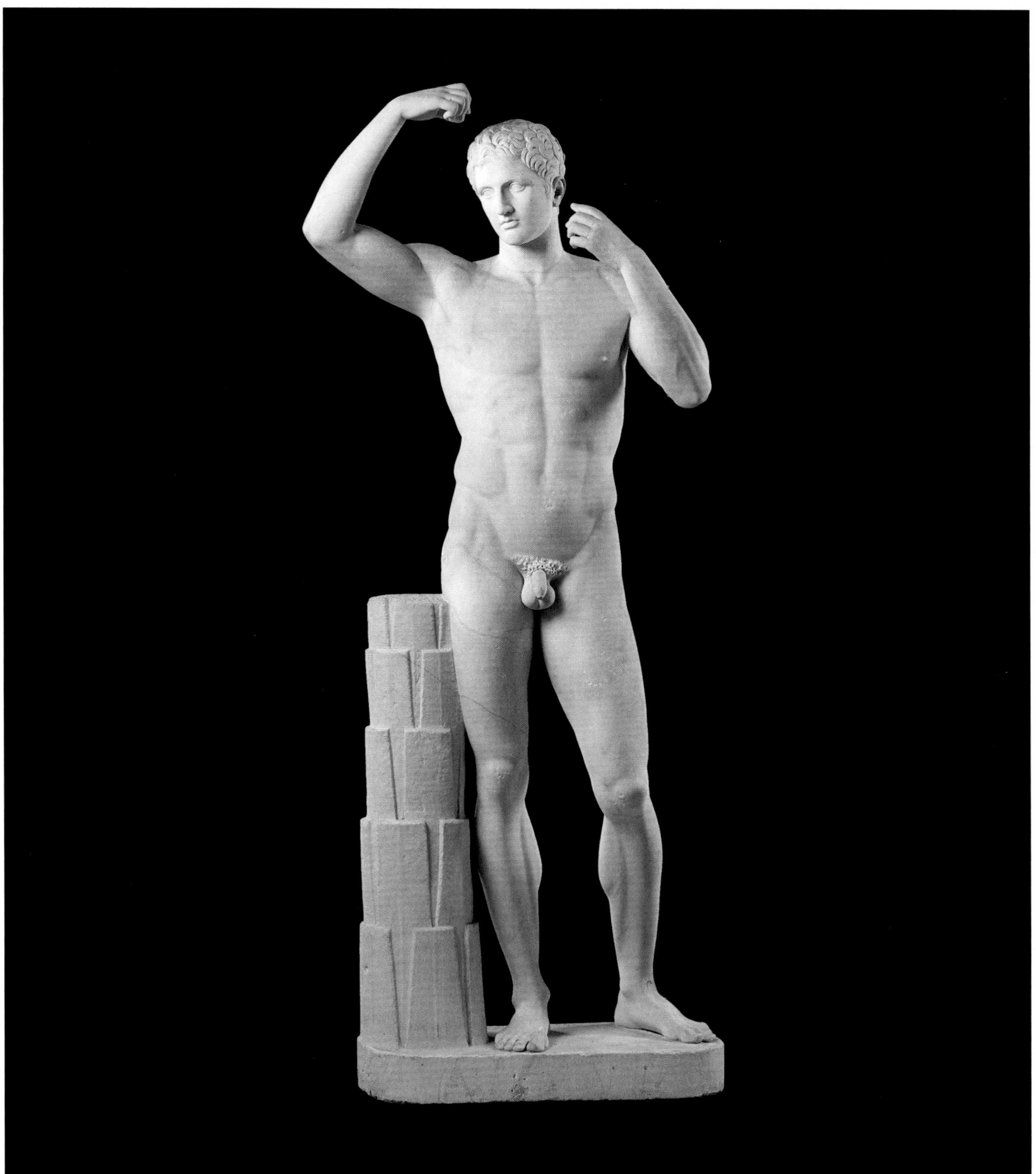

54
Statue of a Youth,
known as the Amelung Athlete
Late 1st–early 2nd century
Marble; 224 × 93 × 53 cm

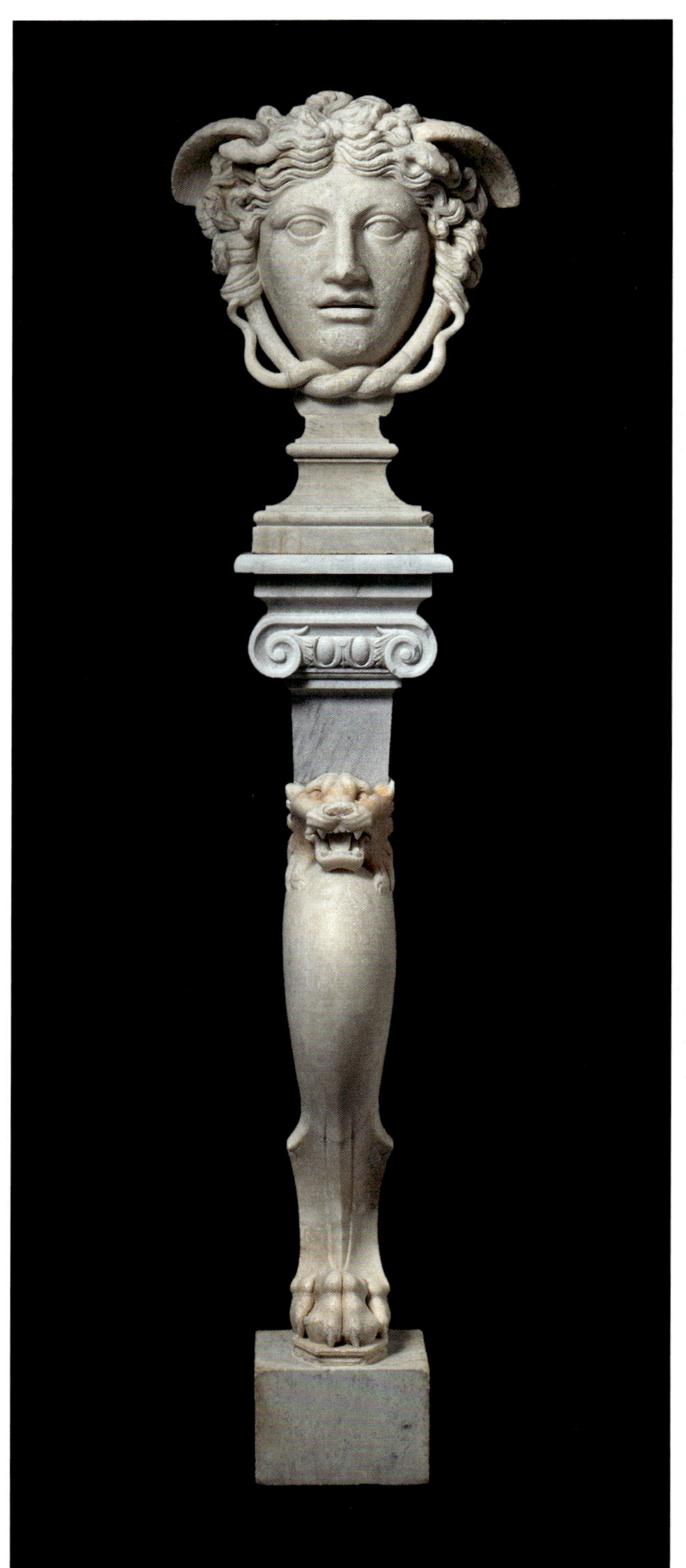

55
Rondanini-Type Medusa on a Trapezophoros (Table Leg) with a Griffin's Head
2nd century
Marble; 173 × 55 × 23 cm

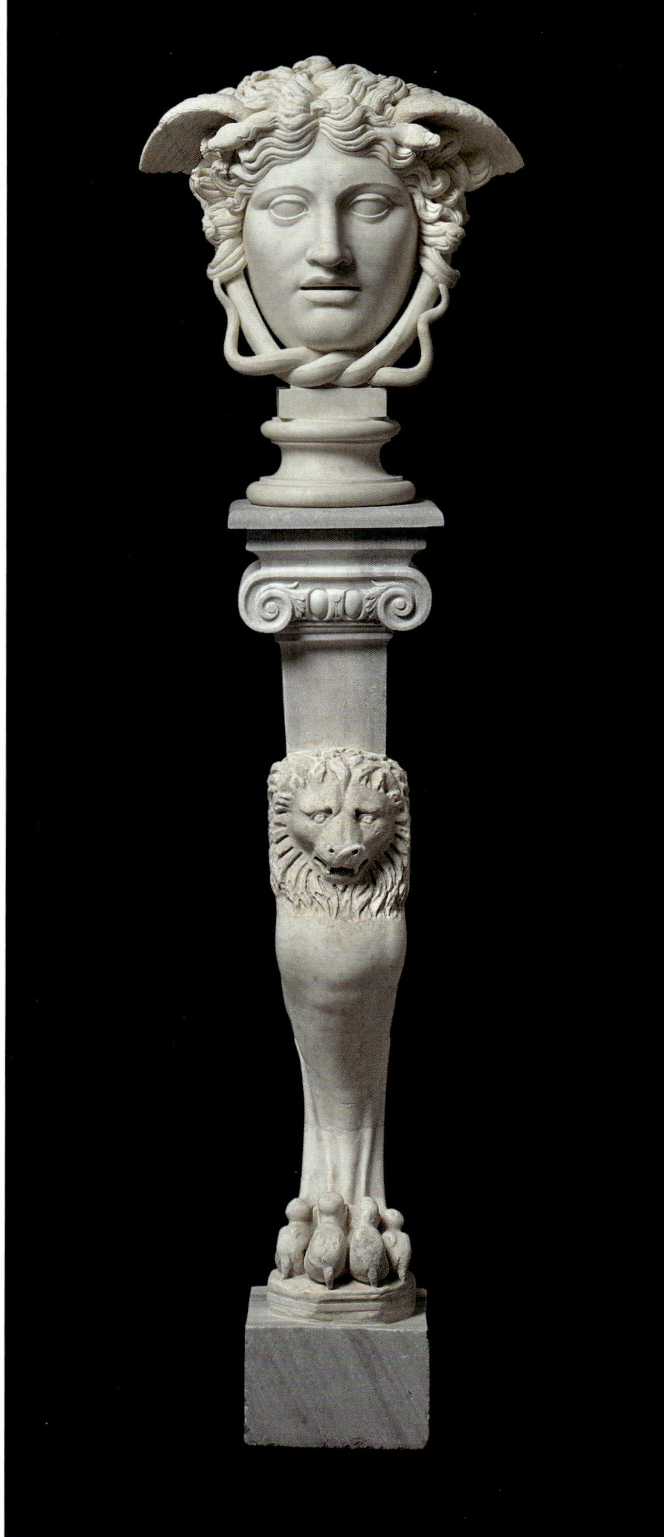

56
Rondanini-Type Medusa on a Trapezophoros (Table Leg) with a Lion's Head
2nd century
Marble; 168 × 60 × 25 cm

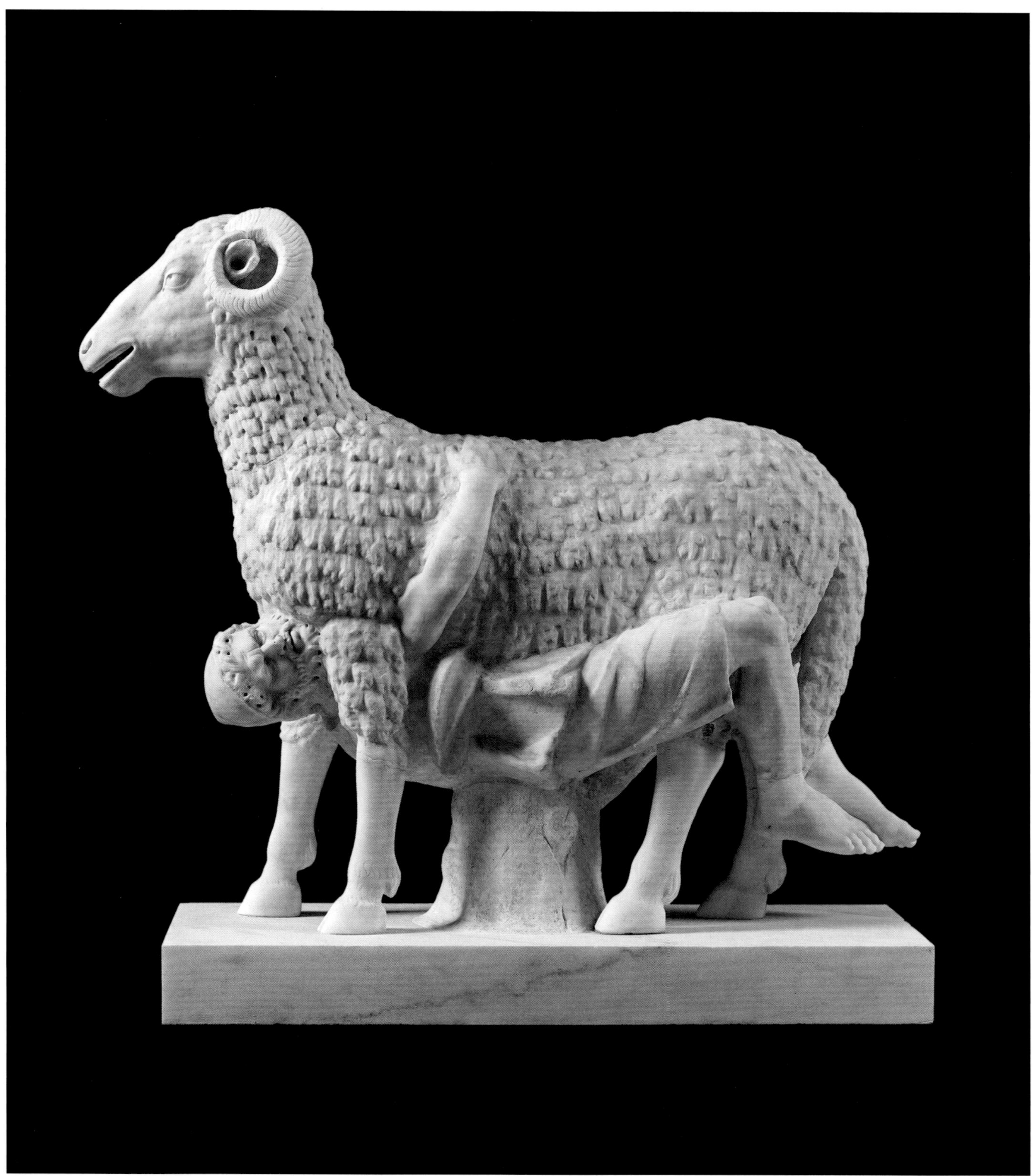

57
Statue of Odysseus Beneath the Ram
Late 1st century
Marble; 77 × 82 × 35 cm

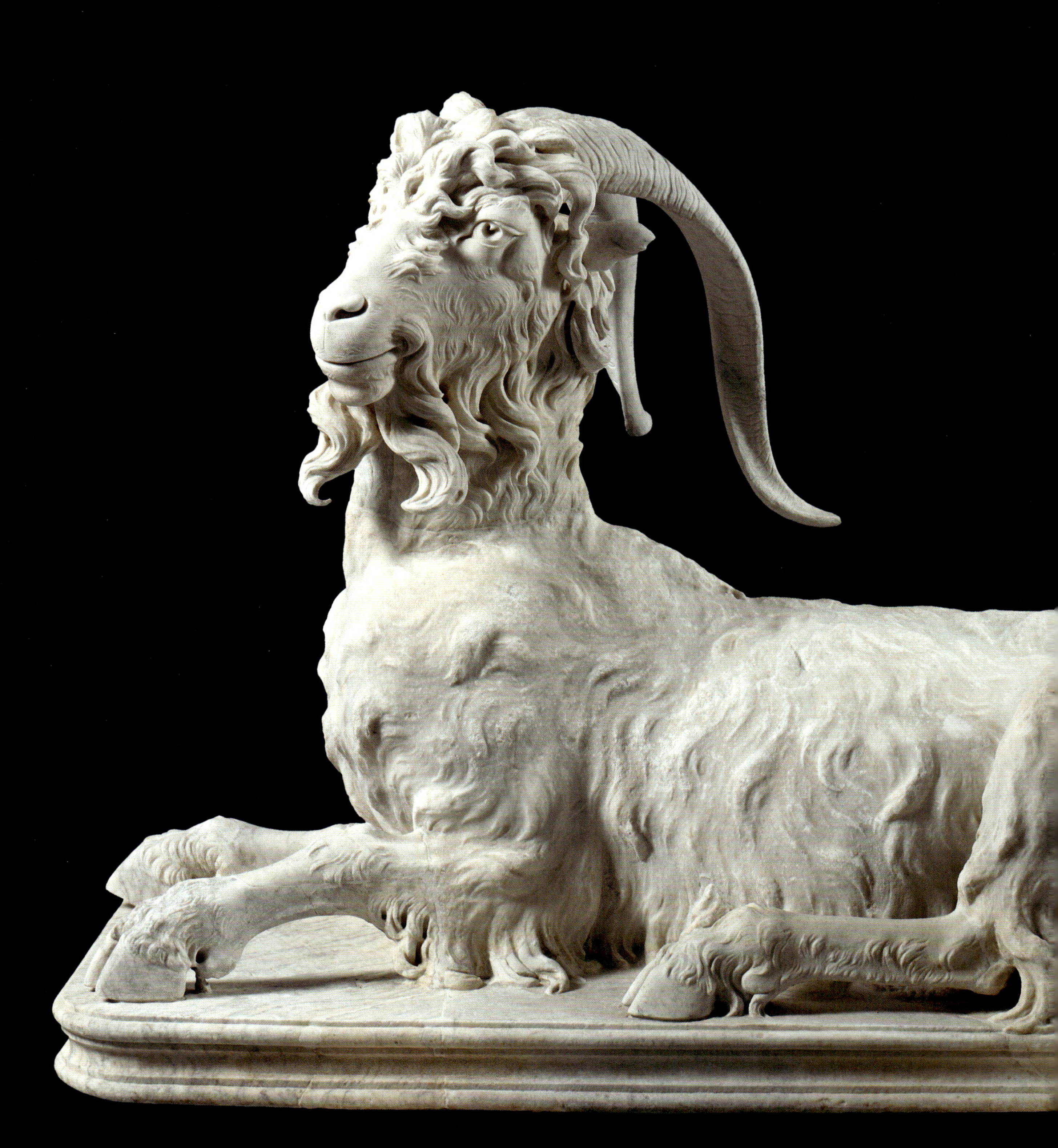

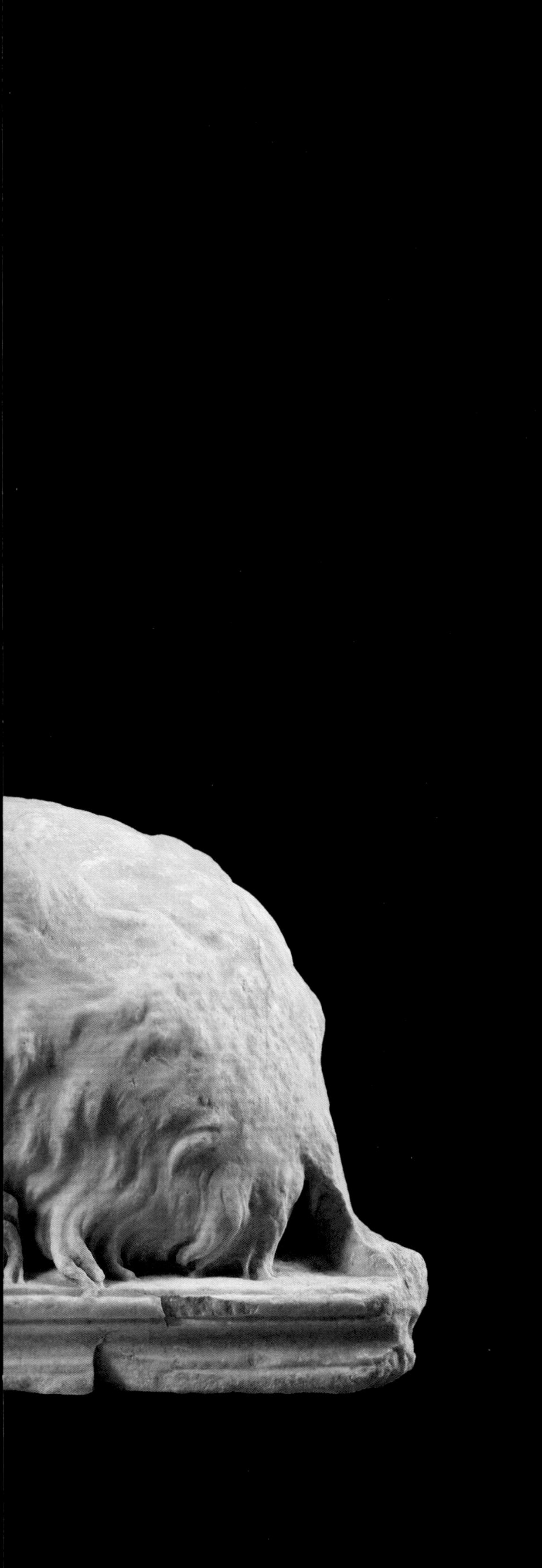

THIS GOAT had the good fortune to come into contact with one of the most famous Italian sculptors of the Baroque period: Gian Lorenzo Bernini. Artists in the seventeenth through nineteenth centuries in Europe, especially in Italy where many antiquities were being unearthed, would often practice their craft by taking ancient sculptural fragments and restoring them to completeness—whether accurately or not.

The first curator of the Torlonia Collection, Pietro Ercole Visconti, attributed the marble head attached to this ancient goat's body to Bernini. Bernini likely came to work on the goat when it was still in the collection of the Italian banker Vincenzo Giustiniani, who had commissioned the sculptor to carve his portrait and who also employed Bernini's father. The goat is regularly mentioned in travel diaries and guides to Rome from the seventeenth and eighteenth centuries; it's hard to imagine a headless goat garnering such attention.

Our bodies accrue scars, piercings, tattoos, wrinkles, and other changes over time, and sculptures—especially those produced two thousand years ago—similarly bear the marks of age and experience. Every work in the Torlonia Collection has lived multiple lives: first as a work commissioned or purchased off the shelf to serve a purpose in a Roman space; another as a fragmented or broken object, rediscovered a long time removed from its creation; and another as a "patient" in the studio of an artist or restorer, such as Bernini, who carefully brought this fragment back to a whole. The sculptures live yet another life in museums, where contemporary viewers can consider each statue's rich story.

58
Statue of a Resting Goat
Body: late 1st century; head: attributed to Gian Lorenzo Bernini (1598–1680)
Marble; 95 × 134 × 71 cm

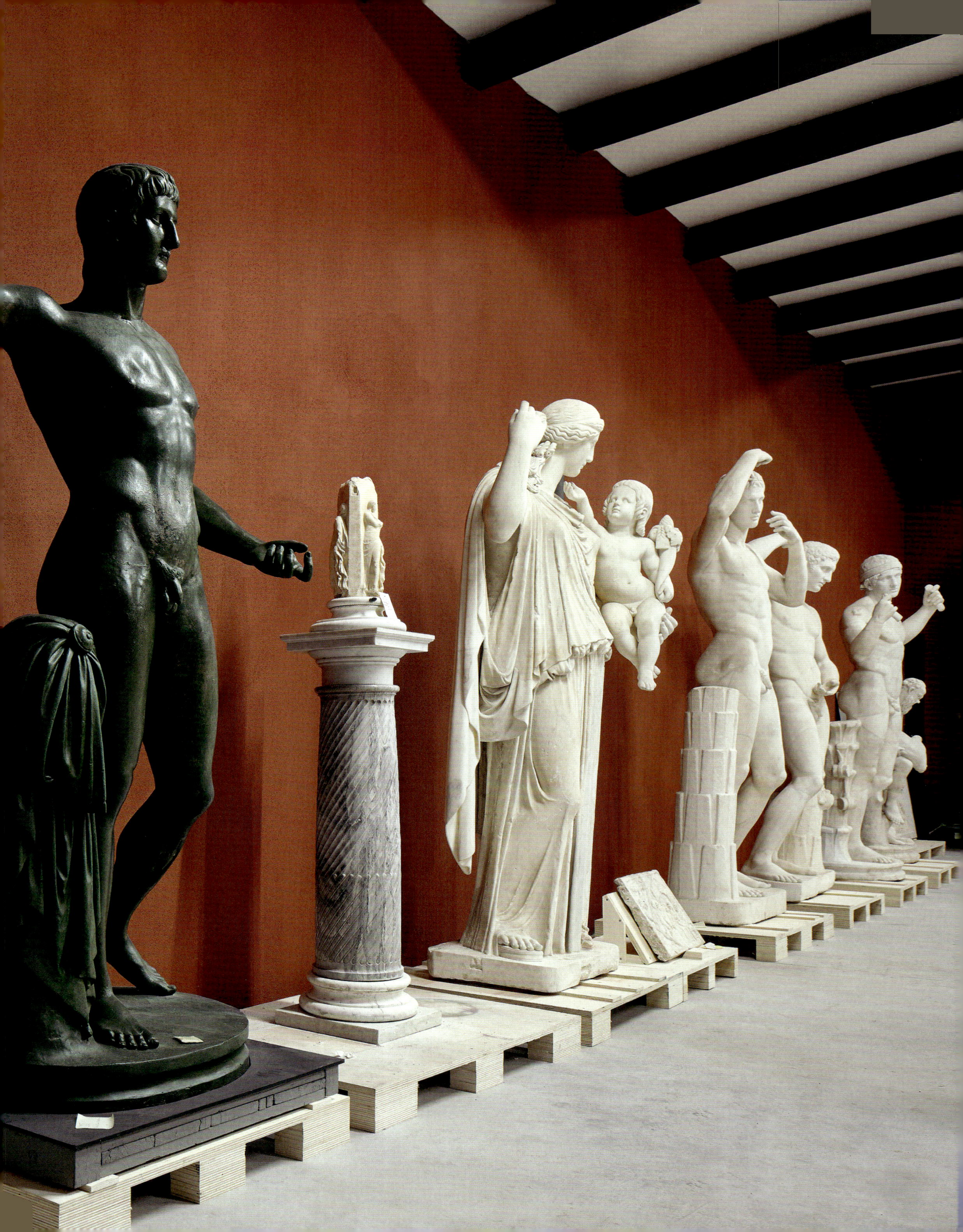

Salvatore Settis

A COLLECTION OF COLLECTIONS: THE TORLONIA MUSEUM & ITS ANTIQUITIES

THE LAST OF THE GREAT princely holdings of Rome, the Torlonia Collection summarizes in itself not only the ambitions and the destiny of those prodigious collections but a much wider history, whose arc extends from the desolation of Rome in ruins to the glory of the great museums of our time. This singular destiny rests with the Torlonia Collection because of the relatively late date at which it took shape (essentially the nineteenth century), but also due to its unusual breadth, the high quality of many sculptures which it contains, and—finally—their frequently distinguished provenance. In sum, these features make the collection of marble sculptures that Prince Alessandro Torlonia wished to assign to a magnificent family museum unique.

Yet this unique character does not fully explain the legendary aura that surrounds the Torlonia Museum in Rome. It is not enough to say that this is the largest collection of sculptures of the classical period in private hands, nor to lay out its many virtues one by one; it must be added that for decades the Collection was not open to visitors. The most representative private collection of antiquities in the city that is richest in them, Rome, has therefore long also been the most hidden: the sharp contrast between its importance and its secrecy explains the legend that came to form around it, and the expectations which, throughout the world, surround its emergence from the shadows.

Ambitions of Excellence

The desire for the Torlonia Museum in Rome and its creation, by bringing together decorations from family palaces with new acquisitions from the antiques market and from excavations, was the solitary project of Prince Alessandro Torlonia (1800–1886) (see fig. 1). His immediate predecessors, in particular his father Giovanni, had gathered numerous antique sculptures in their vast residences, according to a sumptuous decorative taste that continued age-old habits of self-representation by the Roman aristocracy. Alessandro impressed a

This text was adapted from Salvatore Settis's essay in *The Torlonia Marbles: Collecting Masterpieces*, edited by Salvatore Settis and Carlo Gasparri, exhibition catalogue (Milan: Rizzoli Electa, 2021), 20–29.

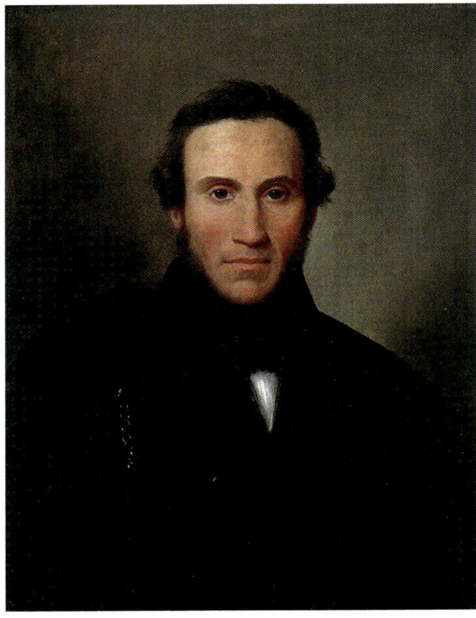

1 Constantino Brumidi (Italian, 1805–1880). *Portrait of Alessandro Torlonia*, before 1849. Oil on slate; dimensions unknown. The Marignoli di Montecorona Foundation, Spoleto, Italy.

decisive turn on Torlonia collecting with the creation of the museum, which, with the very name of *museum*, stated the intention of placing the fruits of a private accumulation of antiquities in a public showcase.

When and how the Torlonia Museum took shape in the prince's mind is not yet completely clear: the research of Carlo Gasparri and Stefania Tuccinardi clarifies that Alessandro began renting an old grain store adjacent to the Palazzo Corsini in Via della Lungara in 1860 and purchased the building in 1864, after the acquisition of the Giustiniani Collection (nominally 1816, in effect probably 1857–59) but before taking possession of Villa Albani (1866). Alessandro transported the 267 Giustiniani sculptures to Via della Lungara immediately and then expanded the building (1881–83); meanwhile, a visitors' itinerary was being created through galleries, aisles, and rooms organized by thematic groups, from sarcophagi to athletes to the Muses to imperial portraits.[1] In order to be worthy of the name, a museum of that time first required a systematic organization of the exhibition sequences, and second, the preparation of a catalogue, which classified the works according to the methods of current antiquarian practice. Two members of the most famous dynasty of antiquarians between the eighteenth and nineteenth centuries, Pietro Ercole Visconti (1803–1880) and then his nephew Carlo Ludovico Visconti (1828–1894), responded to this second requirement in close succession.[2] Pietro Ercole edited the 1876 *Catalogo del Museo Torlonia di sculture antiche* (Catalogue of Museo Torlonia of Ancient Sculpture), which was more of a guide for visitors: printed in small format, without illustrations, and with the briefest description of the 527 pieces then exhibited.[3] Carlo Ludovico edited an enlarged edition of the catalogue in 1883, which was also published in French and English.

So many editions in so few years, even without details of their circulation, signal the success not only of the catalogue, but of the Torlonia Museum. A veritable and conspicuous leap in quality and ambition was marked in 1884–85 by the sumptuous large-format volume *I monumenti del Museo Torlonia di sculture antiche riprodotti con la fototipia*, which contains, in 161 plates, photos of the pieces of the museum (see fig. 2), which had in the meantime grown to hold 622 works, an increase that corresponds clearly to the expansion of the museum spaces of 1881–83. The commentary text on the images in the catalogue was greatly enriched and corrected compared to previous editions; it

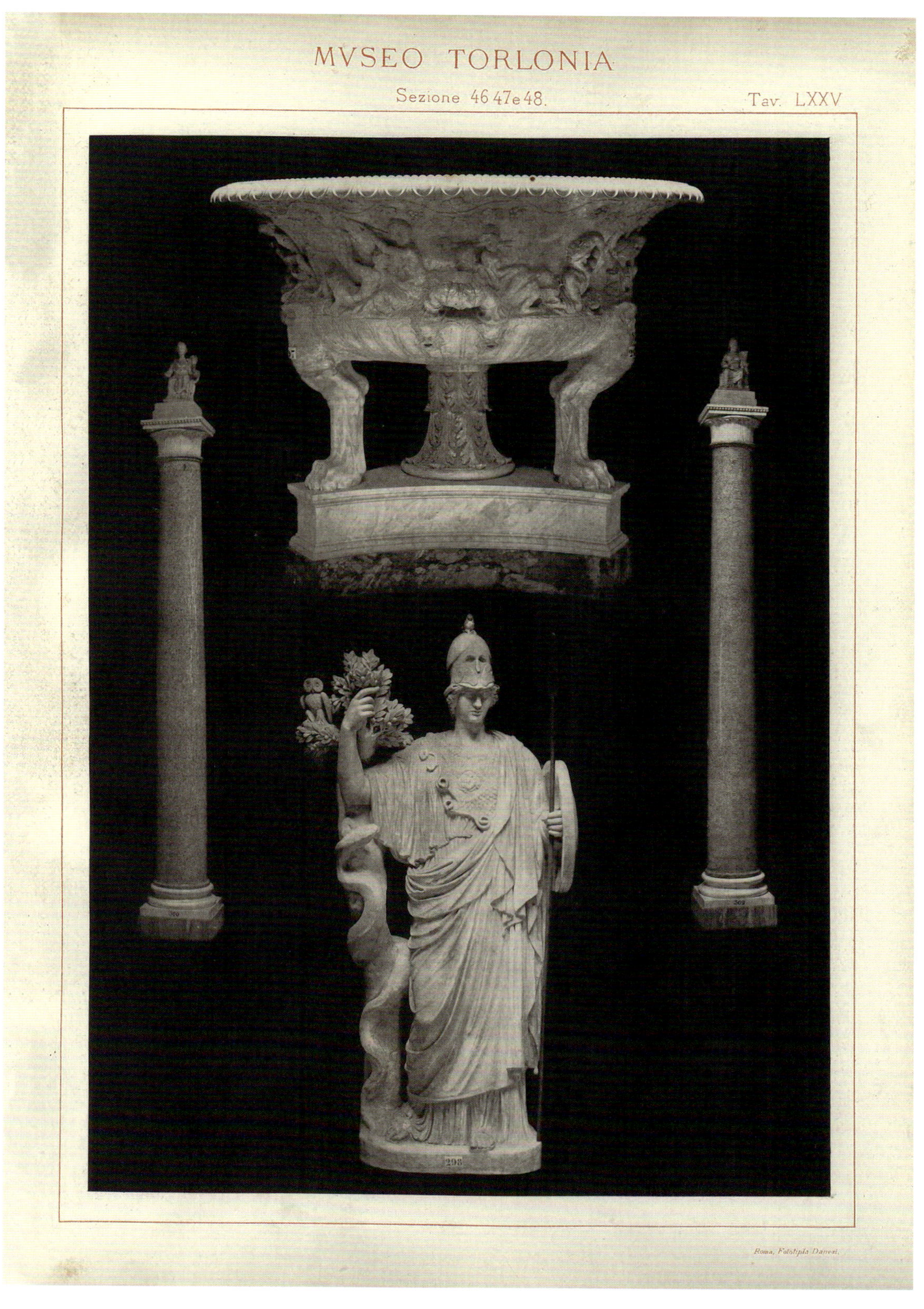

2 Page from Carlo Ludovico Visconti, *I monumenti del Museo Torlonia di sculture antiche riprodotti con la fototipia* (Rome: Stabilimento Fotografico Danesi, 1884–85), pl. 75.

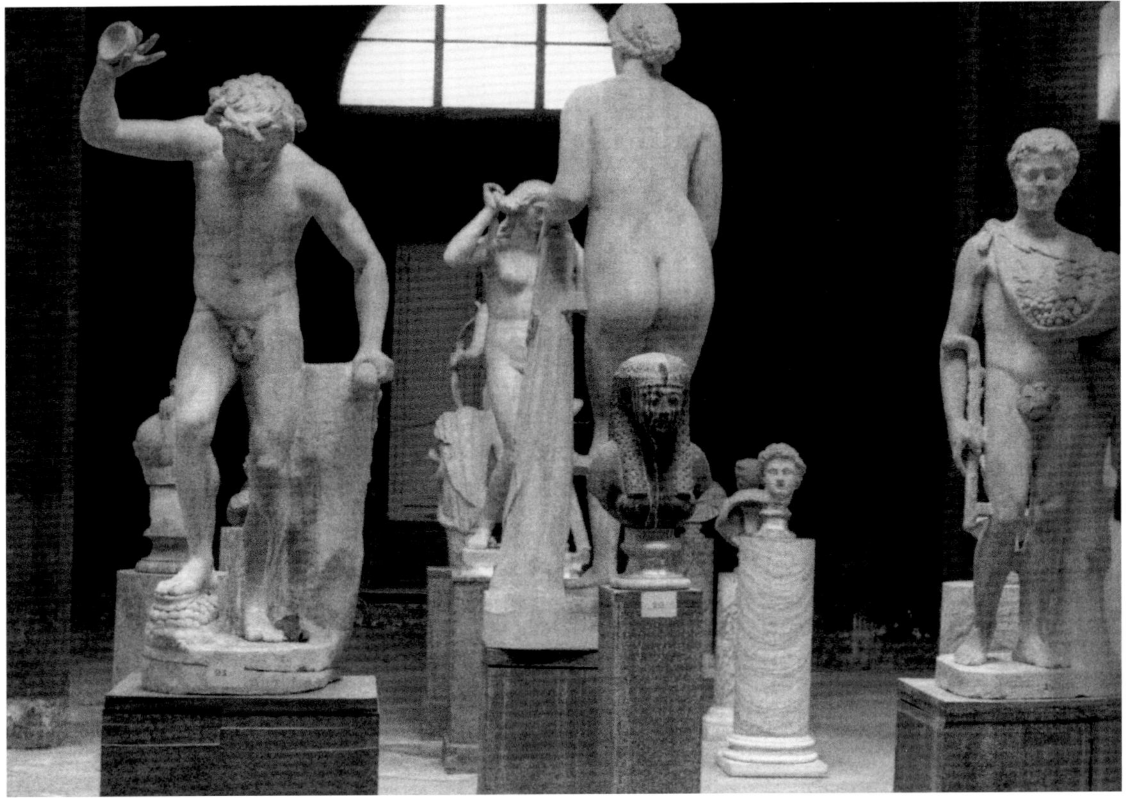

3 Gallery I of the Torlonia Museum, 1930s.

occupied a separate volume, again signed by Carlo Ludovico Visconti, and was published in French (1884) and Italian (1885). There is therefore no lack of indications of continuous transformation and enlargement of the museum, a process that only the death of the prince in 1886 could interrupt; but also of the growth of its fame or, as we would say in today's language, its success. This was such that Carlo Ludovico Visconti could write that "there is no longer an educated person, who does not know, either by sight or by reputation, the Torlonia Museum at Porta Settimiana" (see fig. 3).[4]

The splendid volume with the plates in phototype and the volume of text that accompanied it were not offered for sale but donated: to illustrious recipients, of course, but also to the libraries of the nascent archaeology institutes of universities. This almost regal distribution method, whose academic and cultural aspect is important to note, demonstrates the concern that the Torlonia marbles should enter quickly into the circuit of archaeological knowledge in Europe.[5] This intention is recorded in Carlo Ludovico Visconti's preface to the 1884–85 catalogue:

> Prince Torlonia, not content with having formed this immense treasury of antique sculptures, also wants to bring it in a splendid manner, worthy of him, to the notice of archaeologists, scholars, and all those who lack the opportunity to have it often before them, having had all the monuments published with a magnificent volume of phototype impressions.[6]

The Prince's Intentions

As a date of "foundation" or rather of establishment of the Torlonia Museum, we can tentatively accept 1876, when in the preface to the first printed catalogue Pietro Ercole Visconti boasted of the extent and quality of the "museum of ancient sculpture formed by Prince Don

Alessandro Torlonia," which, "far exceeding the limits of any private collection, has no equal, either in royal or public collections, even those as illustrious as the Vatican and the Capitoline Museums."[7] A few years later Carlo Ludovico went further, recalling in the museum "a series of busts and portraits, which, especially for Roman imperial iconography, surpasses in both number and beauty the well-known collections of the Vatican and the Capitoline Museums."[8]

Alessandro Torlonia, assisted by the two Visconti, was therefore the architect of his museum. But the dates we have lined up above signal a further unique aspect to his undertaking, the fact itself of its having happened straddling the events of 1870 that led to the end of the temporal power of the popes, to the annexation of Rome to Italy, and to its proclamation as the "natural" capital of the young kingdom. In the aftermath of the breach of Porta Pia (September 20, 1870), the agreement for the surrender of the papal troops to the Italian army was signed at Villa Albani-Torlonia: a minute connection, difficult to evaluate, linking the biography of the prince and his antiquities to the political history of Italy. Entering his new capital somewhat reluctantly, the Piedmontese king would soon install himself in the rooms of the pope at the Palazzo del Quirinale, yet not everything fit perfectly with the rhetoric of Rome the capital. It must have seemed strange, for example, that a pope without a kingdom remained the absolute master of the Vatican Museums, and the Capitoline Museums stayed in firm municipal ownership, while the Italian State had no museum of ancient art in Rome. Not even the far-sighted Alessandro Torlonia could have imagined, when he began to collect sculptures to make his museum, that it would be for some time richer in works and fame than any collection of antiquities that the King of Italy himself could boast in his capital.

Acquiring new antiquities and placing them, not in family palaces, but in a museum ordered by rooms and monumental categories, had for Prince Alessandro the double meaning of a powerful act of self-representation and a gesture that implied strong civic intentions and ambitions. A possible precedent in this sense is that of the Marquis Giampietro Campana (1808–1880), a tireless collector in papal Rome in the first half of the nineteenth century and friend of Pietro Ercole Visconti, who from excavations and purchases on the Roman market put together an immense collection of antiquities and promoted it to the status of the Campana Museum, dividing it into twelve "classes" (including eight of antiquity), distributing it among various buildings throughout the city, and allowing access, one day a week, to a select few who came registered in a "golden book" of *Personaggi che hanno visitato il Museo Campana* (Personages who have visited the Campana Museum). Campana was a direct contemporary with Alessandro Torlonia, but his collection had a completely different character, extending with an encyclopedic spirit to more numerous and varied monumental categories (coins, architectural terracottas, jewels, glass, bronzes). We find in it, however, not only the idea of founding a private museum under the family name but also the initiative of documenting its sculptures by photography, as was done in Henry d'Escamps's *Description des marbres antiques du Musée Campana à Rome* (1855–56). Campana's museum ambitions ended in 1857 with his ruinous financial failure, which led him to total collapse and prison. The catalogues of his museum became the inventories of a colossal sale, and his collection was dispersed widely, especially to the Louvre and the Hermitage.[9] But in his feverish accumulation of antiquities, although crushed by misfortune, we ought to recognize a sign of the times, the expression of a national sentiment that manifested itself through the arts. In fact, Campana—although he remained faithful to his sovereign, the pope—had been animated by a manifest Italian patriotism, by love for an Italy that could remain politically divided but had to be aware of its cultural unity. Therefore, his collection was intended to be a "museum of Italian glories."[10]

We must therefore look at the cultural history of Italy in the nineteenth century to better understand in what context and with what aims a Roman prince wanted to mount a new museum, whether the pope or a king reigned in Rome. Prince Alessandro Torlonia's intentions had a very significant role in the founding of the museum, as Carlo Ludovico Visconti writes in the 1884–85 catalogue:

> A continuous and enormous expense, sustained with firm resolve by he who was able and willing to devote it to attain a great objective; *the purchase, either total or partial, of some ancient and distinguished Roman collections*; the opportunity, arisen in recent times, due to many earthworks and construction works, to make new and previously impossible acquisitions—acquisitions that were never allowed to slip from the growth of this museum, whatever sum had to be dispensed on them; the flourishing

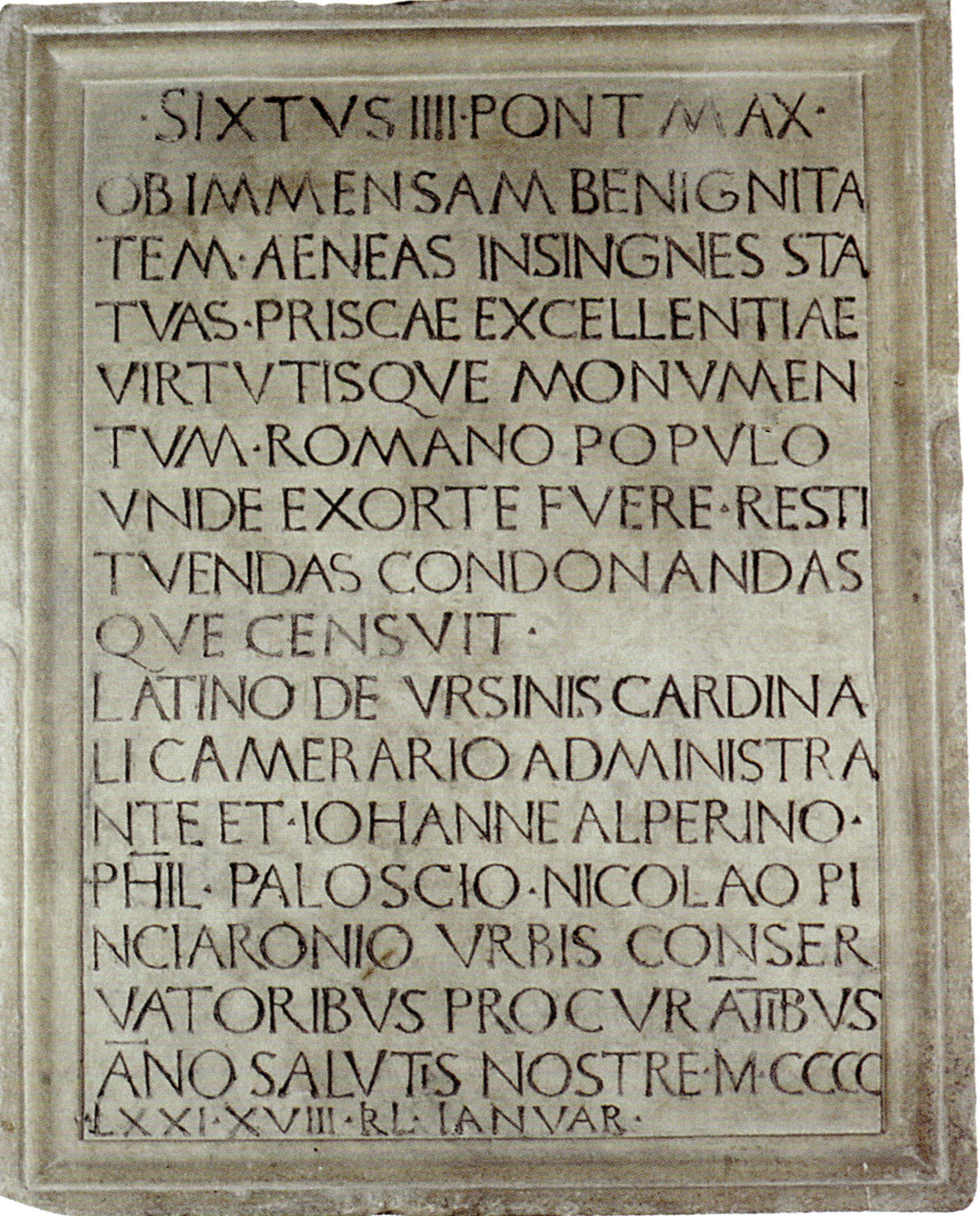

4 Inscription commemorating the donation of Pope Sixtus IV to the Roman people, December 15, 1471. Rome, Capitoline Museums, Palazzo dei Conservatori, staircase, inv. EM220.

> success of excavations carried out among the ruins of ancient cities, or of sumptuous Roman villas, which are now among the numerous large estates owned by Prince Torlonia; such is the complex of causes, which happily contributed to making the formation of such a collection possible, which cannot fail to arouse wonder in anyone who takes a moment to consider it in its remarkable scope.[11]

These words resemble nothing so much as a program for the formation of the museum, with Prince Alessandro himself as its main organizer.

"Some Ancient and Distinguished Roman Collections"

In the 2020–21 exhibition of the Torlonia marbles in Rome, we focused on the most unusual and unexamined characteristic of the Torlonia Museum: its intentional growth and unfolding through the careful annexation of several ancient collections. It is true that archaeological excavations played an important role in the formation of the Torlonia Museum, yet the Collection seems to present itself above all as a collection of collections, having progressively included not only those purchased *en bloc* (such as the Giustiniani), but various other collections formed over the centuries in Rome, which reached the hands of Torlonia through several massive acquisitions: the Giustiniani, Cavaceppi, and Albani Collections. For example, the large Cesi Torlonia Cup (MT 297) came to the Torlonia Museum from Villa Albani, but it had arrived there from the garden of Cardinal Cesi, where it is documented from around 1530; and it was located earlier in a church in Trastevere, where it was drawn in the late fifteenth century.[12] With its travels between the fifteenth and nineteenth centuries, from a medieval church to the garden of a cardinal in the sixteenth century, to the villa of another cardinal in the eighteenth century, and finally to the Torlonia Museum, as well as with the multitude of drawings that follow its fate, the Torlonia Cup thus reflects in itself the guiding thread of collecting in Rome.[13]

The catalogues of the Torlonia Museum insist on provenance from important collections of the past. The text by Pietro Ercole Visconti which prefaces the first 1876 catalogue does not limit itself to mentioning the nuclei from Villa Albani and Cavaceppi Studio and the items that "originate from the famous Giustiniani gallery, formed in the beginning of the seventeenth century by the illustrious Marquis Vincenzo, founder of this family in Rome, and the greatest lover and connoisseur of his time."[14] Alongside these better-known and substantial acquisitions, the *Catalogo* also mentions the marbles "formerly belonging to the Cesarini and known as theirs since the sixteenth century" and "those that around that same time belonged to the Caetani, and then to the Ruspoli." In the preface to the 1884–85 catalogue, Carlo Ludovico Visconti does not mention by name any collection prior to the eighteenth century, but adds to his uncle's text the crucial phrase quoted above—"the purchase, either total or partial, of some ancient and distinguished Roman collections"—as an essential part of Prince Torlonia's "firm resolve" when he was creating his museum.

Even in the descriptive entries on the individual works, both versions of the catalogues give great prominence to the numerous Giustiniani, Albani, and Cavaceppi provenances, but in various cases they give, intentionally or unintentionally, provenance that archival research has proved to be erroneous. Pietro Ercole Visconti cites the Caetani and then Ruspoli Collections, attributing to them what he calls the "Ruspoli Philosopher," namely the so-called Chrysippus (MT 82) in the Torlonia Collection. This information, although repeated such as it is by Carlo Ludovico, remains devoid of any documentary evidence, and the statue is from the Cesarini Collection.[15] Additionally, of the two large sarcophagi that formerly belonged to the Savelli, only one, that with the Labors of Hercules and a dead couple recumbent on the lid (cat. 24), is recorded by the 1884–85 catalogue as being of Orsini provenance. This is correct in that the Orsini residence formerly belonged to the Savelli; while the first version of the *Catalogo* gave it as discovered on the "Via Appia, at the Villa of the Quintili."

The formation and nature of the Torlonia Museum therefore represent, after decades of silence and shadow, the necessary starting juncture for any exhibition of these sculptures; but the oldest collections that are represented are the necessary counterpart to Prince Alessandro's intentions. In researching the Collection, we wanted to translate into a simple narrative framework this tension between the dawn of collecting in the fifteenth century and the complexity of the motivations that led in the nineteenth century to the foundation of the Torlonia Museum. In our original conception in the

2020–21 exhibition, a journey back in time allowed visitors first to appreciate the museum as it was at the death of its founder in 1886. Our exhibition also highlighted these sculptures' provenances, tracing the various routes by which marbles entered the Torlonia holdings: the excavations that contributed to the Collection; the acquisition of the eighteenth-century (Albani, Cavaceppi) and seventeenth-century (Giustiniani) collections; and finally, within these, the surviving marbles from still more ancient collections.

To better understand a narrative sequence like this, linking one extreme to the other, in dates but also along the path of cultural history, we need to examine the origins of antiquity collecting in Rome, which between the fifteenth and sixteenth centuries was the most widespread and meaningful tradition of collecting across all European urban contexts. It is this singular and forgotten story that the Torlonia marbles help illuminate with representative examples.

From the Ruins to the Museum

The starting point of this story must be an absence, an emptiness: that historical phase of over a thousand years, during which there was no collecting, while indeed many thousands of ancient sculptures lay undisturbed in the ruins of Rome. Sometimes a capital, a frieze, or a sarcophagus was laboriously removed to be reused (usually in a church) for prestigious architecture or tombs, but far more often the marbles were torn from the ruins to make lime from them rather than to admire their beauty or understand their meaning.[16] The transition from a situation like this to one in which ancient sculptures were collected and displayed with honor in private homes is far from obvious; and it is important to understand it well, because it is from that very first private collecting that the princely and sovereign collections and then the public museums would be born over time. Because, obvious as it may seem to us, the museum as an institution has only existed for less than three centuries.

So whatever drove people to rummage in the ruins, providing the beginnings for the collections of antiquities? This veritable revolution did not happen in one day. It did not originate only from humanistic culture and aesthetic taste, as may be believed, but had much broader and more varied roots, and was triggered not so much by the artistic or documentary value of the marbles collected, but by purely political motivations, which pushed statues and reliefs to cross the threshold between the indeterminate past of the ruins and the living present of the collections.[17] The decisive moment of this development took place in Rome at the beginning of the fifteenth century, with the return of the popes to their capital after the exile in Avignon and the end of the Western Schism. The newly looming presence of the papal Curia prompted Roman citizens to reaffirm their pride as native Romans, whether they belonged to the old aristocracy or to a new "bourgeoisie" of merchants, lawyers, doctors, notaries, pharmacists, and tax collectors. Some families claimed the ancient Romans as ancestors, as did the Porcari, for example, declaring themselves to be descendants of the Porcii of ancient Rome.[18] This self-ennobling strategy was aimed at guaranteeing and improving their own status in the changed institutional situation of the city. An integral part of this strategy was the recovery of ancient sculptures and inscriptions from the ruins in which they lay and the new sociocultural practice of bringing them into homes as a sign of dignity and distinction, as a strong visual equivalent of a statement such as, "I am a Roman and my family descends from the ancient Roman imperial era."[19]

Scattered traces of this custom can still be seen in the house of Lorenzo Manlio in Piazza Giudea.[20] The building is in itself modest, but on the facade, it displays some fragments of ancient sculptures and a solemn inscription that proclaims it was built in 1476, *Urbe Roma in pristinam formam renascente* ("while the city of Rome is being reborn in its ancient aspect"): very explicit words, which put his Romano-antique sculptures on the side of a political declaration and not an aesthetic choice.[21] Manlio was only an apothecary, but similar methods were also adopted by the high aristocracy and in residences of a very different tone, like that of Cardinal Prospero Colonna, whose collection of antiquities could also boast the Belvedere Torso.[22] That first widespread "collecting" did not in fact have dedicated spaces designed to accommodate sculptures and epigraphs, and therefore, by natural mimetic impulse, adopted the display methods of the medieval reuse of antiquity, almost always in churches; and therefore in the fifteenth and sixteenth centuries people deployed their own antiquities on external walls or sometimes installed them in the courtyards or gardens of their houses. The Greek humanist Manuel Chrysoloras, who visited Rome in 1412, testifies to the frequency of this use, recording that "everywhere in Rome the walls of the houses are full of reliefs and sculptures with mythological scenes, to the point that anyone who walks the streets cannot avoid turning their gaze on them, almost like lovers who admire living beauties by looking at them intensely."[23]

Similar display methods were also used in public places and then gradually employed in museums, in Italy and beyond: for example, the large staircase leading to Santa Maria in Aracoeli was embellished, on the ascending left wall, with eight sarcophagi facades, attested by sixteenth-century sources including a drawing in Stuttgart.[24] Even more often, the ancient sarcophagi were reused as fountain basins, as can still be seen in Rome today (for example in front of the Torlonia palace on Via Bocca di Leone).

Pope Sixtus IV responded to that incipient and improvised "collecting" with a gesture of calculated sovereign generosity. In 1471 he donated to the Roman people the bronzes that had accumulated in the Lateran over the centuries and placed them on the Campidoglio, accompanying them with a sensational inscription (fig. 4): "Sixtus IV Pontiff Maximus, in his immense benevolence, determined *to return and assign in perpetuity* [these] outstanding bronze statues, a perennial testimony of excellence and merit, to the Roman people, *from whose midst they arose* [. . .]."[25] This is a text without precedents or parallels in Europe. With full political awareness, Sixtus IV recognized not only the quality of the bronzes and the excellence of the ancient craftsmen, but above all the right of the Roman people to make them their own, since they had created them (in ancient Rome). By transferring the statues to the Campidoglio, the Ligurian pope surpassed in a single day, because of the rarity and value of the bronze, all that the private citizens of Rome had ever been able to do in their own homes, but he solemnly recognized in them the descendants of the Romans of antiquity. In a certain sense, he thus legitimized the private accumulation of scattered antiquities in the Romans' houses; and yet he claimed for the pontiff full control of that course of events. And in fact, the legislation for the protection of antiquities often enacted by the popes in the following centuries continued to refer to the "precedent" of Sixtus IV, on which would be grafted the foundation by Pope Clement XII of the Capitoline Museums, the first public museum in Europe, and therefore of the world, in 1734.[26] The Torlonia Collection, as a highly representative cross section of artistic and political cultural history, thereby becomes the guiding thread of a narrative, which, from the ruins of the Roman Empire, leads us to the creation of one of the preeminent institutions of eighteenth-century Europe: the public museum.

Notes

1 See Carlo Gasparri, "The Torlonia Museum: The Last Roman Collection of Antique Sculpture," in *The Torlonia Marbles: Collecting Masterpieces*, ed. Salvatore Settis and Carlo Gasparri, exh. cat. (Milan: Rizzoli Electa, 2021), 30–47; and Stefania Tuccinardi, introductions to Sections I and II, in Settis and Gasparri, *Torlonia Marbles*, 134–37, 170–73. On the acquisition of the Giustiniani Collection, see the essay by Gasparri, "The Torlonia Museum," and Laura Buccino, introduction to Section IV, in *Torlonia Marbles*, 218–21. On the thematic groupings of the early museum, see the introduction to Section I in *Torlonia Marbles*. For recent publications on the Collection, see also Stefania Tuccinardi, *Un tesoro di erudizione e arte: Il Museo Torlonia di scultura antica* (Rome: Bardi Edizioni, 2022) and Carlo Gasparri, Salvatore Settis, and Martin Szewczyk, eds., *Chefs-d'oeuvre de la collection Torlonia*, exh. cat. (Paris: Musée du Louvre, 2024). On the history of the Torlonia Museum over the last eighty years, see Lucilla de Lachenal, "Dal Museo Torlonia in via della Lungara alla mostra in Palazzo Caffarelli," *Bollettino d'arte del Ministero per i beni e le attività culturali e per il turismo* 46 (2020): 69–94.

2 See Daniela Gallo, "The Visconti and the Antiquarian Tradition," in Settis and Gasparri, *Torlonia Marbles*, 104–11.

3 This version of the catalogue was reprinted in 1880 and 1881.

4 Carlo Ludovico Visconti, *I monumenti del Museo Torlonia di sculture antiche riprodotti con la fototipia* (Rome: Stabilimento Fotografico Danesi, 1884–85), iii.

5 The precedent is perhaps the distribution, by gift of the King of Naples, of the *Antichità di Ercolano Esposte* (Antiquities of Herculaneum Exposed) more than a century previously.

6 Carlo Ludovico Visconti, *I monumenti del Museo Torlonia*, vi.

7 Pietro Ercole Visconti, *Catalogo del Museo Torlonia di sculture antiche* (Rome: Topografia Editrice Romana, 1876), v. Translation by Jeffrey Nigro.

8 Carlo Ludovico Visconti, *I monumenti del Museo Torlonia*, vi. Translation by Jeffrey Nigro.

9 Francoise Gaultier and Laurent Haumesser, eds., *Un rêve d'Italie: La collection du marquis Campana*, exh. cat. (Paris: LIENART, 2018).

10 Michele Benucci and Susanna Sarti, "Il 'museo delle glorie italiche' di Giovanni Pietro Campana attraverso i documenti dell'Istituto per la storia del Risorgimento italiano," in *Collezionisti, accademie, musei: Storie del mondo etrusco dal XVI al XIX secolo*, ed. Ilaria Bianchi and Giulio Paolucci (Milan: Fondazione Luigi Rovati, 2020); Gaultier and Haumesser, 36.

11 Emphasis mine. Carlo Ludovico Visconti, *I monumenti del Museo Torlonia* (1884–85), iii–iv.

12 See Anna Maria Riccomini, "Before the Torlonia: Antique Sculptures in the Drawings and Engravings of the Sixteenth and Seventeenth Centuries," in *Torlonia Marbles*, fig. 1.

13 Luca Leoncini, "The Torlonia Vase: History and Visual Records from the Fifteenth to the Nineteenth Centuries," *Journal of the Warburg and Courtauld Institutes* 54 (1991): 99–116. See also Riccomini, "Before the Torlonia," in *Torlonia Marbles*.

14 Pietro Ercole Visconti, *Catalogo del Museo Torlonia*, 8.

15 Carlo Ludovico Visconti, *I monumenti del Museo Torlonia*, no. 82.

16 On reuse, see Salvatore Settis and Anna Anguissola, eds., *Recycling Beauty*, exh. cat. (Milan: Fondazione Prada, 2024).

17 Salvatore Settis, "Des ruines au musée: La destinée de la sculpture classique," in *Annales: Économies, sociétés, civilisations* 48, no. 6 (1993): 1347–80; Salvatore Settis, "Collecting Ancient Sculpture: The Beginnings," *Studies in the History of Art* 70 (2008): 12–31; Kathleen Wren Christian, *Empire Without End: Antiquities Collections in Renaissance Rome, c. 1350–1527* (New Haven, CT: Yale University Press, 2010); see also Kathleen Wren Christian, "Collections of Antique Sculpture in Renaissance Rome," in Settis and Gasparri, *Torlonia Marbles*, 52–57.

18 Anna Modigliani, *I Porcari: Storie di una famiglia romana tra Medioevo e Rinascimento* (Rome: Roma nel Renascimento, 1994).

19 Massimo Miglio, "Roma dopo Avignone: La rinascita politica dell'antico," in *Memoria dell'antico nell'arte italiana I, L'uso dei classici*, ed. Salvatore Settis (Turin: G. Einaudi, 1984), 73–111; Arnold Esch, "L'uso dell'antico nell'ideologia papale, imperiale e comunale," in *Roma antica nel Medioevo: Mito, rappresentazioni, sopravvivenze nella 'Respublica christiana' dei secoli IX-XIII* (Milan: Vita e Pensiero, 2001), 3–25.

20 Christian, "Collections of Antique Sculpture in Renaissance Rome," 53, fig. 1.

21 Pier Luigi Tucci, *Laurentius Manlius: La scoperta dell'antica Roma, La nuova Roma di Sisto IV*, Quaderni di Eutopia 3 (Rome: Edizioni Quasar, 2001).

22 Christian, *Empire Without End*, 313–15.

23 "Comparatio antiquae et novae Romae," in Jacques Paul Migne, *Patrologiae Cursus Completus: Series Graeca*, vol. 156, 23–54; Manuel Chrysoloras, *Roma parte del cielo: Confronto fra l'antica e la nuova Roma*, trans. Guido Cortassa (Turin: UTET, 2000), 67. See Michael Baxandall, *Giotto and the Orators: Humanist Observers of Painting in Italy and the Discovery of Pictorial Composition, 1350–1450* (Oxford, UK: Clarendon Press, 1971), 78.

24 Giovanni Agosti, Vincenzo Farinella, Daniela Gallo, and Giovanna Tedeschi Grisanti, "Visibilità e reimpiego: 'A Roma anche i morti e le loro urne camminano,'" in *Colloquio sul reimpiego dei sarcofagi*

romani nel Medioevo: Pisa 5–12, September 1982, ed. Bernard Andreae and Salvatore Settis (Marburg, Germany: Verlag des Kunstgeschichtlichen Seminars der Philipps-Universität Marburg: 1984), 155–70.

25 Emphasis mine. See the complete text of the inscription in Claudio Parisi Presicce, "Antiquities on the Capitol: The Legacy of the Roman People and the Archetype of the Modern Museum," in Settis and Gasparri, *Torlonia Marbles*, 66–77.

26 See Lorenz Wolf, *Kirche und Denkmalschutz: Die päpstliche Gesetzgebung zum Schutz der Kulturgüter bis zum Untergang des Kirchenstaates im Jahr 1870*, Kirchenrechtliche Bibliothek 7 (Münster: Lit Verlag, 2003). See also Parisi Presicce, "Antiquities on the Capitol," 66–77; and Maria Elisa Micheli, "Antiquarian Culture in Eighteenth Century Rome and the Birth of the Public Museum," in Settis and Gasparri, *Torlonia Marbles*, 98–103. The Torlonia Museum represents a vital node in the history of the taste for and relationship with the antique that is linked to the direct artistic patronage of the princes, which involved first and foremost the Italian sculptor Antonio Canova (1757–1822). The museum's history is also connected to the practices of restoration of ancient sculptures and the growing awareness among scholars of that period, such as the Italian banker and art collector Vincenzo Giustiniani (1564–1637), of the existence of multiple copies or variants of the same ancient statuary type. These and other aspects, such as the drawings of antiquities made by later artists, are, each in themselves, of such relevance and so well represented in the collections of the Torlonia Museum that it would be possible to stage an entire exhibition on each of them.

Exhibition Checklist

Conservation research on the twenty-four recently restored sculptures, on view for the first time in this exhibition, was conducted by Laura Buccino, Lucilla de Lachenal, and Stefania Tuccinardi at Torlonia Laboratories. Where relevant, entries distinguish the *ancient*, *original*, or *preserved* parts of a sculpture from its *modern* or *restored* components. *Modern* in this context refers to the early modern period or about the fifteenth through nineteenth centuries, when artists and professional restorers across Europe often re-carved, added new components to, cleaned, or reworked ancient sculptures according to their preferences or the desires of their patrons. Most works in the Torlonia Collection were modified during this era to varying degrees. For all sculptures including those on display for the first time in this exhibition, further information can be found on the Torlonia Foundation website, fondazionetorlonia.org.

Throughout, "left" and "right" refer to the subject's own left or right, respectively.

Pietro Ercole Visconti and Carlo Ludovico Visconti's early comprehensive surveys of the Torlonia holdings, in particular the illustrated catalogue of 1884–85 cited here, remain essential resources for the study of these works. Some of their claims, however, remain unsubstantiated or have been reconsidered by later scholars.

The following abbreviations are used to cite key sources:

Galleria Giustiniana
Galleria Giustiniana del Marchese Vincenzo Giustiniani, 2 vols. Rome, 1631–36. Facsimile with notes by Paolo Parigi, "Le stampe della Galleria Giustiniana nell'esemplare della Biblioteca Casanatense." In *I Giustiniani e l'antico*, edited by Giulia Fusconi, 511–622. Exh. cat. Rome: Palazzo Fontana di Trevi; Rome: L'Erma di Bretschneider, 2001. Page numbers refer to the 2001 edition.

Visconti
Visconti, Carlo Ludovico. *I monumenti del Museo Torlonia di sculture antiche riprodotti con la fototipia*. Rome: Stabilimento Fotografico Danesi, 1884–85.

Settis and Gasparri
Settis, Salvatore, and Carlo Gasparri, eds. *The Torlonia Marbles: Collecting Masterpieces*. Exh. cat. Milan: Rizzoli Electa, 2021.

Tuccinardi
Tuccinardi, Stefania. *Un tesoro di erudizione e arte: Il Museo Torlonia di scultura antica*. Rome: Bardi Edizioni, 2022.

Catalogue numbers in Visconti and Tuccinardi are the same as the MT ("Museo Torlonia") numbers for each work, and therefore are not listed here.

1

Portrait of a Young Woman, known as the Maiden of Vulci

Mid-1st century BCE
Roman, late Republican Period
Very fine-grained white marble; 34 × 22 × 17 cm
MT 489

PROVENANCE: Vulci (Visconti)

SELECTED REFERENCES: Visconti, 357–58, pl. 126; Settis and Gasparri, 138–39, cat. 1; Tuccinardi, 319

CONSERVATION: The portrait bust is largely intact and in very fine condition overall. Only small sections are missing, including the tip of the nose, the lobe of the left ear, and the upper part of the right ear. The eyes would have originally been inlaid, and there are holes in both earlobes for the attachment of earrings as well as behind each ear and at the back of the head for the insertion of a hair ornament. The surface has several abrasions, in particular on the lips and chin; there are short, superficial incisions, like fine scratches, mostly on the right side; the lower part of the bust is rather irregular, especially at the back, while a large chip is missing on the right edge. Shallow chisel marks are visible on the back and on the right side of the bust.

2

Portrait of a Man, known as Euthydemus of Bactria

Late 3rd–early 2nd century BCE
Greek, Hellenistic Period
Pentelic marble; 55 × 33 cm
MT 133

PROVENANCE: Giustiniani Collection

SELECTED REFERENCES: Visconti, 92–93, pl. 34; Settis and Gasparri, 140–41, cat. 2; Tuccinardi, 228

CONSERVATION: The portrait head and neck are largely intact with modern restorations at the edge of the left ear, the tip of the nose, and large parts of the brim of the hat. The only ancient portion of the brim extends from the back to the right side, making its current appearance conjectural. The surface of the hat also appears unfinished or was possibly intended to be finished in stucco. There is a band around the head below the brim of the hat, possibly meant to depict fabric; it may indicate a skullcap or hatband, but is likely not a fillet as there is no knot at the back of the neck. Traces of a small section of fabric are preserved at the right side of the neck, indicating a garment that was later smoothed away.

3
Portrait of a Man, known as the Old Man of Otricoli
Mid-1st century BCE
Roman, late Republican Period
Ancient head: fine-grained white Greek marble; restored bust: Italic white marble; 78 × 61 × 23 cm
MT 533
PROVENANCE: Otricoli (Visconti)
SELECTED REFERENCES: Visconti, 383, pl. 137; Settis and Gasparri, 142–43, cat. 3; Tuccinardi, 330
CONSERVATION: The ancient portrait head ends just above the throat in front, and in back the ancient neck extends down to the join with the bust. It has been set into a modern bust. The tip of the nose and the outer edges of both ears are restored. The hair is softly incised and has been retouched at the back of the head. The modern bust is made of various marble sections pieced together, three of which are ancient but not original to the portrait.

4
Statue of an Emperor on a Throne with a Portrait of Augustus
1st century
Roman, Imperial Period
Ancient: Pentelic marble; restored: white marble and one fragment of gray *bardiglio* marble; 164 × 51 × 101 cm
MT 164
PROVENANCE: Bovillae (Visconti)
SELECTED REFERENCES: Visconti, 114, pl. 41; Tuccinardi, 236
CONSERVATION: The statue was recomposed through a significant campaign of integrative restoration. The main ancient portions of the statue include the torso and the rear portion of the cloak over the left shoulder, and the left bicep and part of the forearm. The section of the legs that is covered by the cloak also features ancient components. These sections of the statue employ numerous modern inserts and restorations to fill in gaps. The torso and lower body have been reintegrated with one another through the insertion of a modern pelvis, extending from the waist to the hips where the drapery begins. Other areas of restoration include the head, most of the right arm and the right hand and globe, the left hand and wrist, a portion of the drapery on the back, the right foot, the left leg and foot, the seat, and the base. The surface has been covered with a whitewash to camouflage the joins, and faux encrustation and scratches were added to simulate an ancient surface on the modern inserts.

5
Portrait of Trajan
17th–18th century
Italian
Luna marble; 85 × 80 cm
MT 541
PROVENANCE: Possibly Giustiniani Collection or Studio Cavaceppi (Tuccinardi)
SELECTED REFERENCES: Visconti, 386, pl. 139; Settis and Gasparri, 236, cat. 59; Tuccinardi, 332
CONSERVATION: The portrait head was long thought to be ancient and attached to a modern bust, with modern restorations to the nose, chin, right ear, one of the eyebrows, and part of the neck. However, recent conservation work carried out since it was included in the 2020–21 exhibition *The Torlonia Marbles: Collecting Masterpieces* in Rome indicates that the head of Trajan has not undergone any integration with the modern bust. Additionally, the head has received an intense surface treatment, the reasons for which are unclear. These problematic elements lead to doubts about the object's antiquity, resulting in its redating as a modern portrait.

6
Statue of a Woman, restored as Plotina
Late 1st–early 2nd century
Roman, Imperial Period
Ancient: Greek marble; restored: Luna marble; 206 × 78 × 81 cm
MT 152
PROVENANCE: Studio Cavaceppi
SELECTED REFERENCES: Visconti, 107–8, pl. 38; Tuccinardi, 233
CONSERVATION: The statue is composed of at least two ancient parts in Greek marble that did not originally belong together: the first includes the right shoulder and the upper part of the chest, descending diagonally across the back; the second includes the left part of the upper body and comprises the entire torso down to below the knees. The veiled head is modern and was based on Plotina's canonical portrait type, which is first attested in 112 on her numismatic portraits. Additional restorations include the left shoulder, a part of the cloak on the left side, the arms holding the attributes of a *patera* and scepter (the latter missing today, but perhaps originally made of metal), the molded base with the hem of the cloak, and the sandal-clad feet.

7
Portrait of a Woman, formerly known as Marciana
120–30
Roman, Imperial Period, Hadrianic Period
Greek marble; 63 × 44 cm
MT 543
PROVENANCE: Studio Cavaceppi
SELECTED REFERENCES: Visconti, 386, pl. 140; Tuccinardi, 332
CONSERVATION: Restorations to the ancient portrait head include the nose and a small portion just below it on the right, which extends downward to the right side of the upper lip; parts of both ears; and a portion of the hairstyle in back, specifically the uppermost part of the center of the braided bun that crowns the top of the head. The entire bust is restored.

8
Portrait of a Woman, formerly known as Matidia
First half of 2nd century
Roman, Imperial Period
Greek marble; 80 × 52 cm
MT 544
PROVENANCE: 1856 excavations at Porto
SELECTED REFERENCES: Visconti, 386–87, pl. 140; Tuccinardi, 333
CONSERVATION: The face and parts of the hairstyle, especially the majority of the crest of overlapping braids in front and the upper part of the braided nest in back, are ancient but have been joined to modern additions, including the remainder of the head and bust. On

the back of the head, much of the hair is restored but is consistent with ancient prototypes, and a thin band of hair has been carved in very low relief to disguise the join between the ancient and modern sections.

9
Portrait of Hadrian
About 130
Roman, Imperial Period, Cuirass-Bust Imperatori 32 Type
White medium-grained crystalline marble from the Greek islands; 79 × 63 cm
MT 545
PROVENANCE: Villa Albani
SELECTED REFERENCES: Visconti, 387, pl. 140; Settis and Gasparri, 157, cat. 14; Tuccinardi, 333–34, pl. VIII
CONSERVATION: The portrait bust is intact with only small chips at the ears, the lower edge of the bust, and the raised border of the armor at the back. The ends of both shoulder straps have been restored; the right one is recomposed from three separate fragments; the left has a reattached strip. The pedestal and base are modern.

10
Portrait of a Woman, formerly known as Sabina
Second half of 2nd century
Roman, Imperial Period
Ancient head: Greek marble; ancient part of bust: fine-grained white marble; restored part of bust: Luna marble; 75 × 48 cm
MT 547
PROVENANCE: Torlonia acquisition
SELECTED REFERENCES: Visconti, 388, pl. 141; Tuccinardi, 333
CONSERVATION: The ancient portrait head is preserved up to the base of the neck, with some chipping visible in the braided hairstyle that wraps around the head. The surface of the face was significantly reworked, likely in the second half of the 19th century: it was smoothed and then camouflaged with some scattered speckling, presumably to imitate the kind of minor surface damage that occurs on ancient sculptures, while the pupils of the eyes were also recarved. The bust is composed of two parts: the ancient part, which runs from the neck to the shoulders and includes the thin tunic and the thicker *himation* (cloak) worn over it; and the modern part, which includes the cloak expanding outward from under the shoulders and also the folds of fabric covering the chest.

11
Portrait of Antoninus Pius
Mid-2nd century
Roman, Imperial Period, Antonine Period, Vatican Sala a Croce Greca 595 Type
Ancient head: fine-grained crystalline marble; restored bust: Luna marble; 81 × 63 cm
MT 549
PROVENANCE: Possibly Giustiniani Collection
SELECTED REFERENCES: Visconti, 388–89, pl. 141; Settis and Gasparri, 158, cat. 15; Tuccinardi, 334–35
CONSERVATION: The portrait head and neck are intact and set into a modern bust. The nose, the left eyebrow, the corner of the right eyebrow, and some locks of hair around the left temple have been restored. There are scratches at the base of the neck. The overall surface is worn and, in several places, quite corroded.

12
Portrait of a Woman, formerly known as Faustina the Elder
Mid-2nd century
Roman, Imperial Period
Ancient: Greek white marble; restored: Luna marble; 88 × 63 cm
MT 550
PROVENANCE: Torlonia acquisition
SELECTED REFERENCES: Visconti, 389, pl. 142; Tuccinardi, 335
CONSERVATION: The ancient portrait head has been cut at an oblique angle below the throat and grafted onto a modern neck and draped bust. Other modern restorations include the nose, a small part of the chin, the knot of braids on the top of the head, and a small portion of the braid on the back left side of the head. The coiffure shows signs of wear on the front, and there are traces of reworking on the chin, perhaps intended to eliminate a flaw on the surface.

13
Portrait of Young Marcus Aurelius
144–47
Roman, Imperial Period, Antonine Period, Uffizi-Toulouse Type
Ancient head: Pentelic marble; restored bust: Luna marble; 85 × 62 cm
MT 552
PROVENANCE: Campus Martius, Piazza Colonna; then possibly Scalambrini Collection (Tuccinardi)
SELECTED REFERENCES: Visconti, 390, pl. 142; Tuccinardi, 335
CONSERVATION: The portrait head is ancient, with restorations to the nose, the upper parts of the ears, and the draped bust with the support. Chipping is evident on the lower right part of the chin, as well as in the ears and the hair. The surface of the face appears to be reworked, perhaps following the removal of a very hard layer of encrustation, traces of which are still visible in two stripes descending along the line of the beard to the jaw. A dark wash was added over the entire bust by restorers in the 19th century to soften the contrast between the ancient patina of the Pentelic marble head and the modern restorations in Luna marble.

14
Portrait of Marcus Aurelius
Late 2nd century
Roman, Imperial Period, Capitoline Imperatori 38 Type
Fine-grained white marble, possibly Pentelic; 92 × 59 cm
MT 553
PROVENANCE: Ardea (Visconti)
SELECTED REFERENCES: Visconti, 391, pl. 142; Settis and Gasparri, 159, cat. 16; Tuccinardi, 335
CONSERVATION: The intact ancient portrait bust is carved from a single block of marble and is missing only a small piece of the right earlobe. The nose, the circular clasp, and some edges of the collar and cloak have been restored. The surface is worn in some places and yet traces of red pigment are visible on the fringe of the tunic. There are no visible signs of modern reworking.

15
Portrait of Faustina the Younger
About 160
Roman, Imperial Period, Antonine Period

Fine-grained Greek marble, possibly Pentelic; 73 × 48 cm
MT 557
PROVENANCE: Acquatraversa (Visconti)
SELECTED REFERENCES: Visconti, 392, pl. 143; Tuccinardi, 336
CONSERVATION: The portrait head and bust are ancient, with slight chipping on the forehead and on the left eyelid and eye. The nose, portions of the drapery, the back support, and the base are all restored.

16
Portrait of Lucius Verus
Second half of 2nd century
Roman, Imperial Period, Antonine Period, Main Type
Fine-grained white crystalline marble; 93 × 80 cm
MT 556
PROVENANCE: Acquatraversa (Visconti)
SELECTED REFERENCES: Visconti, 392, pl. 143; Settis and Gasparri, 160, cat. 17; Tuccinardi, 336
CONSERVATION: The portrait head, which is broken at the neck, belongs together with the bust; they have been reconstituted from several pieces. The lower part of the nose and the front of the neck have been restored. The lower lip and some of the locks of hair are chipped and the surfaces of the beard and hair are worn. The bust itself is reconstituted from various ancient fragments. Much of the drapery has been integrated, as well as the circular clasp, part of the fringe on the right side, and the left shoulder including the vertical folds that descend to the edge of the bust. The pedestal and black marble base are modern.

17
Portrait of a Woman, formerly known as Lucilla
150–80
Roman, Imperial Period, Antonine Period
Ancient head: Greek marble; restored bust: Luna marble; 76 × 52 cm
MT 356
PROVENANCE: Possibly excavations at Roma Vecchia, mid-19th century or shortly after
SELECTED REFERENCES: Visconti, 235, pl. 88; Tuccinardi, 284
CONSERVATION: The portrait head is ancient, and the nose and the entire bust are restored. The surface includes traces of whitewashing in the folds of the garment as well as a small amount of corrosion.

18
Portrait of Young Commodus
170–80
Roman, Imperial Period, Antonine Period, Vatican Busti 368 Type
Ancient head: fine-grained white marble, possibly Greek; ancient part of bust: marble with golden patina; restored: Luna marble; 76 × 57 cm
MT 558
PROVENANCE: Torlonia acquisition
SELECTED REFERENCES: Visconti, 392–93, pl. 144; Tuccinardi, 336
CONSERVATION: The ancient head is mounted on a partly ancient but unrelated bust and exhibits minor chipping, especially on the right side, near the left side of the mouth, and in the hair. Restorations to the head include the nose, the lower part of the left earlobe, a small portion of the right eyebrow, and a small section of hair over the forehead. A large part of the bust is also restored, completing the ancient fragment on the left side.

19
Portrait of Commodus
Late 2nd century
Roman, Imperial Period, Antonine Period
Ancient head: fine-grained marble with a gray tone; ancient (unrelated) bust: fine-grained marble with ivory patina; 93 × 59 cm
MT 559
PROVENANCE: Possibly Studio Cavaceppi (Tuccinardi)
SELECTED REFERENCES: Visconti, 393, pl. 144; Settis and Gasparri, 161, cat. 18; Tuccinardi, 336–37
CONSERVATION: The ancient portrait head has been set into an unrelated ancient bust. The nose and a circular section in the forehead above the right eye have been restored. Several locks of hair on the forehead are missing and the right eyelid is chipped. The surfaces of the beard and hair are worn. There are modern inserts at the base of the neck. The bust is reconstituted from two ancient fragments which do not belong together and are integrated with numerous marble inserts.

20
Portrait of a Woman, formerly known as Crispina
Second half of 2nd century
Roman, Imperial Period
Fine-grained Greek marble; 75 × 50 cm
MT 560
PROVENANCE: Giustiniani Collection
SELECTED REFERENCES: Visconti, 393, pl. 144; Tuccinardi, 337
CONSERVATION: The ancient portrait head is set into a restored, partially ancient bust. The face has some chipping around the left eye, the lips, and the left cheek towards the jaw, and the entire surface has been slightly reworked. The bust, of which the only ancient portion is from the left shoulder to the central area of the chest, has small incisions and inserts that have been covered by a substance to camouflage the restorations. Traces of red appear on the bottom of the folds. Restorations include the nose, the chignon on the nape of the neck, the right section of the bust with the cloak, part of the neck, and the base.

21
Portrait of Septimius Severus
Early 3rd century
Roman, Imperial Period, Severan Period, Serapis Type
Ancient head: Greek marble; restored bust: Luna marble; 92 × 83 cm
MT 566
PROVENANCE: Possibly Giustiniani Collection, or Palazzo Torlonia in Piazza Venezia (Tuccinardi)
SELECTED REFERENCES: Visconti, 396, pl. 146; Tuccinardi, 338
CONSERVATION: The ancient portrait head is set into a modern bust. There are small fractures in the hair at the temples and chips on the locks covering the forehead, as well as surface corrosion on the top of the head. Restorations include the nose, part of the left eyebrow, the lower lip, the left ear, a group of locks right above the right temple, another group of locks near the left temple, and the central, lower part of the beard. Additionally, a thin band was added in the neck under the head.

22

Portrait of Julia Domna

Early 3rd century
Roman, Imperial Period, Severan Period, Leptis A Type
Ancient head: fine-grained white marble; ancient (unrelated) bust: fine-grained white-yellowish marble; 93 × 55 cm
MT 573

PROVENANCE: Veio (Visconti)

SELECTED REFERENCES: Visconti, 398–99, pl. 148; Settis and Gasparri, 163, cat. 20; Tuccinardi, 340

CONSERVATION: The ancient portrait head has been set into an unrelated ancient bust. On the portrait, the nose has been restored and the hair at the back of the head has been recut to allow for the head's insertion into the bust. On the bust, the strip of the cloak that surrounds the shoulders is restored. There are additional restorations in the back and ends of the folds of the cloak. The front part of the pedestal is modern.

23

Portrait Group of Husband and Wife

2nd century
Roman, Imperial Period
Luna marble; 182 × 81 × 38 cm
MT 83

PROVENANCE: Giustiniani Collection

SELECTED REFERENCES: Galleria Giustiniana, 558, pl. 140; Visconti, 56, pl. 21; Settis and Gasparri, 252–53, cat. 69; Tuccinardi, 213

CONSERVATION: The portrait group has been significantly repaired and restored. Modern restorations include the heads, which are both ancient but not original to the statue; the forearms, including the joined hands; the lower part of both figures; and the fingers on the man's left hand that rest on the woman's shoulders. Numerous pieces of marble have been inserted throughout the portrait group, particularly on the man's right shoulder, in the protruding front flap (*umbo*) of the toga, along the entire edge of the U-shaped fold of drapery reaching down beneath the knee (*sinus*), and at various points in the garment, as well as the right breast and abdomen of the female statue and areas of her garment. There is a break at the level of the woman's buttocks at the back. The bodies of the figures are thought to be Trajanic, while the ancient yet unrelated portrait heads are likely later in date. The male head, likely dating to the Severan period, is restored at the tip of the nose, ears, and neck. The female head, possibly Antonine in date, only preserves the ancient face and front part of the hair; the nose, ears, neck, and entire back part of the head are restored. Its surface is very worn with breaks at the left eye, both eyebrows, and the chin; there are various chips. There is a symbol engraved on her forehead: one longitudinal line with three parallel horizontal lines.

24

Sarcophagus Depicting the Labors of Hercules and Lid with Reclining Couple

Second half of 2nd century
Roman, Imperial Period
Asiatic marble; lid: 128 × 239 × 119 cm; sarcophagus: 98 × 242 × 119 cm
MT 420

PROVENANCE: Palazzo Savelli (later Orsini) by the early 16th century

SELECTED REFERENCES: Visconti, 289–93, pl. 106; Settis and Gasparri, 282–83, cat. 83; Tuccinardi, 300–301

CONSERVATION: Both the sarcophagus and the lid are very well-preserved overall and largely intact, with architectural and decorative elements placing their construction around 170. The heads of the reclining couple are unrelated to the rest of the work; the male head may or may not be ancient, while the female head is ancient and probably dates to the Flavian or Trajanic period. The crown of curls on the female head has been added by a modern restorer in a different marble. There are numerous restorations and additions throughout, including the heads of the Erotes on the lid, and the heads and projecting parts of the figures within the aediculae of the sarcophagus. The head of Hercules with the Amazon in the third niche from the left on the back side of the sarcophagus (not illustrated in this volume) is missing. Level with the door on the short left side, a modern wedge has been inserted into a repair hole, which was likely made to explore the inside of the sarcophagus.

25

Sarcophagus Depicting the Labors of Hercules

About 160–70
Roman, Imperial Period, Antonine Period
Thasian marble; lid: 22 × 241 × 96 cm; sarcophagus: 80 × 239 × 98 cm
MT 422

PROVENANCE: Roma Vecchia estate on Via Latina

SELECTED REFERENCES: Visconti, 293–95, pl. 107; Settis and Gasparri, 181–83, cat. 28; Tuccinardi, 302

CONSERVATION: The front side and part of the short sides of the sarcophagus were broken off from the back part and rejoined with a large tufa (limestone) wedge on the right side. The surface is generally worn but without notable losses except for the right side. The last three figures of Hercules have restorations to the legs and arms, as evidenced by a fracture line that crosses the marble diagonally. The narrow bands at top and bottom have been restored in various places, and a whole section seems to be missing at the bottom towards the back. There are other gaps on the lower edge at both sides. The back (not illustrated in this volume), which is blank and roughly hewn with a claw chisel, has a series of horizontal grooves, possibly due to the quarrying process or its placement inside of the tomb. There is significant chipping on the back of the lid at the upper left edge, possibly related to a forced opening of the lid, which was anchored to the sarcophagus with deep braces, the grooves for which are still visible on the border. The original closing slab has been lost and was replaced with two slabs held together by long iron braces. One of the slabs is a modern tombstone of grayish marble, as evidenced by the remains of an inscription and an incised decoration with imbricated leaves and angular acanthus crests; it was cut off at the sides and adapted as a cover for half of the sarcophagus. The front of the lid is currently composed of a series of different fragments, making it difficult to establish how much is original or restored. There are remains of color (including visible traces of red) on the beards of the masks decorating the corners of the lid.

26

Strigilated Sarcophagus with Lions

About 260–70
Roman, Imperial Period
Greek marble; 146 × 266 × 160 cm
MT 417

PROVENANCE: Palazzo Savelli (later Orsini)

SELECTED REFERENCES: Visconti, 288, pl. 105; Settis and Gasparri, 284–85, cat. 84; Tuccinardi, 299–300

CONSERVATION: The sarcophagus is reconstructed from several ancient fragments, and there is a fracture that runs along the whole perimeter of the base, slightly above the plinth. Modern additions on the right side include a section of the lion's belly and its back left leg. On the left side, they include part of the lion's torso and front left paw, the ram's head, and part of its body. The left side is reconstructed thanks to the insertion of a large ancient fragment with a lion's head of comparable scale and style, which once belonged to another ancient sarcophagus. The inscription carved on the body of the central small amphora is modern. It appears that this sarcophagus was once reused as a fountain, a possibility suggested by two holes at the level of the top of the two gorgons' heads carved on the back side. Between the two masks, an image of a sailing ship topped with some numerals was added in the modern era (not illustrated in this volume). Small traces of color and gilding of unidentifiable dates are visible on the surface.

27

Funerary Monument of a Boy, Gaius Marcius Crescens

2nd century
Roman, Imperial Period
White marble; 74 × 94 × 16 cm
MT 413

PROVENANCE: Porto, probably necropolis on Via Portuense

SELECTED REFERENCES: Visconti, 282, pl. 104; Tuccinardi, 298

CONSERVATION: The slab is largely intact except for the two top corners which are broken, and several missing sections along the bottom and sides of the frame. The edges of both sides do not appear to be original, unlike the upper and lower edges of the slab. The central portrait is missing its nose and a portion of the left eyebrow. Various chips and gaps are evident on the two Erotes.

Inscription:
C. MARCIO CRESCENTI VIXIT ANNIS XIIII HOR VIIII FECERVNT PARENTES C MARCIVS THREPTVS ET MARCIA CARPIME FILIO DVLCISSIMO ET SIBI ET LIBERTIS LIBERTABVSQVE POSTE RISQVE EORVM HVIC MONIMENTO ITVS AMBITVS DEBETVR H(OC) M(ONUMENTUM) H(EREDEM) N(ON) S(EQUETUR)

English translation:
To Gaius Marcius Crescens. He lived fourteen years and nine hours. His parents Gaius Marcius Threptus and Marcia Carpime erected (this funerary monument) for their sweetest son, for themselves and for their freedmen and freedwomen and their descendants. Access to this monument is due. This monument will not pass to the heir.

Translation provided by Francesca Tataranni.

28

Statue of a Goddess, known as the Hestia Giustiniani

First half of 2nd century
Roman, Imperial Period, Hadrianic Period
Parian marble; 200 × 78 × 53 cm
MT 490

PROVENANCE: Giustiniani Collection

SELECTED REFERENCES: Galleria Giustiniana, 516–17, pl. 17; Visconti, 358–61, pl. 126; Settis and Gasparri, 243–45, cat. 65; Tuccinardi, 319–20

CONSERVATION: This statue is largely intact with small breaks on the surface. Interventions made in the 17th century include the restoration of the nose, fingers, and parts of the drapery, especially the lower part of the *peplos* and along the edge of the veil. Small metal reinforcing pins were also added. Stucco fillers have been inserted in the face and drapery. The left hand, including the wrist and the support, has been reattached to the forearm. In the 18th century two fingers of the left hand became detached and were repaired. In the 21st century the sculpture was cleaned and the left arm was detached and replaced in the original position; at the same time, some of the 17th-century stucco fillers were removed and the fingers of the left hand were reintegrated. The base is broken around the edges and on the back right corner.

29

Statue of Aphrodite with Eros and Ketos

First half of 2nd century
Roman, Imperial Period
Medium-grained white marble; 191 × 87 × 50 cm
MT 121

PROVENANCE: Giustiniani Collection

SELECTED REFERENCES: Galleria Giustiniana, 524–25, pl. 40; Visconti, 84–85, pl. 31; Settis and Gasparri, 256–57, cat. 72; Tuccinardi, 225

CONSERVATION: The lower half of the body and left hand are ancient. The torso and both arms are restored. The head of Aphrodite is ancient but unrelated and has additions at the ends of the knot of hair on the top of the head, the top of the skull, the chignon, the right eye and the section of the forehead immediately above it, the nose, and the mouth. Other restored portions include the knot of the drapery clasped in the hand, the finger of the left hand, the muzzle and ears of the *ketos*, and the flap of drapery clasped by Eros. The lower limbs and left arm of the Eros are ancient and have been reattached in several places; the nose, the ends of the wings, and the right arm are restored. There are traces of a metal pin on the outer edge of the upper part of the support and the plinth is reworked and resized.

30

Statue of Cupid and Psyche

Second half of 2nd century
Roman, Imperial Period
Ancient: Greek marble; restored: fine-grained white and Pavonazzetto marble; 130 × 81 × 54 cm
MT 174

PROVENANCE: Found in Rome, near Castro Pretorio (Visconti)

SELECTED REFERENCES: Visconti, 122–23, pl. 44; Tuccinardi, 238

CONSERVATION: About two-thirds of Cupid and Psyche's bodies are ancient and intact. The head of Cupid is ancient and original to the figure but has been reattached with small inserts at the base of the neck. Restorations to the figure of Cupid include the nose, a small part of the right wing (with two pins visible) and the entire left wing, the left arm from the torso to the wrist, the right arm from above the elbow, the penis, and the legs from below the knee. On the figure of Psyche the restorations include the nose, wings, right breast, part of the right forearm with the elbow, and the thumb of the right hand (restored in stucco), as well as the lower part of the legs covered in the cloak, extending from under the knee to the base. The base is entirely restored and was made in a single piece with the lower part of both figures and part of the tree trunk support. The quiver hanging from the support includes modern restorations to its upper and lower sections. Incised lines are visible on the restored right wrist and ankles of Cupid, simulating the antiquity of these new additions. Chips are evident on the chest, right arm, belly, and thigh of Cupid, as well as on the left hip of Psyche. The hair above Psyche's ear is corroded and displays loss of detail due to decay.

31
Statue of Crouching Aphrodite
1st century
Roman, Imperial Period, Doidalsas Type
Fine-grained crystalline marble with gray veins; 128 × 45 × 64 cm
MT 182
PROVENANCE: Giustiniani Collection
SELECTED REFERENCES: Galleria Giustiniana, 222–23, pl. 38; Visconti, 128, pl. 46; Settis and Gasparri, 260–61, cat. 74; Tuccinardi, 240–41, pl. IV
CONSERVATION: The ancient portions of the sculpture comprise the torso of the body from the shoulders and upper arms, including the snake armband, to the ankles and a very small section of the base, under Aphrodite's proper right foot. The head and neck; the right arm just below the shoulder and hand, including the perfume jar; the left arm below the bracelet and hand; the front of the left foot; and the entire right foot are all restored. The swan is also almost entirely restored (head, neck, left side, and part of the back). Fracture lines are visible on the goddess's chest and right shoulder. A round piece is inserted in the right thigh. The surface appears remarkably smoothed.

32
Head of Mars
First half of 2nd century
Roman, Imperial Period, Hadrianic Period, Palazzo Borghese-Lecce Type
White marble; 63 × 24 × 26 cm
MT 104
PROVENANCE: Giustiniani Collection
SELECTED REFERENCES: Visconti, 73–74, pl. 26; Tuccinardi, 220–21
CONSERVATION: The head and the neck are original. Restored portions include the nose, part of the lower lip, the chin, a portion of the left side and the upper central part of the visor, and the griffin on the top of the helmet, with the exception of the front legs and the tail. The surface of the marble presents some chromatic alterations, particularly on the right side.

33
Statue of Athena
Late 1st century BCE–early 1st century CE
Roman, Imperial Period, Augustan Period
Pentelic marble; 181 × 70 × 46 cm
MT 62
PROVENANCE: Giustiniani Collection
SELECTED REFERENCES: Visconti, 39–40, pl. 16; Tuccinardi, 208
CONSERVATION: The ancient body is largely intact from the upper chest to the base. Restored portions include the head and neck, sections of the neckline and the left shoulder, both arms including the attributes, the entire upper part of the back down to the waist, and the tip of the right big toe. There are some plugs in the folds of the peplum and in the rear part of the left side of the base. The right arm was probably restored when the work was in the Giustiniani Collection, whereas the left arm is apparently more recent and is made of a different marble. The veins of the marble have been covered in plaster, as was usually the case for the sculptures in the Giustiniani Collection. A small hole, possibly ancient, is visible on the back, on the left shoulder blade. The surface is particularly flat in the central part of the bust, perhaps the result of reworking.

34
Statue of Hercules
Late 2nd century
Roman, Imperial Period, Antonine Period, Trieste or New York Type
Ancient: coarse-grained Greek marble; restored: Luna marble; 100 × 51 × 30 cm
MT 242
PROVENANCE: Torlonia acquisition
SELECTED REFERENCES: Visconti, 167–68, pl. 61; Tuccinardi, 255
CONSERVATION: The ancient torso is well-preserved except for minor chipping and abrasions on its surface. The restored portions include the head surmounted by the jaws of the lion and the neck; the right arm from below the shoulder (in two pieces) up to the hand, including part of the chain; the left hand with the club; the end of the lion skin on the left side and the adjacent support in the form of a trunk; the left leg from below the thigh attachment to the foot; the right leg from above the knee to the foot; and the base with the crouching three-headed Cerberus.

35
Statue of Mercury in the Form of a Herm
2nd century
Roman, Imperial Period, Tralles Type
Ancient body: Greek marble, probably Pentelic; restored: fine-grained white marble; 182 × 61 × 30 cm
MT 504
PROVENANCE: Excavated at Sabina, Italy (ancient Cures) (Visconti)
SELECTED REFERENCES: Visconti, 371, pl. 129; Tuccinardi, 323
CONSERVATION: The body of the statue is largely ancient, with chips on the front and the hem of the cloak, as well as on the bent left arm. The restored portions include the head, the neck, the right arm, and a long portion of the fall of the cloak on the back and side as well as a small part of its edge. The support in the form of a *herm* (the square lower section) is also restored.

36
Statue of Apollo
2nd century
Roman, Imperial Period
Ancient: fine-grained Greek marble; restored: Luna marble; 187 × 75 × 56 cm
MT 237
PROVENANCE: Ostia (Visconti)
SELECTED REFERENCES: Visconti, 164, pl. 60; Tuccinardi, 254
CONSERVATION: The torso and upper left leg are original. The restored portions include the head with the entire neck and a portion in the center of the back under the nape; the entire right arm from below the shoulder and with a portion connecting to the back; the left forearm and *cithara* and the part of the cloak falling onto the support; the right leg from the groin attachment to the foot, including a patch in the upper front part of the thigh; the left leg from below the knee to the base; the entire base with the figure's feet; and the lower part of the support. Chipping is visible on the right side and near the pelvis.

37
Statue of Artemis
Second half of 2nd century
Roman, Imperial Period, Torlonia-Dresden or Millesgården Type
Luna marble; 164 × 65 × 52 cm
MT 48
PROVENANCE: Giustiniani Collection
SELECTED REFERENCES: Galleria Giustiniana, 532, pl. 64; Visconti, 30–31, pl. 12; Tuccinardi, 205
CONSERVATION: The statue is largely intact with an ancient but unrelated head. The nose, chin, and neck; the front of the right hand; the thumb, index finger, and staff in the left hand; and the connecting piece between the right shoulder and arm are all modern. The arms are recomposed from various fragments, with an integrated fragment on the right forearm. The left foot and the lower part of the right calf were also reattached with the supporting tree trunk. To insert the neck, the bust was reworked up to the neckline of the chiton. There is a small missing section between the left hip and left hand. There are fractures on the left breast, the right wrist, and the front edge and the left corner of the base. Part of the upper surface of the base is unfinished. Previously, abrasions extending from the right eyebrow to the lateral band of hair had been enhanced with resin, and putty has been added. Some abrasion is evident at the top of the head and on the underlying bands of hair.

38
Statue of a Boy with Dogs
2nd century
Roman, Imperial Period, late Hadrianic or Antonine Period
White marble; 48 × 59 × 41 cm
MT 442
PROVENANCE: Possibly near the Circus of Maxentius, or the Villa of the Quintilii
SELECTED REFERENCES: Visconti, 319, pl. 113; Tuccinardi, 308
CONSERVATION: The head and body of the child are ancient, including the right leg the portion of the plinth adjacent to it, and the left thigh up to the knee, which was reattached starting from the hip. The right foot, left leg and foot, and both arms of the boy are restored. The rest of the group is modern. The hind legs of the adult dog up to a third of the back, the puppy attached to the mother, and the profiled base are sculpted from one block. A second block of marble was used to sculpt the adult dog's body up to the first third of her front legs. A third block was used to create the end of the mother's right paw, the second puppy, and the child's arms that hold it.

39
Statue of a Girl Holding a Bird
First half of 2nd century
Roman, Imperial Period
Ancient: fine-grained white marble, possibly Luna, with slightly yellow patina; restored: Italic white marble; 96 × 36 × 33 cm
MT 169
PROVENANCE: Found between Via Latina and the nearby Caffarella estate, in the residential area near the Via Appia
SELECTED REFERENCES: Visconti, 117–18, pl. 43; Tuccinardi, 237
CONSERVATION: The head is original to the sculpture and has been reattached at the base of the neck. The outer part of the left ear is damaged. Restorations include the edge of the drapery on the girl's left side, the statue base and tip of the left foot, the middle finger of the right hand, and the bird's beak.

40
Statue of a Boy, restored as Harpocrates
1st–2nd century
Roman, Imperial Period
White marble; 88 × 33 × 28 cm
MT 73
PROVENANCE: Giustiniani Collection
SELECTED REFERENCES: Galleria Giustiniana, 518–19, pl. 23; Visconti, 48, pl. 19; Tuccinardi, 211
CONSERVATION: The head is ancient but unrelated to the sculpture; the head actually depicts a girl, although the reworked sculpture as a whole is meant to depict a young boy in the form of Harpocrates. Both arms below the shoulder have been integrated, along with the cornucopia in the left arm. The club has been assembled from several parts. Other restorations include the lower part of the legs, the tree trunk, and the base. Circle-shaped marks are visible on the left buttock and thigh, perhaps resulting from the carving of the original support. There is some discoloration around the right armpit, on the front of the left shoulder, near the navel, on the inside of the right thigh, and scattered on the torso and thighs. The tip of the nose has been restored, as well as the crown, some locks of hair on the right temple, and part of the right cheek.

41
Statue of the Infant Bacchus on a Ram
1st–2nd century
Roman, Imperial Period
Marble, possibly Grechetto; 60 × 60 × 21 cm
MT 454
PROVENANCE: 1878 excavations at Caffarella (Visconti)
SELECTED REFERENCES: Visconti, 323–24, pl. 116; Tuccinardi, 310
CONSERVATION: The sculpture has been recomposed from two broken sections comprising the center of the body of the ram. Only the body of the ram and the legs of Bacchus are ancient. The entirety of Bacchus's upper body, including the

head, chest, arms, and the objects in his left hand, are restored, as are the left toes. The ram's neck, legs, and tip of the tail; the central support; and the base are later restorations.

42
Statue of the Cesi-Type Silenus (Old Satyr)
1st century
Roman, Imperial Period, Cesi Type
Silenus: white Greek marble; base and panther: Luna marble; 125 × 63 × 56 cm
MT 374
PROVENANCE: Giustiniani Collection
SELECTED REFERENCES: Galleria Giustiniana, 556–57, pl. 138; Visconti, 249–50, pl. 92; Settis and Gasparri, 281, cat. 82; Tuccinardi, 288–89
CONSERVATION: The statue has been placed on an unrelated ancient base with a panther. The Silenus has restorations on the tip of the nose, the left arm from the shoulder joint down to the hand and end of the wineskin, the lower part of the trunk, the right foot, and the left leg from slightly above the knee. The marble surface is worn and shows traces of oxidation.

43
Statue of Isis, restored as Ceres
2nd–early 3rd century
Roman, Imperial Period
Ancient: *bigio morato* gray marble; restored: fine-grained white marble; 198 × 89 × 66 cm
MT 31
PROVENANCE: Giustiniani Collection
SELECTED REFERENCES: Galleria Giustiniana, 552–53, pl. 35; Visconti, 20, pl. 8; Settis and Gasparri, 248–49, cat. 67; Tuccinardi, 200
CONSERVATION: A fracture line just above the breasts clearly demarcates the restoration of the upper part of the sculpture. The sculpture from the fracture line all the way down to the feet appears to be ancient. The front part of the face is ancient but unrelated and the fracture line under the chin and on the forehead is clearly visible. The neck, diadem, forearms, and hands are modern restorations. The feet are both ancient, but unrelated both to one another and to the original sculpture. The base is modern.

44
Statue of Isis
2nd century
Roman, Imperial Period
Body: *bigio morato* gray marble; restored head, arms, and feet: white marble; 151 × 49 × 49 cm
MT 180
PROVENANCE: Giustiniani Collection (Tuccinardi)
SELECTED REFERENCES: Visconti, 126–27, pl. 45; Tuccinardi, 240
CONSERVATION: Only the central portion of the torso is ancient, including the end of the lock of hair on the left shoulder. The top of the knot, the sleeves, and the entirety of the lower part of the garment have been reconstructed in the same *bigio morato* marble. The head and neck, the arms with the attributes (*sistrum* and pail), and the feet have been restored in white marble. The front of the base is reattached. The sleeves of the chiton must have been closed with buttons, which have been retained in the restoration.

45
The Torlonia Nile, formerly the Barberini-Albani Nile
Late 1st century
Roman, Imperial Period, Flavian Period
Bigio morato gray marble; 148 × 230 × 80 cm
MT 427
PROVENANCE: Found in 1633 in the countryside north of Rome; Villa Barberini, Castel Gandolfo; Villa Albani, Rome
SELECTED REFERENCES: Visconti, 302–3, pl. 109; Settis and Gasparri, 204, cat. 38; Tuccinardi, 303
CONSERVATION: Restorations include the top of the head and parts of the crown; the nose of the Nile; the right hand and the reed; a section of the right foot from the heel and the plinth and toes; the upper elements of the cornucopia, including the pinecone and the sheaves of wheat hanging over the side; the head, front paws, and right breast of the sphinx; and the crocodile's head. The left corner of the plinth and the entire lower part of the base are also restored.

46
Statue of Artemis Ephesia
2nd century
Roman, Imperial Period
Body: white marble; head, neck, and hands: black marble, various kinds; 117 × 33 × 37 cm
MT 483
PROVENANCE: Giustiniani Collection
SELECTED REFERENCES: Galleria Giustiniana, 562, pl. 152; Visconti, 351–52, pl. 124; Settis and Gasparri, 270, cat. 79; Tuccinardi, 318
CONSERVATION: The back of the sculpture is well-preserved and includes traces of color on the band that descends vertically from the top of the head. Restorations undertaken during the 17th century include the head and hands in black marble, the animal protomes (heads and torsos) that project from the garment, and the head of a cupid in the third band. Other restorations include the right half of the nimbus surrounding the head, the deers' heads on the left half of the nimbus, the foreparts of the lions on the arms, and a small section at the front of the base and pedestal.

47
Statue of Leda and the Swan
Late 2nd century
Roman, Imperial Period
Marble, possibly Pentelic; 143 × 69 × 49 cm
MT 60
PROVENANCE: 1864 excavations at the Palazzo Imperiale, Porto (ancient Portus)
SELECTED REFERENCES: Visconti, 37–38, pl. 15; Tuccinardi, 98, 208
CONSERVATION: This sculpture has only been partially conserved for educational purposes. It was discovered in poor condition: parts of the arm and cloak were disconnected from the body. The portion from the head to the neck is composed of ancient fragments and 19th-century restorations. Other visible repairs include the right shoulder of Leda and on her left thigh under the body of the swan, whose neck and head are modern. Additional integrations include the right forearm to the hand, parts of the hem and the garment's folds, the toes, and the plinth that surrounds the original base. The surface is quite abraded and the front part of the torso was polished at the end of the 19th century.

48

Statue of Leda and the Swan

First half of 2nd century
Roman, Imperial Period
White marble; 141 × 68 × 43 cm
MT 187

PROVENANCE: Found in 1623 in Piazza di Mario, just south of Velletri; Giustiniani Collection

SELECTED REFERENCES: Galleria Giustiniana, 560–61, pl. 150; Visconti, 131–32, pl. 47; Tuccinardi, 242–43

CONSERVATION: Restorations to the figure of Leda include the head, neck, and left shoulder; the left arm and cascade of drapery; the left thumb and forefinger, and two flaps at the top of the cloak; the sleeve of the chiton; the protruding section of the folds between the breasts; the right arm at the shoulder including the oval connecting piece between the shoulder and arm; the right hand clasping the wing of the swan; and the front part of the left foot and toes and some folds of the drapery. A connecting marble insert has been added to the toes of the right foot. The head and neck of the swan as well as the rear right corner of the rock are also restored.

49

Attic Votive Relief

Late 5th century BCE
Greek, Classical Period
Pentelic marble; 41 × 67 × 11 cm
MT 433

PROVENANCE: Vicinity of the Tomb of Caecilia Metella on Via Appia (Visconti)

SELECTED REFERENCES: Visconti, 313–15, pl. 111; Settis and Gasparri, 174, cat. 25; Tuccinardi, 305

CONSERVATION: The relief is missing its upper part and the surface is worn and chipped. A roughly chiseled area at the center of the lower front of the relief indicates where an element used to secure the relief to a mount or holder was once attached; this backing was removed in antiquity. There are holes of different shapes on both sides of the relief that were used to affix the relief to a wall.

50

Relief of Mithraic Sacrifice

2nd century
Roman, Imperial Period
Marble; 88 × 165 × 18 cm
MT 191

PROVENANCE: Found on the Quirinal Hill (Colonna Garden), near Torre Mesa

SELECTED REFERENCES: Visconti, 134, pl. 48; Tuccinardi, 244

CONSERVATION: Restorations include the head of the torchbearer at the left and his left arm, including the end of the torch; the section between the left torchbearer and the bull, including the tail and bottom drapery of Mithras's cloak; the right arm of the second torchbearer on the right; and much of the space between the bull and the torchbearer on the right. The head of the personification of the sun was completed using another fragment that is probably ancient, but the radiate crown is restored. The back of the relief has been reinforced with a piece of marble molding, which was reused to consolidate the joins between the ancient and modern pieces.

Inscription:
[SOLI I]NVICT[O] MITHRAE FEC(IT) L(UCIUS) AUR(ELIUS) SEVERUS PRA[ES(IDENTE) L(UCIO)] DOMITIO MAR[CEL]LINO PATR(E)

English translation:
To the Unconquered Sun Mithras, Lucius Aurelius Severus made (this) when Lucius Domitius Marcellinus was the presiding Father.

Translation provided by Francesca Tataranni.

51

Unfinished Statue of a Dacian Prisoner

Early 2nd century
Roman, Imperial Period, Trajanic Period
Luna marble; 245 × 111 × 70 cm
MT 412

PROVENANCE: 1859 excavation in Rome at the Vannutelli House, 46 Via del Governo Vecchio

SELECTED REFERENCES: Visconti, 281–82, pl. 103; Settis and Gasparri, 190–91, cat. 33; Tuccinardi, 298

CONSERVATION: The ancient sculpture is unfinished but intact, with only the right hand above the wrist and the fingers of the left hand missing. The nose has been restored and a gap above the left eyebrow has been filled.

52

Portus Relief

Late 2nd–early 3rd century
Roman, Imperial Period
Pentelic marble; 74 × 123 × 15 cm
MT 430

PROVENANCE: 1864 excavations at Porto (ancient Portus)

SELECTED REFERENCES: Visconti, 306–11, pl. 110; Settis and Gasparri, 175–78, cat. 26; Tuccinardi, 304, 306, pl. VII

CONSERVATION: The relief is largely intact. Missing parts include the right side of the frame, the legs of Bacchus from the knees down, a large section between the apotropaic eye and the hull of the ship, and a section of Neptune's right calf and foot. There are two four-centimeter-wide holes for fixing clamps on the long upper side and on the short sides. The back of the relief was relined with a Pentelic marble slab. Significant traces of the original color are visible to the naked eye on the relief's surface, particularly in the red flame of the lighthouse.

53

Statue of Germanicus

1st century
Roman, Imperial Period
Bronze; 219 × 111 × 79 cm
MT 255

PROVENANCE: Estate called "degli Arci" in Sabina, Italy (ancient Cures), February 16, 1874

SELECTED REFERENCES: Visconti, 175, pl. 65; Settis and Gasparri, 144–47, cat. 4; Tuccinardi, 258

CONSERVATION: The torso and flexed left leg are original and the preserved bronze surface shows numerous signs of ancient restoration and repair, including cold-cast repair pieces, hammered after casting, of various sizes and shapes. The head, the left arm from the shoulder, the right arm just above the elbow joints, the right leg from the hem and part of the pubic area all the way down to the foot, the draped support, and the base are all 19th-century plaster additions, coated with a patina to match the color of the ancient bronze. To support the restorations, an iron armature was introduced.

54

Statue of a Youth, known as the Amelung Athlete

Late 1st–early 2nd century
Roman, Imperial Period, Trajanic Period
Medium-grained Greek insular marble; 224 × 93 × 53 cm
MT 470

PROVENANCE: 1864 excavations at the Palazzo Imperiale, Porto (ancient Portus)

SELECTED REFERENCES: Visconti, 339–40, pl. 121; Settis and Gasparri, 185, cat. 30; Tuccinardi, 315

CONSERVATION: The torso and left arm are original, with the latter being reconstituted from ancient fragments. The head and neck; the right arm, shoulder blade, and part of the shoulder; the fingers of the left hand; the left leg from the knee down; and the right leg with the support and base plinth are all restored. The ancient surface is notably worn.

55

Rondanini-Type Medusa on a Trapezophoros (Table Leg) with a Griffin's Head

2nd century
Roman, Imperial Period
Fine-grained white marble, possibly Pentelic; 173 × 55 × 23 cm; Medusa head and base: H. 57 cm; *trapezophoros*: H. 116 cm
MT 294

PROVENANCE: Giustiniani Collection

SELECTED REFERENCES: Visconti, 200, pl. 74; Settis and Gasparri, 254–55, cat. 70; Tuccinardi, 268

CONSERVATION: The Medusa's head and elements of the table leg, including the griffin-headed upper part and the paw-shaped foot, are all ancient but not related to one another. The Medusa head is of Hadrianic date and has visible breaks of ancient date in the hair and in part of the coils of the snakes, which have since been reassembled. There is a large chip missing at the tip of the nose. The tips of the wings and parts of the snakes' coils are restored. Signs of later "antiquing" of the sculpture are evident in the abrasions that have been made on the surfaces but are absent from areas that would have been difficult to reach, including the sides and the areas around the eyes. The table support (*trapezophoros*), which is of Antonine date, shows numerous abrasions. The small base on which the Medusa head rests is modern, as is the small base with volutes (spiral scrolls) applied to the top of the table leg.

56

Rondanini-Type Medusa on a Trapezophoros (Table Leg) with a Lion's Head

2nd century
Roman, Imperial Period
Coarse-grained white marble; 168 × 60 × 25 cm; Medusa head and base: H. 53 cm; *trapezophoros*: H. 115 cm
MT 296

PROVENANCE: Giustiniani Collection

SELECTED REFERENCES: Visconti, 201, pl. 74; Settis and Gasparri, 254–55, cat. 71; Tuccinardi, 268–69

CONSERVATION: The Medusa head and the support with volutes are modern. The table leg, with its lion protome and paw-shaped terminal, is ancient.

57

Statue of Odysseus Beneath the Ram

Late 1st century
Roman, Imperial Period, Flavian Period
Luna marble; 77 × 82 × 35 cm
MT 438

PROVENANCE: Villa Albani

SELECTED REFERENCES: Visconti, 317–18, pl. 112; Settis and Gasparri, 214–15, cat. 47; Tuccinardi, 307

CONSERVATION: The original ancient part of the sculpture is limited to the central portion of the animal and man. The ram's head and the trunk placed under Odysseus's back are ancient fragments from other unrelated sculptures that were reworked in the modern era. Other modern restorations include the ram's left horn, legs, and feet up to the ankles; both of Odysseus's feet; and his right wrist. Small holes on the surface of the fleece of the ram's head may also indicate modern reworking.

58

Statue of a Resting Goat

Body: late 1st century; head: attributed to Gian Lorenzo Bernini (1598–1680)
Roman, Imperial Period, Trajanic Period
White marble; 95 × 134 × 71 cm
MT 441

PROVENANCE: Giustiniani Collection

SELECTED REFERENCES: Visconti, 319, pl. 113; Settis and Gasparri, 268–69, cat. 78; Tuccinardi, 308

CONSERVATION: The ancient surface of the fleece is very worn. The ancient tail is broken. The head, horns, neck, hooves, and most of the base are restored. There are marble wedges inserted in the front of the neck, on the breast, and on the front left hoof at the back. Both horns have been worked separately and inserted and have been broken at the ends. There are abrasions on the goat's chest as well as spots with fake dotting.

Selected Bibliography

Selected Catalogues of the Torlonia Collection

Visconti, Pietro Ercole. *Catalogo del Museo Torlonia di sculture antiche*. Rome: Topografia Editrice Romana, 1876.

Visconti, Carlo Ludovico. *I monumenti del Museo Torlonia di sculture antiche riprodotti con la fototipia*. Rome: Stabilimento Fotografico Danesi, 1884–85.

Gasparri, Carlo, and Ida Caruso. *Materiali per servire allo studio del Museo Torlonia di scultura antica*. Rome: Accademia Nationale dei Lincei, 1980.

Settis, Salvatore, and Carlo Gasparri, eds. *The Torlonia Marbles: Collecting Masterpieces*. Exh. cat. Milan: Rizzoli Electa, 2021.

Tuccinardi, Stefania. *Un tesoro di erudizione e arte: Il Museo Torlonia di scultura antica*. Rome: Bardi Edizioni, 2022.

Gasparri, Carlo, Salvatore Settis, and Martin Szewczyk, eds. *Chefs-d'œuvre de la collection Torlonia*. Exh. cat. Paris: Musée du Louvre, 2024.

Selected Bibliography

Adembri, Benedetta, and Rosa Maria Nicolai. *Vibia Sabina: Da Augusta a Diva*. Exh. cat. Milan: Electa, 2007.

Alexandridis, Annetta. *Die Frauen des römischen Kaiserhauses: Eine Untersuchung ihrer bildlichen Darstellung von Livia bis Iulia Domna*. Mainz, Germany: Philipp von Zabern, 2004.

Bartman, Elizabeth. "The Torlonia Marbles: Rescue, Restoration, Rehabilitation." *American Journal of Archaeology* 126, no. 1 (2022): 151–59.

Beard, Mary. *Twelve Caesars: Images of Power from the Ancient World to the Modern*. Princeton, NJ: Princeton University Press, 2021.

Beard, Mary. *Emperor of Rome: Ruling the Ancient Roman World*. New York: Liveright, 2023.

Beard, Mary, John North, and Simon Price, *Religions of Rome: Volume 1, A History*. Cambridge, UK: Cambridge University Press, 1998.

Becker, Hilary. "Pigment Nomenclature in the Ancient Near East, Greece, and Rome." *Archaeological and Anthropological Sciences* 14, no. 20 (2022): doi.org/10.1007/s12520-021-01394-1.

Beckmann, Martin. *Faustina the Younger: Coinage, Portraits, and Public Image*. New York: American Numismatic Society, 2021.

Bennett, Julian. *Trajan, Optimus Princeps: A Life and Times*. Bloomington, IN: Indiana University Press, 1997.

Birley, Anthony R. *Hadrian: The Restless Emperor*. London: Routledge, 1997.

Boatwright, Mary T. *The Imperial Women of Rome: Power, Gender, Context*. Oxford, UK: Oxford University Press, 2021.

Bowden, Hugh. *Mystery Cults in the Ancient World*. London: Thames and Hudson, 2010.

Bowman, Alan K., Edward Champlin, and Andrew Lintott, eds. *The Cambridge Ancient History: Volume 10, The Augustan Empire, 43 B.C.E.–A.D. 69*. Cambridge, UK: Cambridge University Press, 2008.

Bowman, Alan K., Peter Garnsey, and Dominic Rathbone, eds. *The Cambridge Ancient History: Volume 11, The High Empire, A.D. 70–192*. Cambridge, UK: Cambridge University Press, 2008.

Bowman, Alan K., Averil Cameron, and Peter Garnsey, eds. *The Cambridge Ancient History: Volume 12, The Crisis of Empire: A.D. 193–33*. Cambridge, UK: Cambridge University Press, 2008.

Boyce, George K. "Corpus of the Lararia of Pompeii." *Memoirs of the American Academy in Rome* 14 (1937).

Brennan, T. Corey. *Sabina Augusta: An Imperial Journey*. Oxford, UK: Oxford University Press, 2018.

Burnett Grossman, Janet, Jerry Podany, and Marion True, eds. *History of Restoration of Ancient Stone Sculptures*. Los Angeles: J. Paul Getty Museum, 2003.

Carandini, Andrea. *Vibia Sabina: Funzione politica, iconografia e il problema del classicismo adrianeo*. Florence: Leo S. Olschki, 1969.

Clarke, John R. *The Houses of Roman Italy, 100 B.C.–A.D. 250: Ritual, Space, and Decoration*. Berkeley: University of California Press, 1991.

Daehner, Jens, and Kenneth Lapatin, *Power and Pathos: Bronze Sculpture of the Hellenistic World*. Exh. cat. Los Angeles: J. Paul Getty Museum, 2015.

Daehner, Jens, Kenneth Lapatin, and Ambra Spinelli. *Artistry in Bronze: The Greeks and Their Legacy*. XIXth International Congress on Ancient Bronzes. Los Angeles: J. Paul Getty Museum, Getty Conservation Institute, 2017.

D'Ambra, Eve. "Is Beauty Divine? A Reassessment of the Portraiture of Sabina." *Memoirs of the American Academy in Rome* 65 (2020): 132–71.

De la Bédoyère, Guy. *Domina: The Women Who Made Imperial Rome*. New Haven, CT: Yale University Press, 2018.

Elsner, Jaś. *The Art of the Roman Empire: AD 100–450*. Oxford History of Art. Oxford, UK: Oxford University Press, 2018.

Emerson, Alfred. *Catalogue of a Polychrome Exhibition: Illustrating the Use of Color Particularly in Graeco-Roman Sculpture*. Chicago: Art Institute of Chicago, 1892.

Fejfer, Jane. *Roman Portraits in Context*. Berlin: De Gruyter, 2008.

Fittschen, Klaus. *Die Bildnistypen der Faustina minor und die Fecunditas Augustae*. Göttingen: Vandenhoeck and Ruprecht, 1982.

Fittschen, Klaus. *Prinzenbildnisse antoninscher Zeit*. Beiträge zur Erschliessung hellenistischer und kaiserzeitlicher Skulptur und Architektur 18. Mainz, Germany: Philipp von Zabern, 1999.

Fittschen, Klaus, and Paul Zanker. *Katalog der römischen Porträts in den Capitolinischen Museen und den anderen kommunalen Sammlungen der Stadt Rom*. Vol. 3. Mainz, Germany: Philipp von Zabern, 1983.

Friedland, Elise A., and Melanie Grunow Sobocinski, eds., with Elaine K. Gazda. *The Oxford Handbook of Roman Sculpture*. Oxford, UK: Oxford University Press, 2015.

Fronto, Marcus Cornelius. *Correspondence*. Vol. 1. Translated by C. R. Haines. Loeb Classical Library 112. Cambridge, MA: Harvard University Press, 1919.

Futo Kennedy, Rebecca. *Race and Ethnicity in the Classical World.* Indianapolis: Hackett, 2013.

Galinsky, Karl. *Augustan Culture: An Interpretive Introduction*. Princeton, NJ: Princeton University Press, 1996.

Garnsey, Peter, and Richard Saller. *The Roman Empire: Economy, Society and Culture*. Berkeley: University of California Press, 1987.

Gazda, Elaine K., ed. *The Ancient Art of Emulation: Studies in Artistic Originality and Tradition from the Present to Classical Antiquity*. Ann Arbor: University of Michigan Press, 2002.

Gazda, Elaine K., ed. *Roman Art in the Private Sphere: New Perspectives on the Architecture and Decor of the Domus, Villa, and Insula*, 2nd ed. Ann Arbor: University of Michigan Press, 2010.

George, Michele, ed. *Roman Slavery and Roman Material Culture*. Phoenix Supplementary Volumes 52. Toronto: University of Toronto Press, 2013.

Gradel, Ittai. *Emperor Worship and Roman Religion*. Oxford Classical Monographs. Oxford, UK: Clarendon Press, 2002.

Granino Cecere, Maria Grazia. "Legittimazione e partecipazione al potere: Le donne della domus imperiale durante il principato adottivo." In *Vibia Sabina: Da Augusta a Diva*, edited by Benedetta Adembri and Rosa Maria Nicolai. Exh. cat. Milan: Electa, 2007.

Hackworth Petersen, Lauren. *The Freedman in Roman Art and Art History*. New York: Cambridge University Press, 2006.

Hales, Shelley. *The Roman House and Society Identity*. Cambridge, UK: Cambridge University Press, 2003.

Historia Augusta. Vol. 1. Translated by David Magie. Revised by David Rohrbacher. Loeb Classical Library 139. Cambridge, MA: Harvard University Press, 2022.

Hölscher, Tonio. *The Language of Images in Roman Art*. Translated by Anthony Snodgrass and Annemarie Künzl-Snodgrass. Cambridge, UK: Cambridge University Press, 2004.

Huskinson, Janet. *Roman Children's Sarcophagi: Their Decoration and Its Social Significance*. Oxford, UK: Clarendon Press, 1996.

Huskinson, Janet. "Constructing Childhood on Roman Funerary Memorials." *Hesperia Supplements* 41 (2007).

Huskinson, Janet. *Roman Strigillated Sarcophagi: Art and Social History*. Oxford, UK: Oxford University Press, 2015.

Jackson, Nicholas. *Trajan: Rome's Last Conqueror*. Barnsley, UK: Greenhill Books, 2022.

Joshel, Sandra R. *Slavery in the Roman World*. Cambridge, UK: Cambridge University Press, 2013.

Kampen, Natalie Boymel. *Family Fictions in Roman Art*. Cambridge, UK: Cambridge University Press, 2009.

Kleiner, Diana E. E. *Roman Sculpture*. New Haven, CT: Yale University Press, 1992.

Kleiner, Diana E. E., and Susan B. Matheson, eds. *I, Claudia: Women in Ancient Rome*. Exh. cat. New Haven, CT: Yale University Art Gallery, 1996.

Koch, Guntram, Hellmut Sichtermann, and Friederike Sinn-Henninger. *Römische Sarkophage*. Munich: C. H. Beck, 1982.

Koortbojian, Michael. "*In commemorationem mortuorum*: Text and Image Along the 'Streets of Tombs.'" In *Art and Text in Roman Culture*, edited by Jaś Elsner, 210–33. Cambridge, UK: Cambridge University Press, 1996.

Levick, Barbara M. *Julia Domna: Syrian Empress*. London: Routledge, 2007.

Levick, Barbara M. *Faustina I and II: Imperial Women of the Golden Age*. Oxford, UK: Oxford University Press, 2014.

Ling, Roger, ed. *Making Classical Art: Process and Practice*. Stroud: Tempus, 2000.

Mattusch, Carol C. *Classical Bronzes: The Art and Craft of Greek and Roman Statuary*. Ithaca, NY: Cornell University Press, 1996.

McCoskey, Denise Eileen. *Race: Antiquity and Its Legacy*. Oxford, UK: Oxford University Press, 2012.

Mikocki, Tomasz. *Sub specie deae: Les impératrices et princesses romaines assimilées à des déeses. Étude iconologique*. Rome: Bretschneider, 1995.

Niederhuber, Christian. *Roman Imperial Portrait Practice in the Second Century AD: Marcus Aurelius and Faustina the Younger*. Oxford, UK: Oxford University Press, 2022.

Orr, David G. "Roman Domestic Religion: The Evidence of the Household Shrines." *Aufstieg und Niedergang der römischen Welt* 2, no. 16.2 (1978): 1557–91.

Perry, Ellen. *The Aesthetics of Emulation in the Visual Arts of Ancient Rome*. Cambridge, UK: Cambridge University Press, 2005.

Raff, Katharine A., ed. *Roman Art at the Art Institute of Chicago*. Chicago: Art Institute of Chicago, 2017. artic.edu/digitalroman.

Richlin, Amy. *Marcus Aurelius in Love: The Letters of Marcus and Fronto*. Chicago: University of Chicago Press, 2007.

Rockwell, Peter. *The Art of Stoneworking: A Reference Guide*. Cambridge, UK: Cambridge University Press, 1993.

Rose, Charles Brian. *Dynastic Commemoration and Imperial Portraiture in the Julio-Claudian Period*. Cambridge Studies in Classical Art and Iconography. Cambridge, UK: Cambridge University Press, 1997.

Russell, Amy, and Monica Hellström, eds. *The Social Dynamics of Roman Imperial Imagery*. Cambridge, UK: Cambridge University Press, 2020.

Russell, Ben. *The Economics of the Roman Stone Trade*. Oxford, UK: Oxford University Press, 2013.

Stewart, Peter. *Statues in Roman Society: Representation and Response*. Oxford Studies in Ancient Culture and Representation. Oxford, UK: Oxford University Press, 2003.

Stuveras, Roger. *Le putto dans l'art romain*. Brussels: Latomus, 1969.

Talbot, Margaret. "The Myth of Whiteness in Classical Sculpture." *New Yorker*, October 22, 2018. newyorker.com/magazine/2018/10/29/the-myth-of-whiteness-in-classical-sculpture.

Toynbee, J. M. C. *Death and Burial in the Roman World*. Baltimore: Johns Hopkins University Press, 1971.

Van Voorhis, Julie. *The Sculptor's Workshop: Aphrodisias X*. Wiesbaden: Reichert Verlag, 2018.

Van Voorhis, Julie, and Mark Abbe, eds., with contributions by Juliet Graver Istrabadi. *Imperial Colors: The Roman Portrait Busts of Septimius Severus and Julia Domna*. Lewes, UK: Giles; Bloomington, IN: Sidney and Lois Eskenazi Museum of Art, 2023.

Verri, Giovanni, Thorsten Opper, and Thibaut Deviese. "The 'Treu Head': A Case Study in Roman Sculptural Polychromy." *British Museum Technical Research Bulletin* 4 (2010): 39–54.

Vitruvius. *On Architecture.* Vol. 1, books 1–5. Translated by Frank Granger. Loeb Classical Library 251. Cambridge, MA: Harvard University Press, 1931.

Wallace-Hadrill, Andrew. *Houses and Society in Pompeii and Herculaneum*. Princeton, NJ: Princeton University Press, 1994.

Witt, R. E. *Isis in the Graeco-Roman World*. Ithaca, NY: Cornell University Press, 1971.

Woodhull, Margaret L. "Imperial Mothers and Monuments in Rome." In *Mothering and Motherhood in Ancient Greece and Rome*, edited by Lauren Hackworth Petersen and Patricia Salzman-Mitchell. Austin: University of Texas Press, 2012.

Zanker, Paul. *The Power of Images in the Age of Augustus*. Translated by Alan Shapiro. Ann Arbor: University of Michigan Press, 1988.

Zanker, Paul, and Björn C. Ewald. *Living with Myths: The Imagery of Roman Sarcophagi*. Translated by Julia Slater. Oxford, UK: Oxford University Press, 2012.

Contributors

Silvia Beltrametti
Silvia Beltrametti is senior lecturer in the Department of Art History, Theory, and Criticism at the School of the Art Institute of Chicago. She received a Bachelor of Laws from the University of London and a Doctorate in Jurisprudence from the University of Chicago. Her doctoral thesis explores the legal boundaries of the international trade of antiquities. Her areas of research and teaching include matters at the intersection of art, cultural heritage, and the law. The recipient of numerous awards and grants, Beltrametti has served as a consultant for the UNESCO Cultural Heritage Protection Treaties Section and is a member of the World Monuments Fund's International Council.

Lisa Ayla Çakmak
Lisa Ayla Çakmak is Mary and Michael Jaharis Chair and Curator, Arts of Greece, Rome, and Byzantium, at the Art Institute of Chicago, where she has worked since 2020. She recently led a reinstallation of the Art Institute's galleries of Greek, Roman, and Byzantine art and collaborated with artist Charles Ray on the installation of *A copy of ten marble fragments of the Great Eleusinian Relief* (2017) in those same galleries. She was previously the Andrew W. Mellon Foundation Associate Curator of Ancient Art at the Saint Louis Art Museum, and has held fellowships at the American School of Classical Studies at Athens and the W. F. Albright Institute of Archaeological Research.

Katharine A. Raff
Katharine A. Raff is Elizabeth McIlvaine Curator, Arts of Greece, Rome, and Byzantium, at the Art Institute of Chicago, where she has worked since 2011. Her recent projects include the 2024 reinstallation of the Art Institute's permanent gallery of Roman art and a major 2019 installation on ancient artworks and their modern afterlives. Raff was the editor and primary author of the 2017 digital scholarly publication *Roman Art at the Art Institute of Chicago*, and she has also published on the museum's holdings in Greek, Etruscan, and Byzantine art. She has held fellowships from the United States Fulbright Program and the Metropolitan Museum of Art.

Salvatore Settis
Salvatore Settis is an independent art historian. He was previously director of the Getty Research Institute, Los Angeles, from 1994 to 1999, and of the Scuola Normale Superiore, Pisa, from 1999 to 2010. He chaired the Scientific Council of the Musée du Louvre from 2010 to 2023. Recent exhibitions he has curated include *The Torlonia Marbles: Collecting Masterpieces* at the Capitoline Museums, Rome (2020–21), Gallerie d'Italia in Piazza della Scala, Milan (2022), and the Louvre, Paris (2024); *Recycling Beauty* at the Prada Foundation, Milan (2022–23); and *Serial / Portable Classic* at the Prada Foundation, Milan and Venice (2015). Some of his writings have been translated into as many as eighteen languages.

Index

Page numbers in *italics* refer to illustrations.

Albani, Alessandro, Cardinal, 22. *See also* Villa Albani
Amelung Athlete (cat. 54), 26, *123*, 150
Antonine family
  chronology of imperial figures, 19
  funerary art dating to, 144
  portraits of imperial figures, 31–32, *31*, *60–69*, 62, 64, 142–43
  statues dating to, 146, 147
  table leg dating to, 150
Antoninus Pius (emperor)
  dates of life and reign, 19
  Herodes Atticus and, 43–44
  marriage and family, 31, 64
  portrait of (cat. 11), *60*, 142
Aphrodite
  statue of, crouching (cat. 31), *90*, 146
  statue of, with Eros and Ketos (cat. 29), 26, 34, 35, *88*, 145
Apollo, 26, *96*, 147
Appiah, Kwame Anthony, 42
Appian Way, *32*, 43, 135, 147, 149
Arch of Constantine (Rome), 27, *27*
Artemis
  statue of (cat. 37), *97*, 147
  statue of, Ephesia (cat. 46), 106, *107*, 148
Athena, *92*, 93, 146
Athens, 34, 43–44, 93
athletes, 26, *123*, 150
Attic Votive Relief (cat. 49), 34, 39n75, 43–44, *112–13*, 149
Augustus (emperor, formerly known as Octavian)
  artistic program of, 29, 42, 53
  dates of life and reign, 19
  statue of an emperor on a throne with a portrait of (cat. 4), *13*, 42, *52*, 53, 141
Aureus (Coin) Portraying Empress Faustina the Younger, 31, *31*

Bacchus, *101*, 116, 147–48, 149
Beard, Mary, 41–42
Bernini, Gian Lorenzo, 22, 34, 127, 150
Bernini, Pietro, 34, 127
binders, ancient, 28
Bonaparte family (France), 20, 23n4
bronze
  Greek sculptures, 34, 48, 86
  marble vs., 28, 120
  Sixtus IV's donation of bronzes, 137
  Statue of Germanicus (cat. 53), 28, 120, *121–22*, 149
  statuettes, 27, 36n14
Brumidi, Constantino, *Portrait of Alessandro Torlonia*, *130*

Caecilia Metella, Tomb of, 43, 45n14, 149
Caesar, Julius, 34
Caetani Collection, 135
cameo portrait of Trajanic family, 30, *30*
Campana, Giampietro, 133
Canova, Antonio, 20, 139n26
Capitoline Museums (Rome), 22, 133, *134*, 137
Caracalla (emperor), 19, 32, 33
Cavaceppi, Bartolomeo (Studio Cavaceppi)
  collection of, acquired by Torlonia, 20, 135, 136
  restorations done by, 34
  sculptures previously owned by, 141, 143
Ceres, 31, *103*, 148
Cesarini Collection, 135
Cesi Torlonia Cup, 135
children, depictions of, 33, *82–83*, *98–101*, 145, 147
Chrysippus, statue of, 135
Chrysoloras, Manuel, 136
Civitella Cesi estate, 20, 23n2
Closs, Adolf, *Via Appia, near Rome*, after Bühlmann, *32*
coinage
  Aureus Portraying Empress Faustina the Younger, 31, *31*
  bronzes melted down for, 28
  hairstyles of imperial women on, 30
  Venus depicted on, 34
Colonna, Prospero, Cardinal, 136
Colonna, Teresa, 21, 22
color on sculptures, 28, 36n17, 144, 145, 148, 149
Commodus (emperor)
  assassination of, 32
  dates of life and reign, 19
  portraits of (cats. 18–19), *68*, 143
cosmopolitanism, 41–44
Crispina (wife of Emperor Commodus), 19
  portrait of a woman, formerly known as (cat. 20), *69*, 143
Cupid
  child's funerary monument with cupids, 33, *82–83*, 145
  statue of, with Psyche (cat. 30), 34, *89*, 145–46
  See also Eros and Erotes
Cures (present-day Sabina), excavations at, 120, 146, 149

Dacia and Dacians, 26–27, *27*, 36n16, 41, *115*, 149
decoration of sculptures (gilding, inlays, jewelry, etc.), 28, 48, 140
decorum, 26
Demeter, 86
dextrarum iunctio (joining right hands), 33
dogs, 33, *98*, 106, 147
domus (Roman house), 27

eagles, 34
Emerson, Alfred, 36n19
Ephesus, *27*, 106, *107*, 148
Eros and Erotes, 34, 35, *82–83*, *88*, 144, 145. *See also* Cupid
Escamps, Henry d', 133
Euthydemus of Bactria, 28, 37n28, 44, *50*, 140–41

Faustina the Elder (wife of Emperor Antoninus Pius)
  dates of life, 19
  deification of, 38n54
  personal appearance of, 31
  portrait of woman, formerly known as (cat. 12), *61*, 142
Faustina the Younger (wife of Emperor Marcus Aurelius)
  coin (aureus) portraying, 31, *31*
  dates of life, 19
  marriage and family, 31–32, 38nn59–60, 64
  portrait of (cat. 15), 38n60, 64, *65*, 142–43
  women's "soft power" and, 42
Forum, Roman (Rome), 38n54
Forum of Trajan (Rome), 26–27, 41

freedpersons, 28, 145
Fronto, Marcus Cornelius, 25
funerary sculptures
  along Appian Way, *32*
  ancient Roman customs, overview of, 33
  Funerary Monument of a Boy, Gaius Marcius Crescens (cat. 27), 33, *82–83*, 145
  Portrait Group of Husband and Wife (cat. 23), 33, *74–75*, 144
  reuse of sarcophagi as fountains, 137
  Sarcophagus Depicting the Labors of Hercules (cat. 25), 33, *78–79*, 144
  Sarcophagus Depicting the Labors of Hercules and Lid with Reclining Couple (cat. 24), 33, *76–77*, *77*, 135, 144
  Sarcophagus with Lions, Strigilated (cat. 26), 33, 38n69, *80–81*, 145
  social status and, 28, 77

Gasparri, Carlo, 130
Germanicus, 120, *121–22*, 149
Geta (emperor), 19, 32, 33
gilding, 28, 48, 145
Giustiniani Collection (Vincenzo Giustiniani)
  history of antiquities collecting and, 139n26
  restoration of sculptures in, 35, 127, 146
  sculptures previously in, 22, 43, 86, 93, 127, 140–50
  Torlonia acquisition of, 22, 130, 135, 136
goat, statue of (cat. 58), 22, *126–27*, *127*, 150
gods and goddesses
  Aphrodite crouching, statue of (cat. 31), *90*, 146
  Aphrodite with Eros and Ketos, statue of (cat. 29), 26, 34, 35, *88*, 145
  Apollo, statue of (cat. 36), 26, *96*, 147
  Artemis, statue of (cat. 37), *97*, 147
  Artemis Ephesia, statue of (cat. 46), 106, *107*, 148
  Athena, statue of (cat. 33), *92*, 93, 146
  Bacchus as infant on ram, statue of (cat. 41), *101*, 147–48
  Cupid and Psyche, statue of (cat. 30), 34, *89*, 145–46
  of fertility and childbirth, 31–32, 106
  Harpocrates, statue of (cat. 40), *100*, 147
  Hercules, statue of (cat. 34), *94*, 146
  Hestia (or Vesta), statue of (cat. 28), 34, *40*, 43, *43*, 86, *87*, 145
  Isis, statue of (cat. 44), 34, *103*, 148
  Isis restored as Ceres, statue of (cat. 43), 34, *103*, 148
  Leda and the Swan, statues of (cats. 47–48), *108*, 109, 148–49
  Mars, head of (cat. 32), 34, *91*, 146
  Mercury, herm statue of (cat. 35), *95*, 146
  Nile, personification of (cat. 45), *104–5*, 148
  Roman assimilation of Greek deities, 34, 53, 86, 93, 106
  Silenus, statue of (cat. 42), *102*, 148
gorgons, 35, 93, *124*, 145, 150
Greek art and culture
  Attic Votive Relief (cat. 49), 34, 39n75, 43–44, *112–13*, 149
  deities, Roman assimilation of, 34, 53, 86, 93, 106
  painting competition, 44
  philosophers, 31, 42, 62
  portrait of Hellenistic ruler (cat. 2), 28, 37n28, 44, *50*, 140–41
  Roman interest in, 33–34
  sculpture, Roman copies of, 34, 43, 48, 86, 109
griffins, 34, 35, 106, *124*, 146, 150

Hadrian (emperor)
  as bearded, 31, 62
  dates of life and reign, 19
  marriage and family, 30–31, 37n47
  portrait of (cat. 9), *58*, 142
hairstyles
  beards on emperors, 31, 32, 62, 142, 143
  braided styles, 31, 33, 141–42
  "finger-wave" locks, 64
  hair ornament added to sculpture, 48, 140
  "turban coiffure," 37n36
  of women imitating imperial wives, 30
Harpocrates, *100*, 147
Head of Mars (cat. 32), 34, *91*, 146
Hera, 86
Herculaneum, excavations at, 138n5
Hercules
  Commodus and, 32
  sarcophagi depicting Twelve Labors of (cats. 24–25), 33, *76–79*, *77*, 135, 144
  statue of (cat. 34), *94*, 146
herm (cat. 35), *95*, 146
Herodes Atticus, 43–44
Hestia Giustiniani (cat. 28), 34, *40*, 43, *43*, 86, *87*, 145

idealized forms
  Augustan portraits, 42
  nude male figures, 120, *121–23*
  women's facial features, 28, 30, 48, *49*
Imperial Period. *See* Roman Empire
inscriptions
  display of, in 15th century Rome, 136
  on funerary monument of a boy, 33, 145
  on Mithraic relief, 149
  on portraits, 28
  on Portus relief, 116
  of Sixtus IV, on donation of antiquities, *134*, 137
Isis, 34, *103*, 148
Italy, unification of, 133

Julia Domna (wife of Emperor Septimius Severus)
  dates of life, 19
  marriage and family, 32–33
  portrait of (cat. 22), *71*, 144
  women's "soft power" and, 42
Juno, 31, *31*
Jupiter, 42, 53, 109

ketos (serpent-like sea monster), 35, *88*, 145

lararia (household shrines), 27
Leda and the swan, *108*, 109, 148–49
Liber Pater ("Free Father"), 116
Library of Celsus (ancient Ephesus), *27*
lions
  Artemis and, 148
  Hercules and, 146
  strigilated sarcophagus with (cat. 26), 33, *80–81*, 145
  table leg with head and paw of (cat. 56), *124*, 150
Lucilla (wife of Emperor Lucius Verus)
  dates of life, 19
  marriage and family, 32, 38n60
  portrait of woman, formerly known as (cat. 17), *67*, 143
Lucius Verus (emperor)
  dates of life and reign, 19
  Herodes Atticus and, 44
  marriage, 32
  portrait of (cat. 16), *66*, 143

Maiden of Vulci (cat. 1), 22, 28, *29*, 37n27, 44, 48, *49*, 140
Manlio, Lorenzo, 136
map of Roman Empire, *26*

marble
bronze vs., 28, 120
coatings or washes applied to, 93, 109, 141, 142, 143
decoration of sculptures (gilding, inlays, jewelry, etc.), 28, 48, 140
recycling of sculptures for lime, 136
restoration approaches in the past, 34–35, 109, 127, 140
types of, used for each sculpture, 140–50
as valued by Romans, 25, 43
See also specific sculptures
Marchionni, Carlo, 22
Marciana, Ulpia (sister of Emperor Trajan)
cameo portrait of Trajanic family, 30, *30*
dates of life, 19
deification of, 37n45
portrait of woman, formerly known as (cat. 7), *56*, 141
Marcius Crescens, Gaius, 33, *82–83*, 145
Marcus Aurelius (emperor)
coin (aureus) issued by, *31*
cosmopolitanism and, 42–43
dates of life and reign, 19
Fronto and, 25
Herodes Atticus and, 44
marriage and family, 31–32, 64
portraits of (cats. 13–14), *24*, 62, *62–63*, 142
Mars, 34, *91*, 146
Matidia (niece of Emperor Trajan)
cameo portrait of Trajanic family, 30, *30*
dates of life, 19
portrait of woman, formerly known as (cat. 8), *57*, 141–42
Medusa, 35, 93, *124*, 150
Mercury, *95*, 146
Minerva. *See* Athena
Mithraism, 34, *114*, 149

Neoclassicism, 22
Neptune, 116, 149
Nile, personification of (cat. 45), *104–5*, 148
Nolli, Giovanni Battista, 23n6

Odysseus, *125*, 150
Old Man of Otricoli (cat. 3), 28–29, 37n27, 44, *51*, 141
Orsini Collection, 135, 144, 145
ownership of antiquities, 44, 45n17

Parrhasius, 44
Pausanias, 93
peplos (garment), 86, 145
Piazza Venezia residence (Rome), 20, 23n5, 143
pigments, ancient, 28
Piranesi, Giovanni Battista, 23n6
Pius VI, Pope, 20
Pliny the Elder, 44
Plotina (wife of Emperor Trajan)
cameo portrait of Trajanic family, 30, *30*
dates of life, 19
statue of woman, restored as (cat. 6), 30, *55*, 141
Poma Murialdo, Alessandro, 10–11, 43
Porta Pia (Rome), breach of, 133
Portrait of Antoninus Pius (cat. 11), *60*, 142
Portrait of Commodus (cat. 19), *68*, 143
Portrait of Faustina the Younger (cat. 15), 38n60, 64, *65*, 142–43
Portrait of Hadrian (cat. 9), *58*, 142
Portrait of Julia Domna (cat. 22), *71*, 144
Portrait of Lucius Verus (cat. 16), *66*, 143
Portrait of a Man, known as Euthydemus of Bactria (cat. 2), 28, 37n28, 44, *50*, 140–41
Portrait of a Man, known as the Old Man of Otricoli (cat. 3), 29, 37n27, 44, *51*, 141
Portrait of Marcus Aurelius (cat. 14), 62, *63*, 142
Portrait of Septimius Severus (cat. 21), *70*, 143
Portrait of Trajan (cat. 5), *54*, 141
Portrait of a Woman, formerly known as Crispina (cat. 20), *69*, 143
Portrait of a Woman, formerly known as Faustina the Elder (cat. 12), *61*, 142
Portrait of a Woman, formerly known as Lucilla (cat. 17), *67*, 143
Portrait of a Woman, formerly known as Marciana (cat. 7), *56*, 141
Portrait of a Woman, formerly known as Matidia (cat. 8), *57*, 141–42
Portrait of a Woman, formerly known as Sabina (cat. 10), *59*, 142
Portrait of Young Commodus (cat. 18), *68*, 143
Portrait of Young Marcus Aurelius (cat. 13), 62, *62*, 142
Portrait of a Young Woman, known as the Maiden of Vulci (cat. 1), 22, 28, *29*, 37n27, 44, 48, *49*, 140
Portrait Group of Husband and Wife (cat. 23), 33, *75*, 144
portraiture
imperial portraits, overview of, 29–33
realistic or veristic style, 29, 44
social status and, 28
women's idealized features, 28, 30, 48
See also hairstyles; *and specific titles or subjects of portraits*
Portus Relief (cat. 52), 22, 28, 116, *116–17*, 149
Psyche, 34, *89*, 145–46

rams, 33, *101*, *125*, 147–48, 150
reliefs
Attic Votive Relief (cat. 49), 34, 39n75, 43–44, *112–13*, 149
Portus Relief (cat. 52), 22, 28, 116, *116–17*, 149
Relief of Mithraic Sacrifice (cat. 50), 34, *114*, 149
Unfinished Statue of a Dacian Prisoner (cat. 51), 27, 36n16, 41, *115*, 149
Republican Period
Greek cultural influence, 33–34, 43
portraiture, 28–29, 48, *49*, *51*, 140, 141
Roma Vecchia estate, 23n2, 143, 144
Roman Empire
adoptions, 30, 32, 62
chronology of imperial figures, 19
coinage, 29–30, 31–32, *31*, 34
deification of imperial figures, 32, 37n45, 38n54, 53
funerary sculptures, 28, *32*, 33, *74–83*, *77*
geographic expanse of, 25–26, *26*
Greek influence on art and culture, 33–34, 43, 53, 86, 93, 106, 109
integration of foreigners, 41
portraiture, overview of, 29–33
sculpture's cultural significance, 25–28, 43, 109
women's role in imperial court, 30, 37n43, 38n51, 42
See also specific imperial dynasties and figures
Roman Republic. *See* Republican Period
Rome, capture of (1870), 133
Romulus and Remus, 116
Rondanini-Type Medusa on a Table Leg with a Griffin's Head (cat. 55), 35, *124*, 150
Rondanini-Type Medusa on a Table Leg with a Lion's Head (cat. 56), 35, *124*, 150
Ruspoli Collection, 135

Sabina (wife of Emperor Hadrian)
dates of life, 19
marriage and family, 30, 37n47
personal appearance of, 31
portrait of woman, formerly known as (cat. 10), *59*, 142
Santa Maria in Aracoeli church (Rome), 137
Sarcophagus Depicting the Labors of Hercules (cat. 25), 33, *78–79*, 144

Sarcophagus Depicting the Labors of Hercules and Lid with Reclining Couple (cat. 24), 33, *76–77*, 77, 135, 144
Sarcophagus with Lions, Strigilated (cat. 26), 33, 38n69, *80–81*, 145
Savelli Collection, 135, 144, 145
Severan family, 19, 32–33, *70–71*, 143–44
Severe sculpture style (Greek), 86
Severus, Septimius (emperor)
dates of life and reign, 19
marriage and family, 32–33
portrait of (cat. 21), *70*, 143
Silenus (Old Satyr), *102*, 148
Sixtus IV, Pope, *134*, 137
Statue of Aphrodite with Eros and Ketos (cat. 29), 26, 34, 35, *88*, 145
Statue of Apollo (cat. 36), 26, *96*, 147
Statue of Artemis (cat. 37), *97*, 147
Statue of Artemis Ephesia (cat. 46), 106, *107*, 148
Statue of Athena (cat. 33), *92*, 93, 146
Statue of a Boy, restored as Harpocrates (cat. 40), *100*, 147
Statue of a Boy with Dogs (cat. 38), 33, *98*, 147
Statue of the Cesi-Type Silenus (cat. 42), *102*, 148
Statue of Crouching Aphrodite (cat. 31), *90*, 146
Statue of Cupid and Psyche (cat. 30), 34, *89*, 145–46
Statue of a Dacian Prisoner, Unfinished (cat. 51), 27, 36n16, 41, *115*, 149
Statue of an Emperor on a Throne with a Portrait of Augustus (cat. 4), *13*, 42, *52*, 53, 141
Statue of Germanicus (cat. 53), 28, 120, *121–22*, 149
Statue of a Girl Holding a Bird (cat. 39), 33, *99*, 147
Statue of a Goddess, known as the Hestia Giustiniani (cat. 28), 34, *40*, 43, *43*, 86, *87*, 145
Statue of Hercules (cat. 34), *94*, 146
Statue of the Infant Bacchus on a Ram (cat. 41), *101*, 147–48
Statue of Isis (cat. 44), 34, *103*, 148
Statue of Isis, restored as Ceres (cat. 43), 34, *103*, 148
Statue of Leda and the Swan (cats. 47–48), *108*, 109, 148–49
Statue of Mercury in the Form of a Herm (cat. 35), *95*, 146
Statue of Odysseus Beneath the Ram (cat. 57), *125*, 150
Statue of a Resting Goat (cat. 58), 22, *126–27*, 127, 150
Statue of a Woman, restored as Plotina (cat. 6), 30, *55*, 141
Statue of a Youth, known as the Amelung Athlete (cat. 54), 26, *123*, 150
statuettes, bronze, 27, 36n14
Strigilated Sarcophagus with Lions (cat. 26), 33, 38n69, *80–81*, 145

table legs (*trapezophoroi*), 35, *124*, 150
Thorvaldsen, Bertel, 20
Timotheus, 109
Torlonia, Alessandro, Prince (1800–1886), 20–22, 23n4, 129–35, *130*
Torlonia, Alessandro, Prince (1925–2017), 21, 23
Torlonia, Giovanni Raimondo, Duke of Bracciano, 20–22, 129
Torlonia Collection (Rome)
as "collection of collections," 20–22, 43, 129, 135–36
creation of Torlonia Museum, 20, 22, 129–35
funerary sculptures, overview of, 33
gallery views of, *132*
history of antiquities collecting and, 136–37, 139n26
international exhibitions of, 41, 44
marble vs. bronze sculptures, 28, 120
portraits, overview of, 28–33
restoration of works prior to entering, 22, 30, 34–35, 39n84, 109, 127, 140
Viscontis' catalogues of, 22, 29, 37n36, 130–32, *131*, 135, 140
See also specific sculptures
Torlonia Family
excavations sponsored by, 22, 43, 45n14, 116, 120, 141, 143, 147–48, 150
Family tree, 21
owl as symbol of, 93
real estate holdings, 20, 22, 23n2, 23nn4–5
See also specific family members
Torlonia Foundation, 22–23, 35, 43
Torlonia Laboratories (Rome), 41, *42*, 109, *128*, 140
The Torlonia Nile, formerly the Barberini-Albani Nile (cat. 45), *104–5*, 148
Tourlonias, Marino, 20, 21
Trajan (emperor)
cameo portrait of Trajanic family, 30, *30*
as clean shaven, 31
dates of life and reign, 19
Forum of, 26–27, 41
portrait of (cat. 5), *54*, 141
provincial origins of, 37n45
Trajanic family
chronology of imperial figures, 19
funerary art dating to, 144
portraits of imperial figures, 30–31, *30*, *54–59*, 141–42
relief dating to, 149
Tuccinardi, Stefania, 130, 140

Valadier, Giuseppe, 20
Vatican Museums (Rome), 133
Venus, 31, 33, 34
Vesta and Vestal Virgins, 86
Via Appia, *32*, 43, 135, 147, 149
Villa Albani (Rome)
intellectual circle of, 22, 23n6
papal army's surrender signed at, 133
sculptures previously in collection of, 135, 142, 148, 150
sculptures previously on display at, 37n27
Torlonia acquisition of, 22, 130, 135, 136
Visconti, Carlo Ludovico
collecting practices and, 29, 37n31
numbering system of catalogue, 19, 140
page from catalogue, *131*
on Prince Torlonia's intentions, 132, 133–35
on provenance of sculptures, 135, 140
publication of catalogue, 130–32
scholarly value of catalogue, 132–33, 140
Torlonia Museum's layout and, 22
Visconti, Pietro Ercole
on Bernini's restorations, 127
Campana and, 133
collecting practices and, 29, 37n31
on provenance of sculptures, 135, 140
publication of catalogue, 130–32
scholarly value of catalogue, 132–33, 140
Torlonia Museum's layout and, 22

Western Schism, 136
Winckelmann, Johann Joachim, 20, 22, 23n7, 43, 45n12
World War II, 22

xoanon (wooden cult statue), 106

Zeus, 53, 109
Zeuxis, 44

Myth and Marble: Ancient Roman Sculpture from the Torlonia Collection was published in conjunction with an exhibition of the same title co-organized by the Art Institute of Chicago and the Torlonia Foundation, in collaboration with the Kimbell Art Museum, the Montreal Museum of Fine Arts, and The Museum Box.

EXHIBITION DATES
The Art Institute of Chicago
March 15–June 29, 2025

Kimbell Art Museum
Fort Worth, Texas
September 14, 2025–January 25, 2026

Montreal Museum of Fine Arts
March 14–July 19, 2026

Lead support for *Myth and Marble: Ancient Roman Sculpture from the Torlonia Collection* is provided by Shawn M. Donnelley and Christopher M. Kelly.

Major funding is contributed by the Jaharis Family Foundation, the Boshell Family Foundation, Dwyer Brown and Nancy Reynolds, Marion Cameron-Gray, and two anonymous donors.

Members of the Luminary Trust provide annual leadership support for the museum's operations, including exhibition development, conservation and collection care, and educational programming. The Luminary Trust includes an anonymous donor, Karen Gray-Krehbiel and John Krehbiel, Jr., Kenneth C. Griffin, the Harris Family Foundation in memory of Bette and Neison Harris, Josef and Margot Lakonishok, Ann and Samuel M. Mencoff, Sylvia Neil and Dan Fischel, Cari and Michael J. Sacks, and the Earl and Brenda Shapiro Foundation.

The works of the Torlonia Collection have been restored by the Torlonia Foundation with the support of Fondazione Bvlgari in the Laboratori Torlonia.

The Torlonia Foundation activities are made possible by the support of Chiomenti.

First edition
Printed in Italy

ISBN 978-0-300-27965-8 (hardcover)

Library of Congress Control Number: 2024949488

PUBLISHED BY
The Art Institute of Chicago
111 South Michigan Avenue
Chicago, IL 60603-6404
artic.edu

DISTRIBUTED BY
Yale University Press
302 Temple Street, P. O. Box 209040
New Haven, CT 06520-9040
yalebooks.com/art

Edited by Nora McGreevy with Lisa Meyerowitz
Production by Elizabeth Upenieks with Lauren Makholm
Photography research by Josephine Yanasak-Leszczynski
Proofreading by Juliet Clark
Indexing by Theresa Duran
Design and typesetting by Practise (James Goggin & Shan James)
Typeset in Calvino (James Goggin, 2024, after Algonquin, Photo-Lettering, Inc., 1970s, with thanks to Louise Fili) and Syntax Next (Hans Eduard Meier, Linotype, 2000)
Separations by Professional Graphics, Rockford, Illinois
Printing and binding by Trifolio, Verona, Italy

The Art Institute of Chicago
PUBLISHING
Katie Reilly, Associate Vice President, Publishing
Lisa Meyerowitz, Editorial Director
Lauren Makholm, Director of Production

IMAGING
Bonnie Rosenberg, Director of Imaging
Nathan Keay, Associate Director, Photography
Elyse M. Allen, Associate Director, Production

Photography Credits
Unless otherwise noted, photographs of artworks are in the Collection of the Torlonia Foundation. The works of the Torlonia Foundation are protected by copyright of the Torlonia Foundation. Any commercial use is strictly prohibited. Photographs of works in the Torlonia Collection are by Lorenzo De Masi unless otherwise attributed.

Every effort has been made to identify, contact, and acknowledge copyright holders for all reproductions; additional rights holders are encouraged to contact the Art Institute of Chicago. The following credits apply to all images in this book for which separate acknowledgment is due.

P. 21: Torlonia Family crest © Fondazione Torlonia. P. 26, fig. 1: Mapping Specialists LTD. P. 27, fig. 2: Mark Little / Alamy Stock Photo. P. 27, fig. 3: Album / E. Viader / Prism. P. 30, fig. 5: Office and Photographic Archive of Museo Archeologico Nazionale di Napoli Piazza Museo. P. 31, fig. 6: Image © The Art Institute of Chicago; photograph by Juan Molina Hernández; postproduction by Hayley Hinsberger. P. 32, fig. 7: history_docu_photo_ / Alamy Stock Photo. P. 25, fig. 8: © Fondazione Torlonia, produced by Trasmissione Al Futuro. P. 42, fig. 1, and p. 128: © Fondazione Torlonia, photographs by Agostino Osio. P. 132, fig. 3: Istituto Archeologico Germanico / Deutsches Archäologisches Institut.

Details: Jacket: Statue of Cupid and Pysche (cat. 30); p. 13: Statue of an Emperor on a Throne with a Portrait of Augustus (cat. 4); p. 24: Portrait of Young Marcus Aurelius (cat. 13); p. 40: Statue of a Goddess, known as the Hestia Giustiniani (cat. 28); p. 128: installation view, Torlonia Laboratories, Rome. Photograph by Agostino Osio.

This book was made using paper and materials certified by the Forest Stewardship Council®, which ensures responsible forest management.